Incorporating Sustainability in Management Education

Kenneth Amaeshi • Judy N. Muthuri
Chris Ogbechie
Editors

Incorporating Sustainability in Management Education

An Interdisciplinary Approach

palgrave
macmillan

Editors
Kenneth Amaeshi
University of Edinburgh Business School
Edinburgh, UK

Judy N. Muthuri
Nottingham University Business School
Nottingham, UK

Chris Ogbechie
Lagos Business School
Lagos, Nigeria

ISBN 978-3-319-98124-6   ISBN 978-3-319-98125-3   (eBook)
https://doi.org/10.1007/978-3-319-98125-3

Library of Congress Control Number: 2018968418

This Palgrave Macmillan imprint is published by the registered company Springer Nature Switzerland AG
The registered company address is: Gewerbestrasse 11, 6330 Cham, Switzerland

Contents

Notes on Contributors

Ron Ainsbury was born in South Africa but has studied, worked, and lived around the world including Asia and most recently Australia and New Zealand. He has been a senior executive with a number of global companies including Diageo where he initiated several responsible programmes. He was an associate research professor at Rotterdam Business School when this work was undertaken. He is now based in New Zealand from where he consults to businesses on becoming more responsible.

Kenneth Amaeshi is Professor of Business & Sustainable Development, and Director of the Sustainable Business Initiative, at the University of Edinburgh Business School, UK. His research focuses on entrepreneurship and business model innovation for sustainable development. His other interests include sustainability, corporate responsibility, ethics, and governance. He is widely published.

Frances M. Amatucci is an associate professor in the School of Business at Slippery Rock University of Pennsylvania, USA. She has held adjunct positions at a number of business schools and was Associate Professor of International and Small and Medium-Sized Enterprises (SME) and Director of Graduate Business Studies in the Faculty of Business at the University of New Brunswick/Saint John, Canada. Amatucci is a strong advocate of field-based and experiential learning in business education. She teaches courses related to strategic management, sustainability, and entrepreneurship. Amatucci was the Chair of the United Nations Global Compact's *Principles for Responsible Management*

Education (PRME) initiative at Slippery Rock University and is a member of the PRME Working Group on Gender Equality. She has been a participant in the Business of Humanity® project at the University of Pittsburgh since 2009 and, based on her field research in Russia funded by the project, she wrote the case study *Alcoa Russia*. Her research interests include gender and diversity issues in business, entrepreneurship finance, and sustainability entrepreneurship. She has written articles in peer-reviewed academic journals such as *Entrepreneurship Theory and Practice*, *Venture Capital*, *Journal of Small Business Strategy*, *Journal of Developmental Entrepreneurship*, and the *International Journal of Gender and Entrepreneurship*. She received an MBA and a PhD from the Katz Graduate School of Business at the University of Pittsburgh and was employed for over 16 years in the health care sector.

Andrew J. Angus is Reader (Associate Professor) in Economics, specialising in managerial economics, economic strategy, and environmental economics. He is the full-time Cranfield MBA Director. Angus has worked for the UK Government investigating potential mechanisms for lowering the economic burden of environmental regulation. His other research has focused on investment trends in clean technologies and the economic impacts of commodity price cycles and he has written over 20 papers on these topics in internationally recognised academic journals.

Saulius Buivys has worked in the public sector in between spells in academia first in Kaunas and now in Rotterdam Business School, Netherlands; NEOMA Business School, France; Vilnius University Business School, Lithuania; and ELISAVA Barcelona School of Design and Engineering, Spain. He holds a number of education co-ordination positions and teaches corporate responsibility and sustainability and project management.

George Ferns is Lecturer in Management, Employment, and Organization at Cardiff Business School, UK. His research broadly concerns how organisations engage with issues surrounding the natural environment, focusing on topics such as corporate responses to climate change, corporate social responsibility, and environmental activism. His research has been published by the *Journal of Business Ethics* and in *Business & Society*.

Simon Graham is a sustainability strategist with ten years of experience creating award-winning sustainable innovation both as a practitioner and as a consultant. Following postgraduate research in remote sensing and data mining for tropical coastal and periglacial environments, Graham managed a range of innovative projects in both the public and the private sectors. He was appointed to lead commercial's environmental and corporate responsibility endeavours in 2006, creating a programme that was widely cited by Business in the Community and the Energy Saving Trust for its combination of radical environmental performance, high personnel engagement, and support for business growth. Since 2014, he has been Head of Innovation for De Courcy Alexander (DCA) working with blue-chip clients on projects around the circular economy, low carbon transport, emerging business models, energy efficient innovation, and ethical supply chains. He is the recipient of over 20 national and international awards for projects that have transformed business to become more sustainable.

Rob Gray was, until his retirement in 2015, Professor of Social and Environmental Accounting at the University of St Andrews, UK. He is a qualified accountant and the author/co-author of over 300 articles, chapters, monographs, and books—mainly on social and environmental accounting, sustainability, social responsibility, and education. He founded CSEAR (the Centre for Social and Environmental Accounting Research) in 1991 and for 21 years was its director. He has served on the editorial boards of over 20 learned journals and has worked with a wide range of international and local commercial and non-commercial organisations including collaborations with the United Nations from time to time. In 2001 he was elected the British Accounting Association Distinguished Academic Fellow. He was awarded the Member of the Order of the British Empire in the Queen's 2009 Birthday Honours List and was elected as a fellow of the Academy of Social Science in 2012.

David Roger Grayson, CBE, is a British-European. From 2007 to 2017, he was Director of the Doughty Centre for Corporate Responsibility and Professor of Corporate Responsibility at Cranfield School of Management, UK. He is now an independent commentator on sustainable business and Emeritus Professor of Corporate Responsibility at Cranfield. He is the author of seven books on business, society, and sustainability and a contributor of chapters to many more books. His recent book *All In: The Future of Business Leadership* was published in June 2018.

Teresa Heath is a member of faculty in the Nottingham University Business School, University of Nottingham, UK. She has written articles in a number of leading journals, including the *Journal of Business Ethics*, the *European Journal of Marketing*, and the *Journal of Marketing Management*. Her publications and teaching focus primarily on the fields of sustainability, ethics, critical marketing, and consumption. She is a member of the editorial review board of the *European Journal of Marketing*.

Sally McKechnie is Associate Professor of Marketing at Nottingham University Business School, UK, where she teaches on postgraduate and undergraduate programmes and supervises PhD students. Her research expertise is in the areas of consumer behaviour, marketing communications, and services marketing. She has written articles in a number of leading international journals, including *Psychology & Marketing, Journal of Travel Research, Journal of Business Research, European Journal of Marketing,* and *Journal of Marketing Management.*

Judy N. Muthuri is Associate Professor of Corporate Social Responsibility and the Chair of the Social and Environmental Group at the Nottingham University Business School (NUBS), UK. She has accumulated extensive teaching and programme development expertise in her role as the Director of the MSc in Sustainability and MSc in Corporate Social Responsibility programmes run by the International Centre for Corporate Social Responsibility at NUBS. Her research interests are in business and development, corporate responsibility and sustainability, food poverty, and corporate social innovation. She is widely published.

Joseph G. Nellis is Professor of Global Economy specialising in global economic developments, business environmental analysis, and strategic thinking. He is Deputy Director and the longest serving member of Cranfield School of Management's Executive Board. From 1 January 2014 until 31 January 2015, he served as Director of the School and was Pro-Vice-Chancellor of the University from 2005 to 2008. He also holds visiting professorial appointments at various universities in Germany, Belgium, Austria, the Netherlands, Hungary, the USA, and Ghana. Nellis has written 19 research and subject-based books and over 200 academic and practitioner journal articles. His research encompasses analysis of business developments in a changing world in terms of the macroeconomy, the role of government, the impact of technology, and societal and demographic trends. He is a frequent contributor to a wide range of national and international conferences and is a consultant to a number of international companies in the areas of strategy and business environmental analysis, strategy formulation, and management development. He has also acted as a consultant to several central government departments and public sector organisations.

Chris Ogbechie is Professor of Strategic Management at the Lagos Business School (LBS), Pan-Atlantic University, Nigeria. There, Sir Chris, as he is fondly called, leads sessions on strategy and corporate governance and is also the Head of the Strategy group. He is also a visiting professor at the Strathmore Business School, Nairobi, Kenya, where he teaches the same. He has a PhD in Business

Administration from Brunel Business School, UK, with vast experience in marketing, strategy, and corporate governance. He has several publications in financial services, marketing, strategic planning, and corporate social responsibility and sustainability. He has also presented papers on corporate governance and sustainability at various national and international conferences. He is also the founding Director of the School's Sustainability Centre. His research interests are in strategy in turbulent environments, strategic leadership, board effectiveness, and corporate sustainability. Ogbechie has been involved with several start-ups and a fervent advocate of sustainability practices in business.

Will Oulton is the Global Head, Responsible Investment at First State Investments (FSI), UK, and is responsible for defining and delivering FSI's responsible investment and stewardship strategy globally. In this role, he is tasked with advancing FSI's understanding of how Environmental, Social and Governance (ESG) factors impact long-term investment value. He is also responsible for developing FSI's thought leadership programmes and managing the Responsible Investment governance structure for the business.

Previous to this, he was the Head of Responsible Investment for Mercer Investments across Europe, the Middle East, and Africa, advising institutional asset owners on environmental, social, and corporate governance matters. He has more than 15 years of experience working in sustainable and responsible investment. Before joining Mercer, Oulton was the Director of Responsible Investment at FTSE Group, where he led the development of FTSE's global sustainability services.

In December 2015, he was appointed President of the European Sustainable Investment Forum (Eurosif). He is also a Trustee Director of the Commonwealth Bank of Australia (CBA) (UK) Pension Scheme, a fellow of the Royal Society of Arts, an honorary associate professor at Nottingham University Business School's International Centre for Corporate Social Responsibility, expert panel member of the Prince's Accounting for Sustainability programme, and sits on a number of investment industry advisory boards and committees.

Fred A. Yamoah is a Senior Lecturer at the Department of Management, Birkbeck, University of London, UK. He has considerable teaching and research experience in higher education. Yamoah's multi-disciplinary approach to researching sustainability, supply and value chain management and marketing, informs his teaching on subjects related with responsible business management education. His academic career is driven by a personal passion that teaching and researching sustainability and its related fields can help deliver sustainable interdependence of business and society. Yamoah has also developed an original individual and collaborative research agenda with an output that demonstrates his ability to publish in internationally ranked, peer-reviewed journals. He is an experienced undergraduate and postgraduate research degree supervisor and examiner. He has been involved with various research projects with the UK and international stakeholders in developing countries. He is an experienced curriculum development and enrichment expert. He is a fellow of the Higher Education Academy, UK, and a contributing author of *Developing Skills for Business Leadership*. He also serves as the sustainability co-editor for the *Annual Review of Social Partnership*.

List of Figures

List of Tables

1

Introduction

Kenneth Amaeshi, Judy N. Muthuri, and Chris Ogbechie

Sustainability has become a new mantra, a philosophy of sorts. It does, however, mean different things to different people. If one takes the literary meaning of the word, it could simply suggest longevity or the ability to continue in existence irrespective of counteracting pressures. Another word often used in this regard is resilience. While longevity and resilience are integral to sustainability, they tend to, somewhat, present a narrow and limited view of sustainability.

The broad view of sustainability goes beyond resilience and longevity and emphasises the need to balance environmental, social, and economic considerations in decision-making. It has a direct link with the quest for

K. Amaeshi (✉)
University of Edinburgh Business School, Edinburgh, UK
e-mail: Kenneth.Amaeshi@ed.ac.uk

J. N. Muthuri
Nottingham University Business School, Nottingham, UK
e-mail: judy.muthuri@nottingham.ac.uk

C. Ogbechie
Lagos Business School, Lagos, Nigeria
e-mail: cogbechie@lbs.edu.ng

© The Author(s) 2019
K. Amaeshi et al. (eds.), *Incorporating Sustainability in Management Education*,
https://doi.org/10.1007/978-3-319-98125-3_1

sustainable development—that is, a development that will not inhibit future generations in their quest for development (WCED 1987). It recognises the nested interdependency amongst the economy, society, and environment. In other words, the success of the economy is dependent on the viability of society, and the success of society requires the viability of the environment. As such, without the environment, there will be no society, and without society, there will be no economy. The three are interwoven. Hence, the threat of climate change, whilst an environmental phenomenon, has both social and economic consequences.

Sustainability, therefore, strives to ensure the integrity of this nested interdependency, which is very much at the heart of the United Nations (UN) 2015 sustainable development goals (SDGs). The SDGs are amongst the greatest pursuits of our time. Given the focus of the SDGs on inter-generational equity, the pursuit of sustainable development is, arguably, a normative project, which entails collective responsibility and action from different actors—for example, governments, non-governmental organisations (NGOs), multinational institutions, the academia, and the business community. The SDGs are also fundamental to the contemporary corporate sustainability movement, which emphasises the need to balance environmental, social, and economic considerations in decision-making. This balance has been understood and expressed in many ways including but not limited to *environmental sustainability, economic sustainability*, and *social sustainability*. This is a growing agenda the academia has been called to effectively contribute to.

Business Schools and professional managers, as producers and disseminators of management knowledge, are now being challenged to incorporate this broad view of sustainability into their curricula. The business and management schools (BAMs), in particular, have broad reach and impact on the three pillars of sustainability through their streams of activities—that is, research, teaching, and engagement. Through teaching, for instance, they influence current and future generations of managers and leaders. In this regard, business schools are increasingly seen as a major player in moving sustainable agenda forward while also empowering individuals and organisations to put in place sustainable solutions. This they do by linking together theory and practice of responsible management into their programmes. In addition, there have been initiatives (e.g.

the Grey Principles) and the United Nations Principles for Responsible Management Education (UN-PRME) to promote this agenda. In addition, business education accreditation bodies driving the agenda include EFMD Quality Improvement System (EQUIS), The Association of MBAs (AMBA), and The Association to Advance Collegiate Schools of Business (AACSB), who have started making stringent demands on business schools to reflect sustainability thinking in their curricula.

Since the inception of the UN-PRME in 2007, there has been increased debate as to how to integrate and adapt sustainability into the management education to meet the needs of the twenty-first-century business climate. While there is a seeming consensus by the globally focused management education institutions that sustainability needs to be well ingrained into their management educational curricula, the relevant question is no longer why but how. In spite of the current effort and elegant push on business schools to incorporate sustainability into their operations, some business schools still take for granted how it should be done.

Many BAMs take an insular approach to sustainability in the area of teaching, research, and structure. Shareholder value maximisation and, to a larger extent, meeting the needs of all material stakeholders are projected as the centrepiece of the siloed curriculum, with ethics and societal issues not mainstreamed. In most BAMs, for instance, there is often little support for faculty members to make the transition to a sustainability informed curriculum. This has often resulted to subtle resistance from some faculty members, while others are frustrated and intimidated by the need to incorporate sustainability into their courses and teaching programmes. We (i.e. the editors) face these pressures in our various schools and in practice. However, this traditional approach to management is gradually changing. A growing number of BAMs in the last decade are beginning to respond to the call that management education plays an important role in moving the sustainability agenda forward, and preparing future managers, practitioners, and leaders to meet the challenges of sustainability.

From our experience, higher education institutions (HEIs) are willing to support their faculty members to make the transition to sustainability informed curricula. Unfortunately, there are very few resources available to support the HEIs. In addition, some business schools and management scholars still find it difficult to embed sustainability in their teaching activities. This book is keen to fill this gap. It is intentionally not heavy on theory and academic jargons. The idea is to make it as simple as possible. The chapters provide some examples of, and guides on, how sustainability can be integrated into management education—especially in the MBA modules, as a flagship BAMs programme.

Chapter 2 provides the ample explanation of how sustainability can be embedded into entrepreneurship curriculum with a case study of how it was done in a public university in the United States. Frances M. Amatucci based her argument on the need for a paradigm shift in delivering entrepreneurship education submitting that the recent UN-SDGs offer a platform for exploring and exploiting sustainable entrepreneurial opportunities. Since entrepreneurs employ innovation and creativity in their business models, there is a symbiotic relationship between entrepreneurship and sustainability that can hardly be separated in the twenty-first century.

Rob Gray in Chap. 3 focuses on sustainability accounting and education: *conflicts and possibilities*. Accounting education has a long history of resisting ideas and innovations, which may fundamentally challenge taken-for-granted assumptions. However, these concerns were especially acute when issues such as ethics, social responsibility, social accounting, and now sustainability are being introduced into its curriculum. Sustainability challenges everything about modernity, at least in principle. The chapter shows how the integration process has been challenging as it appears to sit uncomfortably with the accounting conventions and mores. The chapter concludes that integrating sustainability into accounting education will require aggressive and high degrees of disruption, cognitive dissonance, and breaking out of norms. The underlying theme of the chapter, therefore, is that if the educators and students are not feeling importuned and fundamentally challenged, then we are not properly looking at sustainability in accounting.

In Chap. 4, Andrew J. Angus and Joseph G. Nellis explore the embedding of sustainability into business economics. Mainstream economic thinking of sustainability has fused into the field of environmental economics, a sub-discipline of microeconomics. They however propose the need to move beyond this parochial outlook of sustainability. Using the two competing views of sustainability (i.e. weak and strong sustainability), they suggest that sustainability thinking should be infused into business economics education through microeconomics and macroeconomics teaching, rather than being a distinct topic in microeconomics modules. While microeconomics syllabus should view sustainability from firm's perspectives as a means of improving competitiveness and profitability, rather than from the lens of government intervention, the macroeconomic syllabus should focus on how to measure economic growth adjusted for environmental net gain or in a way that is closely linked to human welfare. The chapter also highlights the need to emphasise sustainability-related concepts such as *green economy, circular economy,* and *steady-state economy* in business economics modules.

George Ferns, in Chap. 5, examines the embedding of sustainability into international business (IB) studies. Globalisation, he argues, has changed the world and greatly impacts the business and management education. Thus, to overcome the difficulty, Ferns reflects on two aspects of his experience in integrating sustainability into IB. First, he identifies the limitations in course content in their present structure and discusses how to re-orientate IB towards meaningful inclusion of sustainability. Second, he uses four common students' types by categories to highlight the specific challenges that arise when students are confronted with sustainability issues. The chapter proposes some strategies that may be utilised to effectively rev up sustainability agenda within business and management studies.

Chapter 6 looks at embedding sustainability into marketing. Teresa Heath and Sally McKechnie in this chapter contextualise marketing education for sustainability within the changing higher education landscape, which has been shaped by increasing demands from international and national stakeholders to develop sustainability literacy amongst students. They share their experiences of embedding sustainability within a new marketing course by focusing predominantly on environmental and green issues. The chapter discusses some pedagogical matters and practices in this area. Drawing on a review of literature on marketing and the environment and on examples from practice, the chapter suggests ways to engage students with sustainability issues from the outset and to facilitate their learning. It also reflects on some of the challenges of this endeavour and ways to overcome them.

Chapter 7 describes the integration of sustainability into finance education. Will Oulton, concerned with barrage of questions on his recommendation for someone wanting to move into a career in sustainability and specifically sustainable finance, motivated him to explore the history of sustainable investment and finance. Notwithstanding the laudable effort of several initiatives geared towards embracing sustainability, it is yet to be mainstreamed appropriately into the financial industry. Despite the huge awareness, implementation still lacks depth across many financial institutions. Oulton submits that it is in this aspect that business schools and other higher education can play a leading and huge role to address some of the current gaps.

In Chap. 8, Fred A. Yamoah explores sustainability in supply and value chain management. The chapter argues that supply and value chain management has long been closely related to sustainability because of its direct impact on sustainable development. Yamoah, however, agrees that increased integration of sustainability into supply and value chain management could transform the discipline. He further highlights the challenges encountered in integrating sustainability in the United Kingdom.

In Chap. 9, Simon Graham examines sustainability, management education, and professions from a practitioner perspective. He re-echoes the fact that the business world is changing radically and so the skills needed by people who lead the corporations are also changing. Businesses are seen as positive agents of social, environmental, and economic change and as such, the skills and experiences of practitioners and business leaders must reflect the changing realities. Based on research and years of cumulative experience, it is clear that the business world needs to foster sustainable leadership. The chapter suggests that BAMs can help in this regard through the 6 (six) Cs—Curriculum, Context, Communication, Collaboration, Connection, and Challenge.

Chapter 10 presents a practical inter-university collaboration on teaching sustainability, which is a rare innovation. The chapter examines how three faculty across two European business schools (i.e. Cranfield School of Management, United Kingdom, and Rotterdam Business School, Netherlands) have collaborated over a decade with the single goal of improving the effectiveness and impact of the teaching of corporate responsibility and sustainability amongst graduate management students (MBAs and other management Masters). The chapter suggests the *integrating model* as a potential tool to aid the teaching of business responsibility and sustainability in other business schools both with pre- and post-work experience post graduate students and to form the basis of future research on embedding the principles of responsible business.

In all, the chapters have remained as practical as possible. The essence is to foster a knowledge sharing space and a support mechanism for faculty members of BAMs who want to rethink their teaching through the sustainability lens. Sustainability is a journey. It can only continue to evolve. The evolution, in itself, will present new challenges and difficulties. However, with the right mindset and orientation, adapting to and overcoming the challenges will be much easier than the absence of those. We hope that fellow academics and other management educators will find this book very useful.

Reference

World Commission on Environment and Development (WCED). 1987. *Our Common Future, Report of the World Commission on Environment and Development*. Oxford and New York: Oxford University Press.

2

Embedding Sustainability in the Entrepreneurship Curriculum

Frances M. Amatucci

Introduction

In this chapter the intersection of sustainability and entrepreneurship is explored. There are ample opportunities to introduce sustainability concepts into entrepreneurship education since they employ innovation and creativity in both product and business model applications. The chapter describes these opportunities and why sustainability and entrepreneurship are integrally related. The sustainability revolution requires a paradigmatic shift in the way entrepreneurship education is delivered both in content and in process (Amatucci et al. 2013). A new look at the traditional business plan with sustainability principles included is developed. A case study of sustainability and entrepreneurship as it has evolved in a public university in the United States is provided as an example.

F. M. Amatucci (✉)
Slippery Rock University of Pennsylvania, Slippery Rock, PA, USA
e-mail: frances.amatucci@sru.edu

© The Author(s) 2019
K. Amaeshi et al. (eds.), *Incorporating Sustainability in Management Education*,
https://doi.org/10.1007/978-3-319-98125-3_2

Sustainability in Entrepreneurship Education

Sustainability entrepreneurship has evolved from its earlier forms as eco-preneurship (Ivanko and Kivirist 2008; Schaper 2005; Bennett 1991) and 'green' entrepreneurship (Schaper 2005; Berle 1991). Moreover, it is separate from but related to social entrepreneurship (Short et al. 2009; Tilley and Young 2009). Sustainability and entrepreneurship intersect in many ways, the most important of which is the innovation—the creation of new products, processes, business models, and technologies. Innovation is at the heart of entrepreneurship and sustainability-related innovation is evident in the proliferation of green chemistry, clean energy technologies, organic food, biomimicry, green buildings, and biomaterials, to name a few (Larson 2011, 2012). The sustainability revolution of the twenty-first century has taken hold and is integrally linked to the entrepreneurship revolution of the twentieth century.

Several scholars have proposed a 'call to action' in entrepreneurship education to recognize a paradigmatic shift in the way entrepreneurship is taught (Amatucci et al. 2013; Nadim and Singh 2011). Parhankangas et al. (2015) review the similarities and differences between corporate social responsibility (CSR) and sustainability and conclude that the CSR model is more appropriate for large, established firms, while the sustainability model is better suited for entrepreneurial ventures. Determining factors included the opportunities for new ventures to develop new business models, engage in disruptive innovation, and focus on niche markets. Kuckertz and Wagner (2010) conducted research that suggests that individuals who embrace sustainability have stronger entrepreneurial intentions.

Nearly 10,000 companies from 161 countries commit to the ten principles of the United Nations Global Compact related to human rights, anti-corruption, labor, and environment. Over 600 business schools have committed to the six principles developed by the Principles for Responsible Management Education (PRME) initiative. Evidence strongly suggests the need for issues related to sustainability be embedded in business school curricula. So how has entrepreneurship education evolved to address this need? Have we, as educators, kept up with the sea change caused by sustainability?

There is good news and there is bad news. There is a proliferation worldwide of sustainability-related centers within business schools, many of them associated with entrepreneurship for the purpose of education and outreach. Likewise, many business schools are developing sustainable entrepreneurship courses. A search or inquiry on any of the related list servers will yield numerous responses from colleagues who are eager to share their course syllabi. There is no shortage of information if one seeks it. Moreover, major professional associations involving entrepreneurship, that is, the Academy of Management, the International Council of Small Business and Entrepreneurship, and the US Association of Small Business and Entrepreneurship, chose sustainability for annual conference themes providing opportunities for faculty to participate in teaching seminars, workshops, research presentations, and so on that are useful for tenure and promotion.

The bad news is that we still have much progress to make to create that paradigmatic shift so sustainability is embedded and not stand alone (Laszlo and Zhexembayeva 2011). Most entrepreneurship textbooks still do not incorporate sustainability into the entrepreneurial process of opportunity recognition, industry/market analysis, business modeling, financial reporting, and so on. Templates for business models or business plans typically do not include cues to consider sustainability issues at the time of start-up, with some exceptions (Spinelli and Adams 2016). In the 1990s scholars coined the term 'born global' for new ventures that engage in international growth from the start (Cavusgil and Knight 2009; Oviatt and McDougall 1995). Prior to that, entrepreneurial start-ups were considered primarily for domestic growth, while multinational corporations employed global markets. Today no one questions the 'born global' phenomenon.

Entrepreneurship education needs to progress in the same way. From the beginning many entrepreneurs embrace values related to clean, organic, natural, local, or recyclable. Jeffrey Hollander, founder of Seventh Generation, recognized a market opportunity to create laundry products that were all natural and without harsh chemicals. There is a long list of successful corporations developed by sustainability entrepreneurs who created companies that embrace these values from the start. If sustainability issues are not embedded in entrepreneurship education, they are considered to be optional add-ons that 'maybe' are important. If they are embedded in the models, they are given greater visibility and greater importance.

Sustainability has a justifiable 'place at the table' in entrepreneurship education. But not all entrepreneurship education occurs in universities. Small business counselors need to be given the information they need to inform entrepreneurs and small business owners that practices regarding 'reduce, re-use, recycle' are not the right thing to do but they will also result in cost savings. Yet, many business counselors are not prepared themselves to provide such information. There is an increasing number of organizations that provide information for start-ups regarding water and energy use, recycling, and waste disposal.

A New Look at an Old Friend: The Business Plan

An example of a typical business plan template that is modified to address sustainability issues at each part is provided in Table 2.1 (Amatucci and McKinney 2014). Within the business plan, the entrepreneur has several opportunities to include sustainability. In the Company Overview, typically included in the beginning of the plan, the owner has the opportunity to indicate where sustainability fits into the overall mission and philosophy of the firm. Describing the role of sustainability in business operations, the community impact, employee policies, and products and services reinforces that the philosophy has meaning for the firm.

If the business strategy involves the product(s) to be 'green', the section on Product Description is where this discussion occurs. If the product itself is not 'green', there is also an opportunity to discuss its impact on the environment, reduction of waste in packaging, disposition plans if electronic waste is involved, and other product-related sustainability issues.

The Market Analysis section of the business plan includes the industry overview, market research, and customer and competitor analysis. This section provides several opportunities for highlighting and examining the viewpoints of the industry, in general, toward sustainability. It also presents opportunities where the firm can differentiate itself from competitors,

Table 2.1 Sample business plan including sustainability issues

Business plan section	Traditional overview of contents	Sustainability
Executive summary	• Is NOT an introduction • A mini-business plan in one or two pages • Typically written last	Summarize the role that sustainability plays in your business
Company overview	• Brief Company Introduction • Mission statement: Concise statement of target audience, contribution product makes to customer, uniqueness • Location, size, history • Market and products (Differentiate from others) • Overview of company capabilities	Describe the role of sustainability (people, planet, profit) in your business mission/ philosophy, business operations, products/ services and community relationships. Employees and community as key external stakeholders. Impact of company operations on the environment.
Description of product/service	• What makes your product or service unique? What is your secret Sauce? What 'pain' do you solve? • How is it used? • Has any test marketing been done? • Is there potential for growth? • Do you own any patents, trademarks, copyrights? • Product safety	Discuss sustainability or 'green' aspects of your product or service.

Market analysis: industry overview	• Overview sets the stage for more specific data
	• Industry definition and description
	  – Major players within the industry
	  – Factors driving dynamics
	  – New products and developments
	• Historical and future trends
		• What are legislation and policies driving the industry toward sustainability?
		• Where is industry regarding sustainability?

(continued)

Table 2.1 (continued)

Business plan section	Traditional overview of contents	Sustainability

Market analysis: specific market research	• Market definition
	  – Primary market
	  – Secondary markets
	• Market size and trends
	  – Current total revenues
	• Predicted annual growth rate
		• Market segments for specific product/service.
		• Demand for both product lines (green and traditional)?
		• What sustainability certifications are desirable to obtain (product, firm, staff)

Market analysis: customers	Customer Characteristics • Who are they? • Why do they buy? • How is their need satisfied by the product/ service? • How is this need currently filled? • What are the alternatives? • Who makes the decision to buy? • How frequently do they purchase? • What is size of market?	• In which green segment do customers fall? • Why do they buy 'green'? • How is their need satisfied by the product/ service? • How is this need currently filled? • What are the alternatives?

Market analysis: competitors	• Direct Competitors
	  – Who are they?
	  – Size and product breadth
	  – Revenues and profitability
	  – Strengths and weaknesses
	  – Market shares
	• Indirect Competitors
	• Why is my business better?
		• Why is my business better?—Sustainability is important in this differentiation
		• 'Green' should be a category in the comparison of all facets with competitors

(continued)

Table 2.1 (continued)

Business plan section	Traditional overview of contents	Sustainability
Marketing strategy	Product, Promotion, Price, Place • Product marketplace advantages (warrantees, service policies, incentives, etc.) • How will I tell my customers about my product or service? (advertising, promotions, social media, publicity) • What should I charge for my product? (Price) • How will I get my product to my customers? (Distribution)	Sustainable practices can be an advantage in all of '4 Ps': • Product: Sustainable attributes can be a distinguishable competitive advantage • Promotion: Message that product is Green attracts customers • Price: Often can charge more • Distribution: 'Local' and/or efficiency/ sustainable fuels in transportation can be a favorable message and reduce costs
Operations plan	Manufacturing/Production Plan • Objectives • Facilities (Physical Plant) • Staffing • Subcontractors • Quality Control • Budget/Operating Expense • Concerns for employee health and safety	• 'Cradle to cradle' approach (McDonough and Braungart, 2002) • Sustainability initiatives for Facilities, Processes, Quality Control and Operating expenses. Tax and utility incentives to increase Return on Investment (ROI) of 'green' investments. Include green certifications for staff.
Management and organization	• Describe the key players of your management team, board of directors, advisors, as well as any major investors. • Discuss how your team completes the 'management trinity': production, marketing, and financial expertise. • Discuss what are the holes in the team and how do you plan to fill them	• Hire a team that embraces sustainability principles • Employee reward and compensation that is fair and shows salary equity • Gender equality • A diverse workforce • Safe working conditions • Develop a culture that supports sustainability • Sustainability oriented certifications for staff

(continued)

Table 2.1 (continued)

Business plan section	Traditional overview of contents	Sustainability
Financials	• Sources and uses of financial capital • 3 years of historical and projected income statements, cash flow, balance sheets and assumptions • Projected breakeven analysis • 3 years of tax returns • Personal financial statement	• Triple bottom line principles can be built into the financial plan: monetary profit, environmental impact, and community impact. • Discuss ROI of sustainability initiatives
Social/ environmental impacts	• Historically used when predicting job creation and retention • Also used to describe community relations and environmental stewardship	• There is increasing interest in this component of a business plan. • Job creation (When pursuing public financing, there are often requirements per increment of funding) • Sustainability efforts • Environmental impacts • Community relationships and impacts • Triple Bottom Line (people, planet, profitability) • Stakeholder engagement
Appendices	Show supporting documentation to your business plan in the appendices/exhibits: • Sales to date (customer list) • Pending orders/contracts • Loan/funding commitments • Legal Agreements • Other	Include copies of certifications, publicity received resulting from sustainability efforts, contracts/orders, efforts underway for further greening of the business.

Source: Amatucci and McKinney (2014); McKinney, M. (2013); Amatucci and Grimm (2011)

forge ahead of competition on existing and potential regulatory issues, examine what strategies will attract customers, and determine how sustainability can be a tool to help the firm position itself to excel over competitors.

The Marketing Strategy section provides an opportunity for a sustainable philosophy to benefit the firm in its pricing, distribution, promotion, and product attributes. A growing number of customers have indicated they will buy and pay more for a sustainable product and '4 P' strategies can be identified in the business plan to attract this segment. If a firm chooses to add a green product line, this section will assist the firm to attract customers.

The Operations section of the business plan is ideal for explaining the firm's sustainable processes including such efforts as energy and water reductions, movements toward more sustainable sources of energy, compliance with waste and pollution regulations, quality control processes, conservation of other resources, supplier sourcing, and transportation policies.

The Management section is always a key component of the business plan because the firm's success is dependent upon its management team. For a firm that indicates that sustainability is a priority, it is important to demonstrate this through the Management and Organization section. Information such as management and team commitment to sustainability, gender equity, safe workplace conditions, equity in employee reward and compensation systems, staff sustainability certifications, and the culture that the company promotes internally and externally will convey the firm's commitment and dedication to these principles.

In the Financial section of the plan, the firm can begin the process of indicating not only financial profit projections but also the environmental and social monetary benefits to the firm, completing the pillars of the triple bottom line. Many Fortune 500 companies have been including these components in their annual reports and both national and international organizations such as the United Nations and the Global Reporting Initiative (GRI) have been presenting models of indicators upon which firms can build reporting structures on the three pillars of the triple bottom line. Small businesses can report on savings generated from energy, water, and waste reductions, reductions in carbon footprint, tax and/or utility rebates utilized for improvements, as well as goodwill generated from employee and community interventions and relationships. If the firm has information on how green building or other initiatives have contributed to reductions in employee sick time or has undertaken efforts to increase motivation, this should be reported as well. Eventually a standardized triple bottom line accounting system will be perfected and its use will grow. Businesses that begin developing internal measures will be ahead of their competitors in being able to report their advances.

Historically, the Social/Environmental Impacts section of a business plan focused primarily on jobs created per defined increment of financing and compliance with environmental regulations. With the increasing focus on the triple bottom line, this section can serve as a summary of the company's efforts in the sustainability area which have been portrayed throughout the plan. The firm can display evidence of its greening efforts depicted throughout the plan in the Appendices of the business plan.

Case Study: Sustainability and Entrepreneurship at Slippery Rock University

Slippery Rock University

Slippery Rock University (SRU) is 1 of 14 public universities in the Pennsylvania State System of Higher Education (the State System). It was founded in 1889 as a normal school for teacher training but has expanded to currently include four colleges—the College of Business, College of Education, College of Liberal Arts and College of Health, Environment and Science. Approximately 8500 students are enrolled in a variety of undergraduate and graduate degree programs across the four colleges.

Since its founding in 1889, SRU has a long tradition of embracing core values that are consistent with civic responsibility and sustainability (Slippery Rock University 2018). In 1990, the Robert A. Macoskey Center for Sustainable Systems Education and Research (RAMC) was founded and a unique graduate program, the Master of Science in Sustainable Systems (MS3), the first graduate program focusing on sustainability in the country, was initiated. The Pennsylvania Climate Action Plan detailing what the state will undertake to reduce greenhouse gas (GHG) emissions was completed in 2009. SRU was the first signatory in the State System to commit the university to net climate neutrality.

The SRU Office of Sustainability collects information and coordinates university sustainability initiatives including Earth Day celebrations and the Energy Action Pledge. The President's Commission on Sustainability is comprised of a cross-section of representatives from the SRU community to advise the president on sustainability initiatives, strategies, and policies.

SRU is a member of the Association for the Advancement of Sustainability in Higher Education (AASHE) since 2009. Taking full advantage of its membership, SRU received the Silver rating in its recent submission to Sustainability Tracking Assessment & Rating System (STARS) for its sustainability curriculum and initiatives. SRU has consistently been rated as one of Princeton Review's 'Green Colleges'. The university reduced its GHG emissions by 22 percent from 2005 to 2014 and is committed to achieving carbon neutrality by 2037. It also consistently makes the Sierra Club's Top 100 Cool Schools and the top 100 schools in the University of Indonesia's International Green Metric Survey.

Organizations within the university that facilitate execution of its sustainability initiatives include:

• *Robert A. Macoskey Center*: The RAMC was created in 1990 to promote sustainability at SRU and in the local community. The center is located on 83 acres of the university campus and enacts its mission in three ways: education about sustainability, physical demonstration of sustainable technologies and systems, and supporting sustainability-focused academic initiatives and research. The Harmony House is a newly renovated facility certified LEED-Silver for existing buildings—operation and maintenance—and serves as a classroom and public meeting space.

- *Weather and air quality observatory (WAQO)*: The PA Departmental of Environmental Protection has partnered with SRU to operate a WAQO on the SRU campus. This observatory produces environmental data that is publicly available to the Slippery Rock community and serves as an excellent resource for both teaching and research.
- *McKeever Environmental Learning Center*: Realizing that we have a responsibility for the world in which future generations will live, the Commonwealth of Pennsylvania created the McKeever Center in 1974. The McKeever Center is a public service institute of the State System and is administered by SRU. The McKeever Environmental Learning Center is a facility that runs a variety of environmental education programs including Earthkeepers, Sunship Earth, and Web of Life. Each year, thousands of school-aged students and hundreds of teachers participate in McKeever Environmental Learning Center's environmental education programs that offer residential and non-residential programs for schools throughout the year.
- *Sustainable Enterprise Accelerator (SEA)*: In 2010 the SEA was created from an Entrepreneurial Leadership grant from the State System. The main objective of the SEA is to have student entrepreneurs and established businesses work together to create a world of sustainable businesses. It is described in greater detail in the next section.

A summary of all sustainability initiatives at the university level can be found at http://www.sru.edu/about/sustainability. Thus, it is obvious that the overall university environment contributes to a mindset of sustainability that can easily be transferred to the business school curriculum and entrepreneurship, in particular.

School of Business

Along with the support from various organizations within the university, the School of Business sustainability initiatives are influenced by several external and internal stakeholders. Of particular mention are the PRME and Association to Advance Collegiate Schools of Business (AACSB). These are described in the following paragraph.

Principles for Responsible Management Education (PRME)

The PRME initiative developed by the United Nations Global Compact has had a significant effect on incorporating sustainability into business school curricula. Moreover, PRME's partnerships with accreditation bodies such as AACSB, EFMD Quality Improvement System (EQUIS), and Association of MBAs (AMBA) increase the organization's visibility and credibility. The School of Business became a signatory institution in 2014 and it is the first university in the State System to do so. In 2016 it submitted the first Sharing in Progress (SIP) report, which is publicly available on the PRME website. Multiple presentations at department meetings, retreats, and strategic planning meetings encouraged faculty to adopt PRME principles into the classroom.

As part of the PRME initiative, a repository of sustainability-related teaching materials for each discipline (accounting human resources, management, etc.) was developed and is available to all School of Business faculty. The 2016 SIP contains a curriculum mapping of core courses that include content related to the 17 sustainable development goals (SDGs) promulgated by the United Nations the previous year (see Table 2.2). The PRME initiative has been a major force in the adoption of sustainability within the curriculum.

Sustainable Enterprise Accelerator: CEDBA to SEA

In 2009 the School of Business received a $250,000 grant from the State System for the purpose of developing programs that promote entrepreneurship on the campus. The initial charter of the Center for Economic Development and Business Advancement (CEDBA) was entrepreneurship education and outreach. Very soon after, sustainability was added to the list of priorities and in 2010 the CEDBA became the SEA. The main objective of the SEA is to have students and established businesses work together to create a world of sustainable businesses. The SEA offers three-credit internship opportunities and utilizes a 'hands on', practical approach to teaching entrepreneurship and sustainability.

Table 2.2 2016 UN SDGs and School of Business (BSBA) core curriculum

	A210 Accounting	A340 Law	B303 Statistics	B458 Strategy	E201 Microecon	E202 Macroecon	M320 Op Mgmt	M351 Org Beha	Mk330 Marketing
No poverty			M,TB,A		T,M,C,A	T,M,C	M	M	C
Zero hunger			M,C			TB			C
Good health and well-being	M,T,C,A		M,TB	M,C	M,C,A	T			C
Quality education	C,A		M		M,C	M		C	C
Gender equality				C	TB	M,C		M	C
Clean water and sanitation			C	C		M,C			C
Affordable and clean energy			M,TB,C	T,C	M	M,C			C
Decent work and economic growth	M,T,C,A		T,C,A	C	T,M,C,A		M	M,C	TB
Industry, innovation and infrastructure	M,T,C,A		T,C,A	C	T,M,A	T,M,A	M	C	M,TB,C
Reduced inequalities			M,C	T,C	T,C	T,C		M,C	
Sustainable cities and communities						M,C			C
Responsible consumption and production	C,A		TB,C	T,M		M,C	M	M,C	M,C
Climate action			M	T,C		M,C			C
Life below water			M,TB,C			C			C
Life on land			M,TB,C	T,C					C
Peace, justice, and strong institutions	C,A	T	T,M,C,A		T,M,C,A	T,M,C		T,M,C	C
Partnerships for the goals	C,A		M,C	T		M			C

Source: SRU School of Business Sharing in Progress Report http://www.unprme.org/reports/SRUPRMESIP2016.pdf
T, Text Chapter; M, Module within a Chapter; TB, Topic Box; C, Current Events; A, Assignment; A210, Managerial Accounting; A340—Legal Env. of Business; B303, Issues in Global Business; B458 Business Capstone; E201, Macroeconomics; E202, Microeconomics; M320, Operations Management; M351, Organizational Behavior; Mk330, Principles of Marketing

Curriculum Design and Development

In addition to the SEA internships, there are the following four three-credit courses that have a primary focus on sustainability: (1) economics of sustainable development; (2) management and society; (3) sustainability, entrepreneurship, and innovation; and (4) sustainable business consulting. This chapter focuses on the last two since they are directly related to entrepreneurship.

Sustainability, Entrepreneurship, and Innovation

There are several pedagogical approaches to teaching a course related to sustainability and entrepreneurship. When this course was first developed in 2011, there were few entrepreneurship textbooks that included sustainability concepts. The most one could find is a chapter at the end of the textbook on social entrepreneurship. That has somewhat changed as traditional entrepreneurship textbooks are incorporating sustainability cases such as TOMS Shoes, Warby Parker, d.light, and LuminAID (Barringer and Ireland 2016). There are several instructional design approaches an instructor can adopt:

1. *Use a mainstream entrepreneurship textbook and sustainability text*: While this approach provides breadth and comprehensiveness in content for both fields, it can be expensive. An example would be using an entrepreneurship text such as Barringer and Ireland (2016) with sustainability texts (Gittell et al. 2012; Larson 2011; Dean 2014).
2. *Use a mainstream entrepreneurship textbook with supplementary sustainability references*: There are many entrepreneurship textbooks on the market that provide sufficient coverage of the entrepreneurial process. The text is then supplemented with articles about sustainability that can be downloaded for free from the university library and/or cases. This cuts the costs for students but may take additional time for the instructor to source the supplementary materials. The text may also be supplemented with cases that incorporate issues related to sustainability and entrepreneurship (Moroz et al. 2014; Rothaermel and Janovec 2012; Laszlo et al. 2012).

3. *Use a mainstream sustainability text with supplementary entrepreneurship references*: Unlike entrepreneurship, there are fewer texts that focus just on sustainability. However, availability is increasing (Blackburn 2015; Larson 2011; Laszlo and Zhexembayeva 2011). There is a plethora of entrepreneurship resources available on the Internet as well as free downloads from the university library.
4. *Use online references for both sustainability and entrepreneurship*: While this may be the least expensive option for students, it takes more time for the instructor to source and organize these classroom materials.

These approaches have been adopted for a typical 13–15-week semester, but can be modified for shorter semesters. However, it is difficult to require a full business plan in a semester that is less than eight weeks in length. This depends on whether the students are graduates or undergraduates and their level of preparation coming into the course. Regardless of which approach the instructor chooses, it is useful to include an experiential exercise, usually involving a feasibility analysis, business modeling, or business plan. Through a faculty member, the School of Business has a relationship with the Business of Humanity® Project (www.boh.pitt.edu) at the University of Pittsburgh, which organizes a new venture case competition during the semester. Student teams develop their ideas which include elements of 'humanism' in the business model and compete against teams from other universities. The competition took place in the middle of the 15-week fall semester and was ideally timed for students to submit a shorter version of their feasibility analyses. An example of a typical course module for a 13-week semester is provided in Exhibit 5.1.

Regardless of such a competition, student teams are required to develop a feasibility analysis on a new venture involving sustainability. Students become highly engaged in the project during the semester. Because the assignment requires a great deal of research using a computer, the course is typically held in a computer laboratory. The course is only available as an elective to management and marketing majors. Due to prerequisites, only students outside the School of Business who minor in business are able to enroll.

Sustainable Business Consulting

The Sustainable Business Consulting class is an elective for seniors who are management or marketing majors. The course is designed for student field-based consulting and follows the guidelines of the Small Business Institute® (http://smallbusinessinstitute.org). This type of experiential learning where student teams work on specific problems of clients who are from the local business community provides an opportunity to apply classroom learning to real-world situations. The course design effectively addresses aspects of the School of Business mission involving engagement, impact, outreach, and service learning. In addition to the consulting projects, there are supplemental resources such as a small business text and sustainability cases like the sustainability consulting case InterfaceRAISE (Rothaermel and Janovec 2012) and the Clarke pesticide case (Laszlo et al. 2012).

Anyone who has taught a course like this knows some of its challenges since it is not a typical lecture course, but an experiential exercise involving a real-world problem and a client—not 'just' a professor. Students work in teams with clients who have problems with their firms. We typically try to find projects that involve sustainability but that is not always possible. If the project does not involve sustainability, the students are required to draft a sustainability plan for the client that involves the usual 'reduce, re-use, recycle' processes. The course is best offered with prerequisites that include some basic coursework covering entrepreneurship and sustainability.

Although students often encounter challenges related to coursework application, more common issues are related to teamwork, time management, and communication. It forces the students, and sometimes the inexperienced professor, outside their comfort zones due to the lack of structure and control. For instance, team meetings not only have to be synchronized with students but also with business owners who have limited time and often do not respond to e-mails. It is important to choose a client who will work well with the students and be available when needed. That is not always an easy task. Clients can be found in a variety of ways, including contacting the local Chamber of Commerce. It is also important to create as much structure as possible by developing a tentative course schedule that provides topic areas and deadlines so students have some sense of stability and certainty about deliverables.

Still, students enjoy the experience and the opportunity to gain a strong recommendation in the job market and another line of achievements on their resume.

> I would just like to first start off by saying how much we enjoyed working with our client (sustainable microbrewery) this semester, and how much this project helped me in figuring out my career path in life. I hope that he will take our ideas seriously and implement them to increase the market share that he wants for his company.
>
> After we took a look at her business plan, we realized that it could be better. The problems included the lack of financials, disorganization, repetitiveness, and missing sections. I think the two most valuable things I learned during the completion of this assignment are important and will follow me through my life. The first would have to be patience with working with other students and the client, and the second is the overwhelming importance of organization and communication.

Successes and Failures

While the program in the School of Business at SRU has made great progress during the past five years, there have been challenges and there are still opportunities for growth. *First*, the entrepreneurship curriculum is not a cross-campus, cross-disciplinary initiative. In fact, it is not available to all business majors. Many schools have made great headway in expanding entrepreneurship outside the business school (Welsh 2014). There are numerous sustainability and entrepreneurship issues in health care, engineering, the performing arts, and other areas within the university. An action which would make the course more accessible to non-business majors is to eliminate the prerequisites. *Second*, these initiatives mostly depend on a few faculty who serve as champions for the cause. While many faculty claim to support sustainability, it takes a real effort to change pedagogical approaches and adopt the 'green lens' in all aspects of the curriculum. As with any change effort, this will take time.

A *third* challenge is to leverage the use of the 17 SDGs as a means to embed sustainability into the curriculum. It is necessary to communicate and reinforce to both faculty and students that the SDGs are entrepreneurial opportunities that create innovative solutions to world problems. Members of the PRME task force have been instrumental in communicating the PRME principles and SDGs throughout the school.

Conclusion

The purpose of this chapter is to review sustainability and entrepreneurship education. Both are integrally related because of their common dependence of innovation. While much progress has been made with regard to embedding sustainability in entrepreneurship courses, there is much more work to be done. The chapter includes a case study of sustainability and entrepreneurship at a university in the United States. The case study of embedding sustainability in entrepreneurship education at SRU shows the benefits of having higher-level support from the university and from external organizations. Academics in business schools from less supportive contexts can leverage the principles promulgated by the United Nations Global Compact and the PRME. Moreover, major accreditation bodies such as AACSB, Accreditation Council for Business Schools and Programs (ACBSP), and EFMD/EQUIS are supportive and can assist faculty in convincing administrators that sustainability initiatives, in curriculum and research, can be rewarding. Entrepreneurship and sustainability have a symbiotic relationship that can hardly be separated in the business school curriculum in the twenty-first century.

Sustainability in Entrepreneurship

Proposed Module

Week One	Course introduction. What is entrepreneurship? Who are entrepreneurs? Trends in global entrepreneurship. What is sustainability entrepreneurship? (Tragedy of the commons, limits to growth theory, anthropogenic changes in the environment, cradle to cradle)
Week Two	Sustainability entrepreneurship (continued) Opportunity recognition Case: 'Andrew Kellar and Simply Green Biofuels'
Week Three	Opportunity recognition (industry/market gaps and trends) Opportunities emanating from sustainability (clean energy, clean products, green supply chains, biomimicry, green chemistry, building design, water usage, etc.) in ALL sectors of the economy around the world. Case: 'Clarke: Transformation for Environmental Sustainability'
Week Four	Introduction to feasibility analysis feasibility analysis Sustainable business idea generation (develop a half page description of a business venture that incorporates sustainability issues)
Week Five	Product service analysis. What is your value proposition? How does it address an environmental trend, solve a problem, or fill a gap in the marketplace? Develop preliminary market research survey.
Week Six	Industry/market analysis (industries related to sustainability, trends, growth rate, market segmentation) Case: Clean energy, organic/natural food, and so on
Week Seven	Marketing strategy (sustainability and pricing, packing, advertising and sourcing) Radical transparency Case: 'Jeffrey Hollender and Seventh Generation'

Week Eight	Present feasibility analyses
Week Nine	Business modeling for sustainable businesses Case: 'Ray Anderson and Interface'
Week Ten	Management strategy (vision, mission, core values, building a team that embraces sustainable business practices, culture, human resource strategy.) Case: 'Growing tentree: Social Enterprise, Social Media, and Environmental Sustainability'
Week Eleven	Green Supply Chain Management (local sourcing, water and energy conservation, cradle to cradle) Case: 'Green Mountain Coffee'
Week Twelve	Financial and Accounting Issues, financial statement analysis, sources of funding, CERES, GRI Case: Timberland and Vanity Fair
Week Thirteen	Present final business plans

Adopted from Barringer and Ireland (2016) and Gittell et al. (2012)

References

Amatucci, Frances, and Mary McKinney. 2014. Sustainability and the Business Plan. Paper presented at the 38th annual meeting of the Small Business Institute®, Las Vegas, Nevada, February, 14–16.

Amatucci, Frances, Nelson Pizarro, and Jay Friedlander. 2013. Sustainability: A Paradigmatic Shift in Entrepreneurship Education. *New England Journal of Entrepreneurship* 16 (1): 7–18.

Amatucci, Frances, and Richard Grimm. 2011. Re-Inventing the Business Plan Process for Sustainable Start-Ups. *Journal of Strategic Innovation and Sustainability* 7 (1): 154–159.

Barringer, Bruce, and R. Duane Ireland. 2016. *Entrepreneurship: Successfully Launching New Ventures*. 5th ed. Boston, MA: Pearson.

Bennett, Steven J. 1991. *Ecopreneuring: The Complete Guide to Small Business Opportunities from the Environmental Revolution*. New York: Wiley.

Berle, Gustav. 1991. *The Green Entrepreneur: Business Opportunities that Can Save the Earth and Make You Money*. Blue Ridge Summit, PA: Liberty Hall Press.

Blackburn, William R. 2015. *The Sustainability Handbook: The Complete Management Guide to Achieving Social, Economic and Environmental Responsibility*. 2nd ed. Washington, DC: The Environmental Law Institute.

Cavusgil, S. Tamer, and Gary Knight. 2009. *Born Global Firms: A New International Enterprise*. New York: Business Expert Press, LLC..

Dean, Thomas. 2014. *Sustainable Venturing: Entrepreneurial Opportunity in the Transition to a Sustainable Economy*. New York: Pearson.

Gittell, Ross, Matt Magnusson, and Michael Merenda. 2012. *The Sustainable Business Casebook*. Irvington, NY: Flatworld Knowledge. isbn:978-1-4533-4677-8.

Ivanko, John, and Lisa Kivirist. 2008. *ECOpreneuring*. Gabriola Island, Vancouver: New Society Publishers.

Kuckertz, Andreas, and Marcus Wagner. 2010. The Influence of Sustainability Orientation on Entrepreneurial Intentions—Investigating the Role of Business Experience. *Journal of Business Venturing* 25 (5): 524–539.

Larson, Andrea. 2011. *Sustainability, Innovation and Entrepreneurship*. Irvington, NY: Flatworld Knowledge. isbn:978-1-4533-2725-8.

———. 2012. The New Strategic Frontier: Environment, Sustainability and Entrepreneurial Innovation. University of Virginia. UV2001, Darden Business Publishing.

Laszlo, C., and N. Zhexembayeva. 2011. *Embedded Sustainability: The Next Big Competitive Advantage*. New York: Routledge.

Laszlo, Chris, Katy McCabe, Eric Aheam, and Indrajeet Ghatge. 2012. Clarke: Transformation for Environmental Sustainability. Case Western Reserve University Fowler Center for Sustainable Value W12820, Ivey Publishing.

McDonough, William, and Michael Braungart. 2002. *Cradle to Cradle: Remaking the Way We Make Things*. New York: North Point Press.

McKinney, Mary. 2013. Writing a Business Plan Which Includes Sustainability Perspectives. Presentation at the 15th Annual Entrepreneur's Growth Conference, Duquesne University, Pittsburgh, PA, May 10, 2013.

Moroz, Peter, Simon Parker, and Edward Gamble. 2014. Growing Tentree: Social Enterprise, Social Media and Environmental Sustainability. Paul Hill School of Business, W14047, Ivey Publishing.

Nadim, Abbas, and Parbudyal Singh. 2011. A System's View of Sustainable Entrepreneurship Education. *Journal of Strategic Innovation and Sustainability* 7 (2): 105–114.

Oviatt, Benjamin, and Patricia McDougall. 1995. Global Start-Ups: Entrepreneurs on a Worldwide Stage. *Academy of Management Executive* 9 (2): 30–43.

Parhankangas, Annaleena, Abagail McWilliams, and Roy Shrader. 2015. Doing Well by Doing Better: Entrepreneurs and Sustainability. *Journal of Small Business Strategy* 24 (2): 1–20.

Rothaermel, Frank T., and Michael Janovec. 2012. InterfaceRAISE (in 2010): Raising the Bar in Sustainability Consulting. McGraw Hill Education MH0005, Harvard Business School Publishing.

Schaper, Michael. 2005. *Making Ecopreneurs: Developing Sustainable Entrepreneurship*. Hampshire: Ashgate Publishing Ltd.

Short, Jeremy, Todd Moss, and G.T. Lumpkin. 2009. Research in Social Entrepreneurship: Past Contributions and Future Opportunities. *Strategic Entrepreneurship Journal* 3: 161–194.

Slippery Rock University. 2018. Sustainability website accessed March 15, 2018. http://www.sru.edu/about/sustainability/legacy-of-sustainability; http://www.sru.edu/about/sustainability.

Spinelli, Stephen, and Rob Adams. 2016. *New Venture Creation: Entrepreneurship for the 21st Century*. McGraw Hill.

Tilley, Fiona, and William Young. 2009. Sustainability Entrepreneurs: Could They Be the True Wealth Generators of the Future? *Greener Management International* 55: 79–92.

Welsh, Dianne. 2014. *Creative Cross-Disciplinary Entrepreneurship: A Practical Guide for a Campus Wide Program*. New York: Palgrave Macmillan.

3

Sustainability Accounting and Education: Conflicts and Possibilities

Rob Gray

Introduction

The accounting literature has a long engagement and concern with educational issues: not least because of the critical tensions that seem inevitable in any approach to studying accounting. These tensions arise as a consequence of accounting's *apparently* procedural, technical and "neutral" nature, which is so frequently reinforced through an emphasis on rote learning, on getting answers "correct" and, broadly, in not encouraging a questioning approach to the subject (Lucas 2000; McPhail 2004; Thomson and Bebbington 2004, 2005). In more recent years, these tensions have been thrown into relief as a result of pedagogic studies, which have found that accounting students are inclined to emphasise shallow rather than deep learning (Gray et al. 1994; Thomson and Bebbington 2004).[1] These concerns are especially acute when matters such as ethics, social responsibility, social and environmental accounting and, now, sustainability have been brought to the accounting curriculum. Such topics

R. Gray (✉)
University of St Andrews, St Andrews, Fife, UK
e-mail: rhg1@st-andrews.ac.uk

© The Author(s) 2019
K. Amaeshi et al. (eds.), *Incorporating Sustainability in Management Education*,
https://doi.org/10.1007/978-3-319-98125-3_3

have not only struggled to find any place in the central accounting curriculum but have experienced degrees of resistance from educators and students alike as their often personal and challenging nature appears to sit so uncomfortably with normal conventions of accounting and its educational mores (see, e.g., Deegan 2016; Collison et al. 2014). After all, for many, education is not just about dispensing knowledge in a didactic fashion, it is much more about helping us understand who we are and how we should conduct ourselves in society (Thomson and Bebbington 2005, 508).

This short chapter will introduce a few of the key issues that have arisen when seeking to bring sustainability to the accounting classroom and although there are many ways in which aspects of sustainability might be introduced to the curriculum, I will argue that the fundamental questions relate to what you—as a teacher and/or student—believe to be the purpose of education (in accounting as elsewhere) and the extent to which education *must* carefully consider the implications of the very different conceptions of what sustainability actually means.

The chapter comprises four sections following this introduction. The section entitled "What is Accounting and Its Limits" looks broadly at accounting education, whilst "What Are We Actually Talking About?" explores differences in beliefs about sustainability and the very fundamental implications which these different beliefs have on how we approach accounting and its education. The section entitled "Sustainability Accounting?" then looks at what is meant by "sustainability accounting" and the final section, "Education", concludes with reflections upon the education process itself.

What Is Accounting and Its Limits?

At its simplest, accounting is typically seen as a series of integrated processes by which organisational activity is captured and then represented by financial numbers: which numbers are then subject to adjustment and consolidation in order to produce comprehensive financial summaries through which intelligent and informed persons—typically managers and investors—might make sensible economic decisions. These processes, adjustments and summaries are complex, numerous, intricate and often obscure and, without question, learning and applying these is undeniably demanding. Consequently accounting "education"—or more accurately "training"—can so frequently be entirely absorbed by this (undoubtedly important) detail and minutiae. But, this is not the whole story by any means. Accounting does not just describe events such as assets or profit; it creates them: in a crude sense they often do not exist until accounting recognises them (Hines 1988). Equally, accounting may appear to be a technology—a series of techniques—but it is a technology with considerable layers of ethics and political judgement embodied in it (McPhail 1999). Furthermore, the consequences of accounting are by no means simply economic—they are also social and environmental and stretch well beyond the conventional boundaries of the accounting entity (Gray et al. 2014). As if this were not enough, the techniques, their application and their justification are not always coherently articulated: at their worst they simply do not make sense and at their best they are open to manipulation, misunderstanding and mistake (Tinker 1985; Gambling 1978). And finally, the elephant in the room, believe it or not, is the question "what is (and by implication what is not) accounting?" This is a far from obvious question and whilst professional examinations and the predominant views of the accounting firms' clients are typically accepted as defining what accounting is, this is very highly contestable. In essence, accounting is whatever one decides it *should* be (Hines 1988; Gray and Collison 2002; Hopwood 2007) and what it *should* be is heatedly contested by "those in power, those seeking power and those opposing power" (Thomson and Bebbington 2004, 610).

In these circumstances, it is easy to see why there might be so many areas of potential conflict within education in accounting. Is the educators' duty to train the student or to develop independent enquiry? Is it appropriate to expose the ethical and political layers embedded in accounting? And what should one do when students find that their personal values conflict with the tenets and principles of accounting? How far should educators go in challenging the taken-for-granted assumptions about the limits of accounting? To what extent do accountants need to be equipped with the capacity to handle ethical matters and embrace—or at least critically assess—innovations? and so on (see e.g., Gray et al. 1994;

Lucas 2000; McPhail 1999, 2001, 2004). The challenge here is that whilst we might argue that a "good" education should encourage students to embrace different and conflicting points of view (Coulson and Thomson 2006), there is often little or no room for such difference in the classroom and such difference can be an anathema within professional examination and practice (Lee 1990).

One might have thought that there was room for such cognitive dissonance—even a requirement for such difference—in university accounting education. And yet, despite the very obvious inter-connectedness between social, ethical and environmental (notably sustainability) issues and accounting, there remains clear evidence that such matters are simply not entering mainstream accounting education (Deegan 2016; Humphrey et al. 1996; Gray and Collison 2002; Collison et al. 2014).

There are a range of reasons mooted in the literature as why this might be. First, there is the assertion that such matters are "not accounting": for whatever reason teachers, students and practitioners often have fairly fixed views as to what accounting is and is not. Why would one teach subjects not relevant to the curriculum? Second, in a number of related arguments, teachers observe that (i) there is more than enough in a conventional curriculum to keep one fully occupied; and/or (ii) of all the potential new (or peripheral) matters, why privilege issues such as sustainability?; and/or (iii) why introduce new material on which the teacher has little or no prior knowledge and diminish the areas of tuition in which they are relatively adept? (see, e.g., Gray et al. 2001)

These arguments, which derive, on the whole, from innate conservatism and self-disciplining amongst academics, can often find justification and support from the observation that "such matters" are being handled elsewhere. Whether it be a course in business ethics, environmental law, corporate social responsibility (CSR) or sustainability and society (e.g.), a conscientious teacher can legitimately infer that the students are getting the breadth needed elsewhere in the programme. Such views are by no means limited to accounting (Gray et al. 2001).

Perhaps the most rigorous explanation for accounting's resistance to these areas of "novelty" was initiated by Tom Lee (1990) and Fenton Robb (1989). They developed the argument that accounting acted as an autopoietic system which, essentially, embraced and absorbed those ideas which "coded" to its central architecture and rejected those which did not. In essence, if a notion fitted into existing accounting mores, the idea could be accepted; if it did not, it was rejected by the discipline. This argument has been developed in the literature (Power 1992). It has persuasive logic—even if it has proved difficult to substantiate empirically. Autopoiesis has certainly been useful in articulating many of the difficulties that have faced attempts to introduce sustainability into the accounting curriculum (Lawrence et al. 2013; Khan and Gray 2016) and it can easily be seen to encompass the more prosaic and conservative arguments we saw earlier.

There is now a considerable literature demonstrating the important reflexive relationship that accounting has with ethics, environment, society, justice, sustainability and so on (Gray et al. 2014; Bebbington et al. 2014). Whilst accounting may wish to avoid a consideration of life-threatening issues such as sustainability, it is more and more difficult to justify such a position (ICAEW 2004; Hopwood et al. 2010). And yet, there is more than enough evidence to suggest that accounting education continues to ignore sustainability. A simple observation of the number of courses within an accounting degree or professional education which do not mention it and/or the number of graduate accounting students who would not have met the notion in their studies is arguably evidence enough. It suggests that accounting can be thought to continue to act autopoietically, regardless of the critical and potentially life-threatening nature of the issues.

Only when we have some substantial understanding of this resistance might we begin to consider how sustainability could be embedded into the accounting curriculum. From a practical point of view, there is little value in innovative and exciting suggestions for sustainability education if those ideas are simply going to be ignored, rejected or, even, scorned.

What Are We Actually Talking About?

The context in which we might consider the inter-twining of sustainability and education is well summarised by Deegan (2016, 65–66). Essentially, despite 30 years of wide-ranging, often global initiatives, the inequalities of humanity and the desecration of the planet simply keep on getting worse. There is no longer much doubt that international financial capitalism, financial markets, corporations and accounting are all inescapably implicated in this situation.

What remains unclear—or, at least unresolved—is whether the *problematique* represented by un-sustainability can be resolved by humankind's current systems of organisation (international financial markets, profit, growth, corporations, etc.) or whether un-sustainability is actually the *result* of these very systems. At the risk of simplifying somewhat, the literature identifies the former view with something called "weak" sustainability and the latter point of view with what it calls "strong" sustainability. This distinction matters—and matters acutely in accounting and related business and economic studies. Crudely, if weak sustainability holds, then our existing systems of management and accounting may need tweaking and adjustment, but they can be considered essentially sound. If strong sustainability holds, then there is a very good chance that only through a drastic uprooting and fundamental surgery of our taken-for-granted systems might humanity manage to approach anything that looks like a sustainable future. Under strong sustainability, it is not at all obvious that anything we currently recognise as accounting, business, growth, profit or finance might be able to exist. That is a truly daunting prospect. It is one that many observers seem unable to accept (Hamilton 2010).

It is in this context that we now begin to see why questioning the very nature of education becomes so very important if we are to sensibly address sustainability. If one subscribes to the views of (e.g.) Thomson and Bebbington, then, at a minimum, one must look to education to help students—and subsequent practitioners—understand the differing points of view; to help them interrogate the arguments and evidence of the different world views (Spangenberg 2017); and to encourage and support them in coming to a (however tentative) conclusion. It is difficult to conclude that this is happening currently. It is as though accounting (and business and management education) is proving to be autopoietic and consequently only able to embrace the less drastic notions of sustainability—is only able to embrace the implications of a weak sustainability. Dyball and Thomson (2013) argue that accounting education for sustainability must extend beyond weak sustainability and it must recognise the possibilities of major social and economic transformations (303–304). Education crucially helps us to frame the issues (see, e.g., Longman 2015) and helps us to assess whether "our intellectual commitments are justified" (Thomson and Bebbington 2005, 511).

As far as one can tell, there seems to have been more exploration of how management and business education is responding to sustainability than there has in accounting. The management surveys are telling. For example, Landrum and Ohsowski (2017) find that the emphasis in sustainability in management education is on the weak form: the form which does not challenge existing models of business and management practice (Gray 2013). Isil and Hernke (2017) come to the same conclusion and argue that weak sustainability dominates in management education—in a manner which offers no challenge to conventional management thinking. And Cullen (2017) argues that there is a tendency to muddle ideas of sustainability with notions such as social responsibility or ethics and to rather miss the point of sustainability education. Indeed, Cullen argues, attempts to implement any sustainability education really require a broader systemic change within mindsets and the curriculum. My experience suggests that there is no reason not to generalise these views across to accounting (Gray et al. 2001; Collison et al. 2014).

The challenge to introduce a richer notion of sustainability into a possibly autopoietic system like accounting is considerable. History does not favour a positive outcome. Indeed, major attempts in the UK to develop environmental awareness throughout the curriculum—most notably the Toyne Report and HE21 in the 1990s—are remarkable in the minimal observable effect they had on disciplines (see, e.g., Gray et al. 2001; Gray and Collison 2002; Collison et al. 2014).

So, unless one is going to seek to fundamentally challenge the existing mores of accounting (and business) and actively seek to change mindsets and worldviews (Spangenberg 2017; Cullen 2017), education is going to either ignore sustainability altogether or only consider the weakest forms of sustainability (much as it seems to do now).

There is, however, some serious challenge to this rather stark binary choice.

There appears to be a growing awareness that the exigencies associated with strong sustainability are actually rather terrifying and something that many people in the modern world actually find unthinkable (Hamilton 2010; Marshall 2014; Adams 2015). Briefly, it seems that contemplation of strong sustainability can challenge an individual's sense of self and their place in society; it can instil sensations of hopelessness and futility and can set up seriously dysfunctional cognitive dissonance (see also Landrum and Ohsowski 2017). It may well be that an initial purpose of sustainability education is to help educators overcome such ennui and, possibly, that a major purpose of any education is to increase the potential to handle cognitive dissonance.

A more pragmatic approach is counselled by Stefan Schaltegger who, explicitly aware of the futility of counsels of despair, focuses exclusively on the positive messages of what might be—or indeed can be—achieved (Schaltegger et al. 2017). This is a project to "open up new spaces" as Baker and Schaltegger (2015) argue. So, for example, Etxeberria et al. (2017) take an explicitly corporate point of view and explore what new accountings might move the organisation closer to a sustainable direction. In doing so, they neatly side-step the unresolved conundrum as to whether they are simply adopting a weak sustainability position (which they would deny) or adopting an iterative and pragmatic approach to discovering strong sustainability through current possibilities and practices. The attractions of this sort of approach are very clear: whether they can or will deliver anything as radical as strong sustainability remains unresolved.

Sustainability Accounting?

If there are disagreements concerning the nature of sustainability and if the question of what is (or what is not) "accounting" is contestable, it will come as no surprise to learn that there is a considerable range of different things which find themselves labelled "sustainability accounting". This is not the place to review this range of possible "sustainability accountings" (but, see, e.g., Gray et al. 2014): all we can do is provide a brief idea of what this "accounting for sustainababble"[2] might look like.

In very simple terms, we might think of there being three very broad approaches to "sustainability accounting": those which fit relatively neatly into extant accounting practices (and extant accounting courses); those which take current accounting methods and practices and extend them in order to turn the ideas back onto themselves; and those approaches which try and capture a more holistic sense of sustainability which may, or more usually may not, find expression in the conventional accounting entity. These categories are intended simply to be illustrative and are certainly neither complete nor discrete.

Extant Accounting

There is little or no problem for accounting and for accounting education with the first of these approaches: in essence, some of the elements of ideas associated with sustainability are simply inserted into existing notions and programmes. So, management accounting has long recognised the notion of efficiency and the need to support management decisions: the integration of environmental management, investment appraisal for environmental risk and the pursuit of "eco-efficiency" (see, e.g., Gray et al. 2014, 172) is relatively straightforward (see, e.g., Collins et al. 2011). Similarly, financial accounting is not especially challenged by either recognising environmental liabilities arising from (say) polluted land or considering the limited disclosure requirements concerning employees, environment or human rights issues, for example. Even the relatively lukewarm contemplation of "integrated reporting" (see, e.g., Thomson 2015) has hardly had a seismic impact on financial accounting (although the "capitals" framework might change this—see later). Equally, in finance, as Deegan (2016) notes, sustainability can be considered as just another risk or niche variable.

Extending Accounting Possibilities

More disruption is promised—in principle at least—when long-established components of accounting are re-interpreted and/or expanded in an attempt to capture more than the immediately economic impacts of the organisation. We might see three broad themes here.

The first theme is, arguably, the Stefan Schaltegger project of exploring innovative ways in which management accounting (in particular) might embrace a longer-term perspective, planetary boundaries or, for example, the sustainable development goals (Schaltegger et al. 2016; Etxeberria et al. 2017). This approach stays within accounting but seeks to cajole the organisation into more interesting and less un-sustainable waters.

The second theme re-addresses "capital". Capital is a crucial notion in conventional accounting and maintaining organisational capital intact is one of its few immutable desiderata. How might accounting be extended to incorporate not just economic capital but social and environmental capital as well? Then one can use accounting, in theory at least, to ask the question whether the organisation of interest to us contributes to, maintains or destroys economic, social and environmental capital: a useful first approximation of the organisation's potential "sustainability". Something called "full cost accounting" was amongst the first attempts at this idea and sought ways of internalising (at least theoretically) the different external costs imposed by economic activity on society and the environment (see Bebbington et al. 2001 for a summary of these ideas). Full cost accounting overlaps with an idea known as "sustainable cost" which asks the question "what would the organisation have had to spend if it had maintained environmental capital during an accounting period?" (Gray 1992; Bebbington and Gray 2001). Neither of these approaches has found much enthusiasm within the accounting profession or companies themselves—almost certainly because they show (suggest?) that, in all probability, current companies are significantly un-sustainable.[3] Somewhat more enthusiasm was shown for variations on these themes which were developed through Forum for the Future (Howes 2004), the Prince of Wales "Accounting for Sustainability" project (Hopwood et al. 2010) and the "multiple capitals project" (Coulson et al. 2015). All of these sought to use elements of the idea of different capitals but in a manner more sympathetic to corporate interests and, perhaps more significantly, in a way which weighted economic contributions and certain social contributions (like employment) over other detriments like inequality and environmental degradation.

The third of these themes is perhaps the most widely recognised initiative around corporate sustainability: John Elkington's "Triple Bottom Line" sought to recognise that a sustainable organisation needed to be performing socially and environmentally as well financially (Elkington 1997). That is, an organisation needed to recognise (and report upon) its social and environmental performance alongside its financial performance. This basic idea has been institutionalised—albeit at a fairly undemanding level—in the Global Reporting Initiative (GRI), which has been moderately successful in encouraging a significant minority of large companies to voluntarily adopt some elements of these three components of disclosure (Buhr et al. 2014).

It seems likely that each of these themes could take us closer to what an "accounting for sustainability" might actually look like but it is highly contestable whether the current practice in any of these areas actually tells one anything at all about whether or not the organisation has contributed to or detracted from its own un-sustainability (Milne and Gray 2013). It is not insignificant to note that, as Thomson and Bebbington (2004) tell us, it is not *what* you teach but *how* you teach it. Each of these methods can be subsumed within a weak sustainability framework and can be treated as if it were compatible with current means of organising. Or they can be used to expose a strong sustainability point of view which radically challenges the extant practice. It depends not so much on the vehicle we use as the person who is steering it.

Addressing Sustainability Directly

The difference between the forgoing approaches and addressing sustainability directly is the level of resolution we bring to the analysis. The foregoing suggestions all have two basic characteristics in common. First, they each take the organisation as the accounting entity and even when willing to soften those boundaries still have the entity at the heart of the accounting when, in fact, neither society nor ecology is organised in the same way as corporations. The second characteristic they share is that they take, to a greater or lesser extent, the conventional ideas of accounting, finance and business and attempt to shoe-horn notions of sustainability into them. The notions are basically incompatible: *ecology and society simply have no place in conventional accounting and are much, much larger concepts.* Even expanding the notions can run the risk of still (often unconsciously) adopting the taken-for-granted assumptions. This conundrum is reflected at its most basic in the contrasting questions: do we take accounting, management and corporations and ask "how can they contribute to sustainability"? Or do we take society and ecology as our starting point and ask "what must be done to approach sustainability?" The first takes corporations and accounting as essential to our discussion; the second allows for the possibility that accounting and corporations may be the problem and any answer may decide that we need no accounting or corporations—at least as we currently know them (Milne et al. 2009; Russell et al. 2017).

Approaching accounting for sustainability with this frame of mind is necessarily more speculative for at least two reasons. First, organisations are, perhaps understandably, reluctant to engage with methods which might challenge the organisation's very existence (and, incidentally, expose the vacuity of many of their claims about sustainability and social responsibility). Consequently, the practicability of the methods is unlikely to have been tested. Second, there are the problems of collating data and crossing disciplinary boundaries to offer new forms of accounting that adopt different perspectives (Lewis and Russell 2011; Christ and Burritt 2017). Despite these difficulties, perhaps the most promising initiatives in this area have involved the employment of the notion of ecological footprints to measure, in effect, the amount of planetary space that individuals, nations and organisations use. Ecological footprints offer amongst the most persuasive evidence that mankind's ways of organising are far from sustainable (see, e.g., Gray 2006), but data at the organisation level is not currently available. Similar experiments with "social footprints" have also been explored (Thomas and McElroy 2016).

Other approaches have included direct attempts to re-configure organisational boundaries (see, e.g., Antonini and Larrinaga 2017). There is also a considerable movement to de-centre the (social and/or environmental) accounting through what are typically known as external social audits (Thomson et al. 2015). And in innovative and challenging developments, there is a growing experimentation with both accounts of social issues

(Cooper et al. 2005) and accounts of both species and extinction (Jones and Solomon 2013).

So, it is obvious, even from this briefest of reviews, that there is a considerable diversity within "accounting for sustainability". The very diversity can be a very encouraging sign (as our modern minds struggle with this most bewildering of concepts, Gray 2010) but, simultaneously, it is so very important to keep one's eye on the issues of planetary and societal sustainability. This array of different approaches could be in danger of occasionally obscuring the central point and allowing a student (or teacher or practitioner) to become distracted by the elegance and detail of the form over the function.

Education

Hopefully this short essay has illustrated that what comprises education for accounting and sustainability is unlikely to be ever adequately covered by a single—or a simple—approach to the subject (Brown 2009; Deegan 2016). Hence, the importance of one's beliefs about the nature of education. I share with many the commitment that education cannot ever be about single, didactic notions. Our primary task is, I believe (I stress "believe" as this is not a fact or a provable position), to embrace what John Keats called "negative capability", which might be paraphrased as "*believing strongly in X whilst accepting, without reservation that not-X may be the case*". It is a notion which does not deny the role of belief but embraces the notion that all knowledge, belief and facts are conditional. That is, as Brown (2009, 308) suggests, accounting education should not be about seeking out and inculcating definite "truths" and single "correct" accountings around sustainability, but rather it must be about the facilitation and broadening of debate. By this means, we are constantly challenged to *change our mind*. This is at least as much a challenge to the "teacher" as it is to the "student". Different folk will come to different conclusions, but any conclusion should only be acceptable if it is arrived at for transparent reasons and/or that the values that underpin the conclusion are clearly articulated (Tinker and Gray 2003). My central contention is that, as far as I can see, the current situation in accounting education falls some considerable way short of this ideal. A lecturer in financial accounting, for example, is unlikely to be willing to have the core themes of the course challenged and exposed—if only for reasons of time and space. But an educational approach based on negative capability would encourage careful examination of taken-for-granted assumptions on growth, corporations, capital, capitalism, finance, financial markets, monetarisation, accounting entity boundaries, consumption and so on. It would be profoundly disruptive and disturbing.

At least part of the problem is psychological as we have seen: difficulty in coping with notions which seem to challenge one's taken-for-granted assumptions and which require one to explicitly handle cognitive dissonance (see, e.g., Hamilton 2010).[4] It seems to me that education is failing—and possibly even worthless—if it cannot help an individual address conflicting and difficult notions: otherwise what is education for?

So, it is hopefully obvious that the only approach I can see for an education for accounting and sustainability that makes any sense lies in embracing a multitude of approaches which challenge how we teach, rather than what we teach (Coulson and Thomson 2006; Dyball and Thomson 2013; Thomson and Bebbington 2004, 2005; Lucas 2000; Brown 2009). Challenge, conflict and analysis become the *sine qua non* of the classroom (Gray et al. 2014, 325–327; Collison et al. 2014).

This is not to say, though, that either there are no "facts" to be shared (e.g., levels of species extinction; levels of inequality, ecological footprints), nor are there no arguments that need to be deconstructed (Does accounting serve the public interest? Is growth essential? What are the strengths and weaknesses of international financial capitalism?). Equally, our selection of approaches will always reflect our own preferences and beliefs. Education is never neutral, nor should it be so. It might approach an open-mindedness and an even-handedness though. Such an approach might encourage students to actively challenge the teacher whilst equipping the student with capacities for research and argument. I would seriously maintain that humility on the part of both student and teacher is crucial: opinions need substance behind them. We must recognise that we may simply not know enough about an issue; we may simply not have spent enough time in thinking about and analysing an issue to have a view worthy of attention (even if that view is to ignore sustainability).

I tend to believe that largely un-informed opinions may actually be valueless.

What seems clear, however, is that the treatment of sustainability and the challenging nature of education should not sit in specialised electives where the bulk of students can ignore it and where the challenge to the core of accounting is isolated (Gray and Collison 2002). Whilst new issues might, very properly, be experimented with in minor electives, it is only when sustainability sits at the core of mainstream classes and disrupts them accordingly that we might begin to see that we are genuinely educating accountants for sustainability.

Guidance on specifically how to approach such a challenge exists in the literature (although, arguably, each teacher needs to develop their own unique embracing of the challenge). Perhaps the most widely suggested approach is the employment of *dialogics* associated most vividly with the work of Ian Thomson and Judy Brown (see the references). Their attachment to democratic principles leads them to adopt an approach which seeks to empower students and to break down the traditional teacher/student relationship.

To the extent that there is any collective view on the subject, teachers are well-advised to look carefully at the dialogics approach—but that does necessarily exclude consideration of other initiatives. We have seen how many academics would encourage the introduction of sustainability-related notions into the core curriculum without, necessarily, disrupting the core technologies (Schaltegger et al. 2017; Collins et al. 2011), whilst others might encourage students to explore and imagine new accountings in a range of different settings (Coulson and Thomson 2006; Collison et al. 2014). We also should not ignore ideas from other disciplines (see, e.g., Sidiropoulos 2014; Cullen 2017; Landrum and Ohsowski 2017; Andersson and Öhman 2016).

My own preferred approach is predicated upon the assumption that if you understand sustainability, it stops you from sleeping at night (Gray 2013): sustainability is a profoundly disruptive notion. It is important to stress, though, that as an educator, I see my duty as allowing students the opportunities to commit to (say) weak sustainability or even (say) to extreme forms of liberalism *but only* if they have addressed and can seriously address the weight of evidence and argument that a strong sustainability position would demand. Of course, the opposite is also true: everyone committing to a deep ecologist position equally must be subject to a deliberate pounding of arguments from, *inter alia*, an undiluted free-market finance specialist.

I sought to achieve this in a module I ran for a number of years—latterly at the University of St Andrews—and I tried to summarise the thinking that went into the course and the experience of living with such a course in a piece in *Accounting Education: An International Journal* (Gray 2013). The basic lecture outline is shown in the following text box: a structure obviously based on Gray et al. (2014). However, the list itself is rather bland and uninspiring. It only makes sense (to me at least) when the other issues in the course are wrapped around it (Gray 2013). The subtext of the module was "Helping students come to a well-informed view about the relationship between business, accounting and society". This is not obvious from the lecture list and this rather emphasises the point that it matters less what you teach than how you go about "teaching" it.

A Lecture Course for Sustainability Topics

1. Overview of business, society, sustainability, accountability and responsibility
2. Systems thinking, liberal democracy and social accounting
3. Accountability, neo-pluralism and theories of organisational accountability
4. Social responsibility and sustainability
5. Profit and responsibility: conflict or harmony?
6. Social, environmental and "sustainability" reporting
7. Environmental management and "win-win"
8. Socially responsible investment?
9. External social audits
10. The practice and theory of discharging social, environmental and sustainability accountability
11. Practical options for the future?

My personal belief remains that if sustainability fits into the curriculum, it is not sustainability but rather a form of sustainababble comprising some gentle mix of environmental management and CSR-lite. It is not at all clear that such a commitment tells us anything at all about sustainability. Sustainability challenges everything about modernity—at least in principle—and so an absence of disruption and an absence of cognitive dissonance suggest to me an absence of sustainability.

Education in accounting, as elsewhere, should, I believe, be dedicated to high degrees of disruption, cognitive dissonance and discomfort. When we embrace sustainability, I am unable to see any value in any other approach.

Notes

1. Shallow or surface learning emphasises memory, regurgitation and passivity; deep learning emphasises understanding, engagement and critical analysis (Gray et al. 1994).
2. "Sustainababble" was a colourful and illustrative term coined by Engelman (2013) to capture the range of chatter around what purported to be sustainability which, largely, failed to ever address sustainability itself.
3. Which is probably the correct answer (Gray 1992, 2010).
4. Gray et al. (2001) report an interview with an academic who stated, "I am aware of sustainability but it is scary…".

References

Adams, Matthew. 2015. Apocalypse When? (Not) Thinking and Talking about Climate Change. *Discover Society*, March 1. Accessed January 10, 2018. http://discoversociety.org/2015/03/01/apocalypse-when-not-thinking.

Andersson, Pernilla, and Johan Öhman. 2016. Logics of Business Education for Sustainability. *Environmental Education Research* 22 (4): 463–479.

Antonini, Carla, and Carlos Larrinaga. 2017. Planetary Boundaries and Sustainability Indicators: A Survey of Corporate Reporting Boundaries. *Sustainable Development* 25: 123–137.

Baker, M., and S. Schaltegger. 2015. Pragmatism and New Directions in Social and Environmental Accountability Research. *Accounting, Auditing and Accountability Journal* 28 (2): 263–294.

Bebbington, Jan, and Rob Gray. 2001. An Account of Sustainability: Failure, Success and a Reconception. *Critical Perspectives on Accounting* 12 (5, Oct.): 557–587.

Bebbington, Jan, Rob Gray, Chris Hibbitt, and Elizabeth Kirk. 2001. *Full Cost Accounting: An Agenda for Action*. London: ACCA.

Bebbington, Jan, Jeffrey Unerman, and Brendan O'Dwyer, eds. 2014. *Sustainability Accounting and Accountability*. London: Routledge.

Brown, Judy. 2009. Democracy, Sustainability and Dialogic Accounting Technologies: Taking Pluralism Seriously. *Critical Perspectives on Accounting* 20: 313–342.

Buhr, Nola, Rob Gray, and Markus J. Milne. 2014. Histories, Rationales, Voluntary Standards and Future Prospects for Sustainability Reporting: CSR, GRI, IIRC and Beyond. Chap. 4 in *Sustainability Accounting and Accountability*, ed. Jan Bebbington, Jeffrey Unerman, and Brendan O'Dwyer, 51–71. London: Routledge.

Christ, Katherine L., and Roger L. Burritt. 2017. What Constitutes Contemporary Corporate Water Accounting? A Review from a Management Perspective. *Sustainable Development* 25: 138–149.

Collins, Eva, Stewart Lawrence, Juliet Roper, and Jarrod Haar. 2011. *Sustainability and the Role of the Management Accountant*. Research Executive Summary Series 7(14). London: Chartered Institute of Management Accountants.

Collison, David, John Ferguson, and Lorna Stevenson. 2014. Sustainability Accounting and Education. Chap. 3 in *Sustainability Accounting and Accountability*, ed. Jan Bebbington, Jeffrey Unerman, and Brendan O'Dwyer, 30–47. London: Routledge.

Cooper, Christine, Phil Taylor, Newman Smith, and Lesley Catchpowle. 2005. A Discussion of the Political Potential of Social Accounting. *Critical Perspectives on Accounting* 16 (7): 951–974.

Coulson, Andrea B., Carol A. Adams, Michael N. Nugent, and Kathryn Haynes. 2015. Exploring Metaphors of Capitals and the Framing of Multiple Capitals: Challenges and Opportunities for <IR>. *Sustainability Accounting, Management and Policy Journal* 6 (3): 290–314.

Coulson, Andrea, and Ian Thomson. 2006. Accounting and Sustainability: Encouraging a Dialogical Approach; Integrating Learning Activities, Delivery Mechanisms and Assessment Strategies. *Accounting Education: an International Journal* 15 (3, Sep.): 261–273.

Cullen, John G. 2017. Educating Business Students About Sustainability: A Bibliometric Review of Current Trends and Research Needs. *Journal of Business Ethics* 145 (2, Oct.): 429–439.

Deegan, Craig. 2016. Twenty Five Years of Social and Environmental Accounting Research Within Critical Perspectives of Accounting: Hits, Misses and Ways Forward. *Critical Perspectives on Accounting* 43: 65–87.

Dyball, Maria Cadiz, and Ian Thomson. 2013. Sustainability and Accounting Education. *Accounting Education: An International Journal* 22 (4): 303–307.

Elkington, John. 1997. *Cannibals with Forks: the Triple Bottom Line of 21st Century Business*. Oxford: Capstone Publishing.

Engelman, Robert. 2013. Beyond Sustainababble. In *State of the World 2013: Is Sustainability Still Possible?* ed. Erik Assadourain and Tom Prough, 3–18. Washington: Island Press.

Etxeberria, Igor Álvarez, Eduardo Ortas, and Stefan Schaltegger. 2017. Innovative Measurement for Corporate Sustainability. *Sustainable Development* 25: 111–112.

Gambling, Trevor. 1978. *Beyond the Conventions of Accounting*. London: Macmillan.

Gray, Rob. 1992. Accounting and Environmentalism: An Exploration of the Challenge of Gently Accounting for Accountability, Transparency and Sustainability. *Accounting Organisations and Society* 17 (5, July): 399–426.

———. 2006. Social, Environmental, and Sustainability Reporting and Organisational Value Creation? Whose Value? Whose Creation? *Accounting, Auditing and Accountability Journal* 19 (3): 319–348.

———. 2010. Is Accounting for Sustainability Actually Accounting for Sustainability … and How Would We Know? An Exploration of Narratives of Organisations and the Planet. *Accounting Organizations and Society* 35 (1): 47–62.

———. 2013. Sustainability and Accounting Education: The Elephant in the Classroom. *Accounting Education: An International Journal* 22 (4): 308–332.

Gray, Rob, Carol Adams, and David Owen. 2014. *Accountability, Social Responsibility and Sustainability: Accounting for Society and the Environment*. London: Pearson.

Gray, Rob, Jan Bebbington, and Ken McPhail. 1994. Teaching Ethics and the Ethics of Accounting Teaching: Educating for Immorality and a Case for Social and Environmental Accounting Education. *Accounting Education* 3 (1, Spring): 51–75.

Gray, Rob, and David Collison. 2002. Can't See the Wood for the Trees, Can't See the Trees for the Numbers? Accounting Education, Sustainability and the Public Interest. *Critical Perspectives on Accounting* 13 (5/6): 797–836.

Gray, Rob, and David Collison with John French, Ken McPhail, and Lorna Stevenson. 2001. *The Professional Accountancy Bodies and the Provision of Education and Training in Relation to Environmental Issues.* Edinburgh: ICAS.

Hamilton, Clive. 2010. *Requiem for a Species: Why We Resist the Truth about Climate Change.* Oxon: Earthscan.

Hines, Ruth D. 1988. Financial Accounting: In Communicating Reality, We Construct Reality. *Accounting, Organizations and Society* 13 (3): 251–261.

Hopwood, Anthony G. 2007. Whither Accounting Research? *The Accounting Review* 82 (5): 1356–1374.

Hopwood, Anthony, Jeffrey Unerman, and Jessica Fries, eds. 2010. *Accounting for Sustainability: Practical Insights.* London: Earthscan.

Howes, Rupert. 2004. Environmental Cost Accounting: Coming of Age? Tracking Organisation Performance Towards Environmental Sustainability. In *The Triple Bottom Line: Does It All Add Up?* ed. Adrian Henriques and Julie Richardson, 99–112. London: Earthscan.

Humphrey, Christopher, Linda Lewis, and David Owen. 1996. Still Too Distant Voices? Conversations and Reflections on the Social Relevance of Accounting Education. *Critical Perspectives on Accounting* 7 (1/2): 77–99.

Institute of Chartered Accountants in England and Wales. 2004. *Sustainability: The Role of Accountants* (in the *Information for Better Markets* series). London: ICAEW.

Isil, Osgur, and Michael T. Hernke. 2017. The Triple Bottom Line: A Critical Review from a Transdisciplinary Perspective. *Business Strategy and the Environment* 26 (8): 1235–1251.

Jones, Michael John, and Jill Frances Solomon. 2013. Problematising Accounting for Biodiversity. *Accounting, Auditing and Accountability Journal* 26 (5): 668–687.

Khan, Tehmina, and Rob Gray. 2016. Accounting, Identity, Autopoiesis + Sustainability. *Meditari Accountancy Research* 24 (1): 36–55.

Landrum, Nancy E., and Brian Ohsowski. 2017. Content Trends in Sustainable Business Education: An Analysis of Introductory Courses in the USA. *International Journal of Sustainability in Higher Education* 18 (3): 385–414.

Lawrence, Stewart Raymond, Vida Botes, Eva Collins, and Juliet Roper. 2013. Does Accounting Construct the Identity of Firms as Purely Self-Interested or as Socially Responsible? *Meditari Accountancy Research* 21 (2): 144–160.

Lee, T.A. 1990. A Systematic View of the History of the World of Accounting. *Accounting, Business and Financial History* 1 (1): 73–107.

Lewis, Linda, and Shona Russell. 2011. Permeating Boundaries: Accountability at the Nexus of Water and Climate Change. *Social and Environmental Accountability Journal* 31 (2): 117–123.

Longman, Philip. 2015. Why the Economic Fates of America's Cities Diverged. *The Atlantic*, November 28. Accessed January 10, 2018. https://www.the-atlantic.com/world/.

Lucas, Ursula. 2000. Worlds Apart: Students' Experiences of Learning Introductory Accounting. *Critical Perspectives on Accounting* 11 (4): 479–504.

Marshall, George. 2014. *Don't Even Think About It: Why Our Brains are Wired to Ignore Climate Change*. London: Bloomsbury.

McPhail, Ken. 1999. The Threat of Ethical Accountants: An Application of Foucault's Concept of Ethics to Accounting Education and Some Thoughts on Ethically Educating for the Other. *Critical Perspectives on Accounting* 10 (6): 833–866.

———. 2001. The Dialectic of Accounting Education: From Role Identity to Ego Identity. *Critical Perspectives on Accounting* 12 (4): 471–499.

———. 2004. An Emotional Response to the State of Accounting Education: Developing Accounting Students' Emotional Intelligence. *Critical Perspectives on Accounting* 15 (4–5): 629–648.

Milne, Markus J., and Rob Gray. 2013. W(h)ither Ecology? The Triple Bottom Line, the Global Reporting Initiative, and Corporate Sustainability Reporting. *Journal of Business Ethics* 118 (1, Nov.): 13–29.

Milne, Markus J., Helen Tregidga, and Sara Walton. 2009. Words Not Actions! The Ideological Role of Sustainable Development Reporting. *Accounting, Auditing & Accountability Journal 22* (8): 1211–1257.

Power, Michael. 1992. After Calculation? Reflection on Critique of Economic Reason by André Gorz. *Accounting, Organizations and Society* 17 (1): 477–499.

Robb, Fenton. 1989. The Application of Autopoiesis to Social Organizations—A Comment on John Mingers: An Introduction to Autopoiesis: Implications and Applications. *Systems Practice* 2 (3): 343–348.

Russell, Shona, Markus J. Milne, and Colin Dey. 2017. Accounts of Nature and the Nature of Accounts: Critical Reflections on Environmental Accounting and Propositions for Ecologically Informed Accounting. *Accounting, Auditing & Accountability Journal* 30 (7): 1426–1458.

Schaltegger, Stefan, Igor Álvarez Etxeberria, and Eduardo Ortas. 2017. Innovating Corporate Accounting and Reporting for Sustainability— Attributes and Challenges. *Sustainable Development* 25: 113–122.

Schaltegger, Stefan, Florian Lüdeke-Freund, and Erik G. Hansen. 2016. Business Models for sustainability. A Co-evolutionary Analysis of Sustainable Entrepreneurship, Innovation and Transformation. *Organization and Environment* 12 (1): 1–26.

Sidiropoulos, Elizabeth. 2014. Education for Sustainability in Business Education Programs: A Question of Value. *Journal of Cleaner Production* 85 (15, Dec.): 472–487.

Spangenberg, Joachim H. 2017. Hot Air or Comprehensive Progress? A Critical Assessment of the SDGs. *Sustainable Development* 25: 311–321.

Thomas, Martin P., and Mark W. McElroy. 2016. *The MultiCapital Scorecard: Re-thinking Organizational Performance*. White River Junction, Vermont: Chelsea Green Publishing.

Thomson, Ian. 2015. But Does Sustainability Need Capitalism or an Integrated Report' a Commentary on 'The International Integrated Reporting Council: A Story of Failure' by Flower, J. *Critical Perspectives on Accounting* 27 (Mar.): 18–22.

Thomson, Ian, and Jan Bebbington. 2004. It Doesn't Matter What You Teach? *Critical Perspectives on Accounting* 15: 609–628.

———. 2005. Social and Environmental Reporting in the UK: A Pedagogic Evaluation. *Critical Perspectives on Accounting* 16 (5, July): 507–533.

Thomson, Ian, Colin Dey, and Shona Russell. 2015. Activism, Arenas and Accounts in Conflicts Over Tobacco Control. *Accounting, Auditing and Accountability Journal* 28 (5): 809–845.

Tinker, Tony. 1985. *Paper Prophets: A Social Critique of Accounting*. Eastbourne: Holt Rinehart and Winston.

Tinker, Tony, and Rob Gray. 2003. Beyond a Critique of Pure Reason: From Policy to Politics to Praxis in Environmental and Social Research. *Accounting, Auditing and Accountability Journal* 16 (5): 727–761.

4

Sustainability in Business Economics

Andrew J. Angus and Joseph G. Nellis

Introduction

The widely quoted definition of sustainable development, 'development that meets the needs of the present without compromising the ability of future generations to meet their own needs' (World Commission on Environment and Development 1987), requires that society carefully considers how best to use scarce resources that have competing uses. This is the mission of economics and for centuries economists have been considering the challenges of sustainable development, beginning with the work by Thomas Malthus on limits to growth (Malthus 1798), with prominent later additions such as Hotelling's work on the optimal extraction of non-renewable resources (Hotelling 1931), Ronald Coase on the problem of social cost (Coase 1960), and more recently work by David Pearce on the Green Economy (Pearce et al. 1989).

Mainstream economic thinking on sustainability has coalesced into the field of environmental economics, a branch of welfare economics

A. J. Angus (✉) • J. G. Nellis
Cranfield School of Management, Bedford, UK
e-mail: a.angus@cranfield.ac.uk; j.g.nellis@cranfield.ac.uk

© The Author(s) 2019
K. Amaeshi et al. (eds.), *Incorporating Sustainability in Management Education*,
https://doi.org/10.1007/978-3-319-98125-3_4

(Perman et al. 2011). In keeping with the tradition of welfare economics, environmental economics is more comfortably taught as part of a syllabus that focuses on social, rather than private decisions. This legacy has meant that teaching sustainability in business economics has mostly focused on how governments change market signals, via green taxes, emissions trading, or subsidies, to coerce business into more sustainable modes of operation. Hence, sustainability in business economics is taught as a distinct topic within a business microeconomics module/course, focusing on the rationale and logic of government environmental policy intervention.

This chapter proposes that practice has now moved beyond this view of sustainability in business economics. Sustainable action is often led by business as a means of gaining competitive advantage, creating, or destroying barriers to entry, or creating new markets. We suggest that sustainability thinking should be infused through both microeconomic and macroeconomic teaching, rather than being a distinct topic on a microeconomics module or course. This thinking follows the philosophy of the 2012 United Nations Conference on Sustainable Development, also known as 'Rio+20', which proposed that macroeconomic policy should be designed for sustainability in a 'top down' approach, known as the *green economy*, and firms should incrementally improve their environmental performance in a 'bottom up' approach, known as *green growth* (Barbier 2011, 2012).

Accordingly, we propose that a microeconomics syllabus should view sustainability from a firm's perspective, as a means of improving competitiveness, creating new barriers to entry, or disruptive innovation, rather than viewed entirely through a lens of government intervention. A macroeconomics syllabus should include questions around how to measure economic growth, adjusted for environmental gains and losses, or in a way that more closely links to human wellbeing. Consideration should also be given to what concepts such as the *green economy*, *circular economy* (Ghisellini et al. 2016), and *steady state economy* (Daly 1973) mean in the context of macroeconomic planning.

To date, environmental economics, by definition, has focused on markets and the environment. However, in practice firms must also consider their effect on employees and surrounding communities: the other pillar of sustainability. In this respect, theory and teaching can lead practice. While firms clearly understand and act upon their environmental responsibilities, they are less clear how best to add value to local communities and measure impact. Business economics courses can help build best practice in this respect. However, this chapter focuses on the current body of literature, so is more focused on environmental than social sustainability.

Sustainability in Business Economics

Following the Brundtland Commission's work (World Commission on Environment and Development 1987), economists set about understanding how economic concepts could be applied to help society achieve sustainable development. This led to two competing views of sustainability: *weak* and *strong*, which can be distinguished by the pattern of consumption of three types of capital (Hanley et al. 2006):

- *human capital*—the knowledge level, skills, and experience within society;
- *man-made capital*—the stock of goods that can be used to create other goods; and
- *natural capital*—stocks of natural resources, including biophysical cycles and biodiversity.

Weak sustainability allows human or man-made capital to be substituted for natural capital, as long as aggregate capital remains constant over time (stemming from work by Solow 1986 and Hartwick 1977). This is consistent with the requirements of welfare maximisation where ecological degradation is accepted as long as this creates compensating net benefits to society across generations. For instance, a habitat could be used for development as long as the gain in human and man-made capital exceeds the loss of natural capital. But, if taken to the extreme, this does raise tricky questions as to how we compare the value of the different forms of capital (Bordt 2018; O'Niell 1993)—how many textbooks compensate for the loss of a panda bear? Indeed several economists have questioned the long-term sustainability of weak sustainability (Ekins et al. 2003).

Strong sustainability differs in that natural capital is sacrosanct and society cannot be compensated for its loss (Aslaksen et al. 2013; Daly and Cobb 1989). Every capital vector must remain intact and stay above a critical minimum level of over time (Rao 2000). This is a more restrictive view of sustainable development and suggests economic development should only take place when it requires no natural capital, or where natural capital can be directly replaced. This view is precautionary, where natural capital levels are maintained to avoid any risks of permanent, catastrophic ecological damage (Aslaksen et al. 2013).

Thus, it should be appreciated that weak and strong sustainability are very different views, with the former becoming associated with environmental economics, the latter with ecological economics (Ang and Van Passel 2012). Environmental economics broadly studies the interdependence of business and the environment, with a focus on how markets can be used to manage environmental issues, whereas ecological economics is concerned with the management of ecological critical limits (Hanley et al. 2006). Hence ecological economics bridges economics and biophysical sciences, while environmental economics bridges business and the environment. This chapter focuses on environmental economics and weak sustainability, because it is more relatable to business studies. This does not mean that ecological economics is any less important, just that it will be studied in different educational contexts.

Teaching Sustainability in Business Economics

Environmental economics can be broadly understood and taught through the concept of optimal pollution (Fig. 4.1). The curve representing *marginal benefit of production (MB)* of a good or service is downward sloping, reflecting consumer willingness to pay: each successive unit of output is valued less highly than the previous unit. The *marginal damage cost of production (MDC)* is proportionate with output: more production causes more pollution and associated costs to society (e.g., health impacts associated with poor air quality). Where the MB curve crosses the MDC curve,

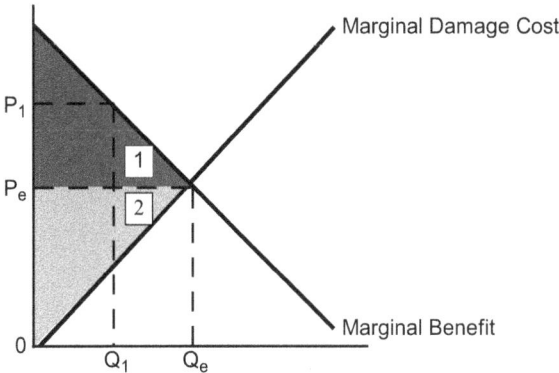

Fig. 4.1 The concept of optimal pollution

the benefits of production are equal to the costs such that any further increase in output will mean that social costs exceed benefits.

Similarly, any decrease in output will lower social wellbeing. For instance, a reduction in output from Q_e to Q_1 will reduce the number of transactions that could be made where benefits exceed damage costs, resulting in a deadweight loss of areas 1 and 2. Area 1 represents the loss of *consumer surplus*, transactions where consumers' willingness to pay (represented by MB) would have been above the price they would have actually had to pay (P_e). Area 2 represents lost supplier surplus, transactions where the revenue received (P_e) would have been in excess of MDC. Therefore, output at Q_1 is socially too low: the point of optimal pollution is a Pareto-optimal outcome.

The objective of environmental economics is to help society recognise and achieve optimal pollution. As a branch of welfare economics, environmental economics assumes that a perfectly functioning market will provide a Pareto-optimal allocation of resources, but recognises that markets fail in several ways, collectively termed *market failures*. *Market failures* are particularly pertinent for environmental goods and services, which tend to generate indirect value, but are not traded in the market place. For instance, wetlands offer flood protection to surrounding villages and towns, which would otherwise be periodically flooded, resulting in households paying higher insurance premiums. But as the wetland's function is a *public good*, it is not valued by the market. Therefore, the loss of environmental functions often manifest themselves as external costs (often referred to as *externalities*), lying outside the property rights system and the market.

Welfare economics views it as government's role to correct the market system so that damage costs are internalised in market price and costs (Johansson 1991). Therefore, achieving optimal pollution requires a monetised estimate of the environmental loss associated with MDC. To this end economists have developed several techniques, such as the *hedonic pricing method*, which derives a demand curve for the environmental characteristics of market goods, based on observations of user behaviour. For example, the decision to buy a house is partly related to the quality of the environment—Hedonic pricing isolates the element of the final sale price that is the buyer's desire to live within a particular environment (Rivas Casado et al. 2017; Glen and Nellis 2010). Another technique is the *contingent valuation method*, which asks people how much they would be willing to pay to attain an improvement in environmental quality, or how much they would be willing to accept in compensation for the loss of environmental amenity (Kahneman and Knetsch 1992). Through statistical analysis these methods construct a demand curve for an environmental amenity.

The second element of achieving optimal pollution is the design of instruments that correct market failures. This is usually achieved by changing the nature of incentives that firms and individuals face when transacting (Burtraw and Woerman 2013; Parson and Kravitz 2013; Hahn 2000). To this end several economic instruments have been proposed, such as environmental taxes, or emissions trading, which increase the cost of using the environment, while other instruments, such as subsidies, make it less expensive for firms to install technology that reduces pollution (Taylor et al. 2012; Jordan et al. 2003).

Thus, a session on sustainability in business economics can introduce the high-level concepts of weak sustainability and how markets can be corrected to provide sustainable development. This view on the topic is usually well received by students, broadening their thinking on sustainability and how government interventions affect industry profitability and competitiveness. The subject matter can be used to develop class debate about whether markets can be used to manage the environment or markets only damage the environment. However, many students fail to see the application of concepts to day-to-day business and this has been a frequent criticism in student feedback.

This criticism is difficult to avoid. Environmental economics treats sustainability from a societal viewpoint, focusing on how governments can intervene to correct markets. The mainstream textbooks say comparatively little about the organisational changes and economic trade-offs that occur inside a business when they have to respond to changes in government sustainability policy. In business education it is arguably more important for managers to understand how to respond to market changes, rather than the broad governmental drivers, although both clearly matter. Over the years we have found that increasingly, many students' interest goes beyond a broad understanding of weak sustainability to what businesses gain from sustainable action. A session on the basic drivers misses some crucial elements of the opportunities that arise from sustainable business. Therefore, there is scope for thinking more widely about how sustainability is applied to business.

A Conceptual Framework for Teaching Sustainability in Business Economics

Figure 4.2 presents a conceptual framework of how businesses interact with sustainability. The 'Societal Reference Point' can be interpreted as government's vision of sustainable development. It represents society's expectations of business environmental and social performance. The reference point is not static, but moves according to the attitudes of society at that time. Generally the direction has been upwards, moving the minimum acceptable standard higher. Traditional teaching on sustainability in business economics has been around the setting of this reference line: examining the drivers of sustainability, government sustainability targets, and what mechanisms are used to achieve these targets.

Below the reference line are the compulsory actions that businesses must take to meet the reference line and in so doing reduce operational

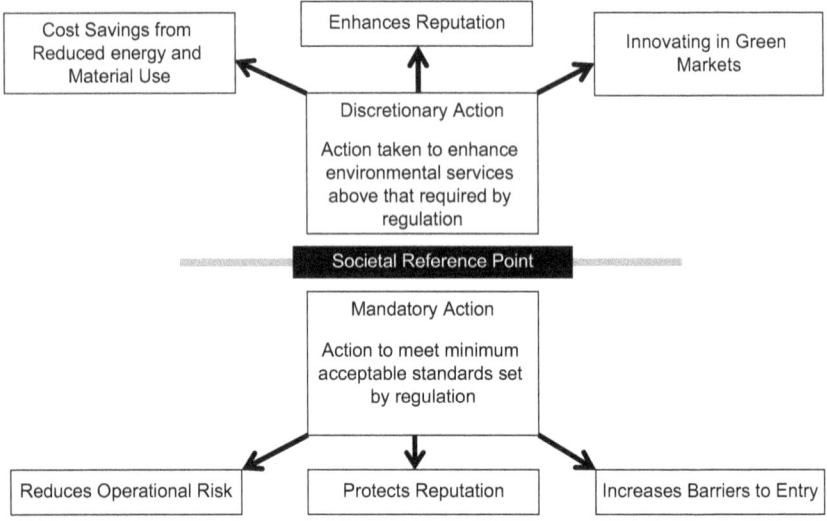

Fig. 4.2   The environmental reference level (Adapted from Hodge 1989)

risk, including mandatory shutdowns, legal action, and associated reputational impact. This is reactive. Business must comply with regulation to escape prosecution. However, this has some positive externalities, where increased compliance burdens raise the barriers to entry in particular industries. Furthermore, by complying with regulation the firm will avoid the reputational damage of any sustainability scandals.

Above the reference point are discretionary actions above minimum acceptable standards, where businesses perceive advantages of sustainable action. In other words, businesses are taking action beyond that required by regulation, motivated by a desire to reduce expenditure on energy or resources, to innovate and to defend existing market share or differentiate their products from competitors.

The foregoing describes a broad spectrum of activity that goes beyond the traditional focus on the reference line. It highlights three areas of business activity: compliance activity, resource efficiency, and market exploitation. Crucially these are important managerial competencies providing a more relevant focus for teaching sustainability in business economics. The following sections discuss how teaching can be focused on these managerial competencies.

Focusing Teaching on Business Compliance

The bulk of business sustainability activity will be organising compliance with government regulation, which usually requires firms to limit their emissions of a pollutant to the required standard, or remove dangerous processes or systems (reference line in Fig. 4.2). Sessions focused around regulatory compliance can be useful in equipping managers with a framework for understanding the operational implications of sustainability, while at the same time allowing the exploration of additional economic concepts such as cost-effectiveness. This teaching mode also makes the subject more relevant to managers than teaching based on optimal pollution.

Compliance with regulation entails a series of managerial and technical responses, all of which have a financial cost. To minimise the impact on a firm's competitiveness, it is imperative for the company to comply at least cost. *Cost-Effectiveness Analysis (CEA)* identifies management options capable of achieving a specified target at least cost, or making the best return from a specific input (Perman et al. 2011). CEA provides a framework for identifying, prioritising, and applying the emission reduction measures that achieve regulatory compliance at least cost. The output of CEA is a cost-effectiveness ratio, which provides a measure, for a given pollution reduction technology, of how much cost is required to achieve a unit reduction in pollution. In this way CEA does not require the calculation of the social benefits of an abatement action, which can be a difficult and expensive process.

A company can plan its most cost-effective response to regulation by arranging the cost-effectiveness ratios of all available abatement options in ascending order, known as a *Marginal Abatement Cost Curve (MACC)*. A MACC graphically represents the relative costs of achieving successive increases in pollution reduction over a specified timeframe (over and above some counterfactual) by successively adopting interventions in order of least marginal cost (Yin et al. 2018; Morris et al. 2009). Of course this requires that a manager has first collected information from specialists within a firm on the techniques available to reduce pollution, their reduction potential, and costs. Costs include additional investment costs, spread over the relevant investment life to give an annual equivalent cost, plus changes in annual operating costs such as fuel, maintenance, and other costs like training where relevant. MACCs are derived from models focused on emission reductions from industrial plants, but can be expanded to industrial sectors or countries (Liu and Feng 2018).

Table 4.1 shows example data for a MACC. The first column lists the various pollution (in this case CO_2) reduction techniques, the second lists the cost-effectiveness ratio of each abatement technique (expressed in $000/tonne), and the third lists the abatement potential of each technique. This can be visualised as a MACC (Fig. 4.3).

Figure 4.3 shows that some initial pollution abatement options, such as energy efficiency, which could include things like motion detecting lights, offer 'win-win' opportunities, with negative marginal abatement costs. Here, the avoided costs (energy bills) from energy efficiency exceed the cost of adopting the intervention. Beyond the 'win-win' options, which can collectively reduce emissions by 6 tonnes, achieving further emission reductions will involve extra net costs per unit of emission. Marginal abatement costs might be expected to be relatively small for small-scale options, but higher for methods that require large capital expenditure.

The MACC allows a manager to determine the most cost-effective way to respond to regulation. For instance, if this particular firm was required to reduce emissions by 18 tonnes then the most cost-effective response would be to install all techniques from energy efficiency to chemical scrubbers. Installing carbon capture and retrofitting machinery would be unnecessary.

Table 4.1 Example of marginal abatement cost data

	$000/tonne CO_2 reduced	Tonnes reduced
Energy efficiency	−5	1
Product lightweighting	−3	2
Solar panels	−1	3
Reconfigure build process	1	4
Chemical scrubbers	5	8
Carbon capture	7	2
Retrofit machinery	10	6

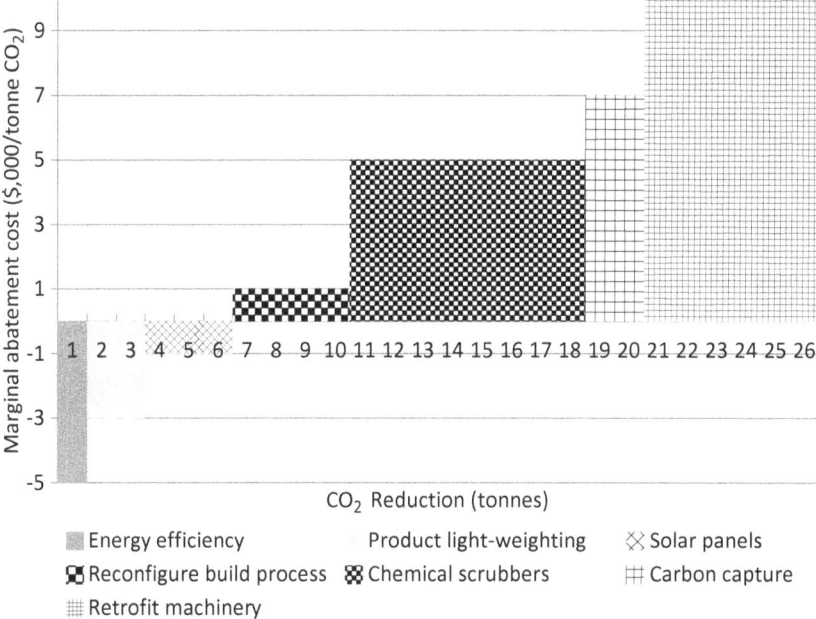

Fig. 4.3 A marginal abatement cost curve

Using multiple MACCs allows a more subtle insight into how regulation affects competitiveness. By comparing Figs. 4.3 and 4.4 it can be seen that the firm represented in Fig. 4.4 has higher abatement costs, so it will be more expensive for this firm to comply with the regulatory standard that requires a reduction of 18 tonnes CO_2, relative to the firm represented in Fig. 4.3.

This demonstration can be used as an entry point to a discussion of how environmental regulation could change the competitive nature of the sector. The firm in Fig. 4.3 could see environmental regulation as a low-cost way of reducing the market power of the firm in Fig. 4.4. This is why we see some firms lobbying for more stringent environmental regulation, because it disproportionately disadvantages their competitors.

MACCs can also be used to help managers understand the most cost-effective response to economic instruments, such as an emission tax. For instance, if a tax rate was set at $5000 per tonne of CO_2 emitted, then the firm represented in Fig. 4.4 would choose to install all techniques from

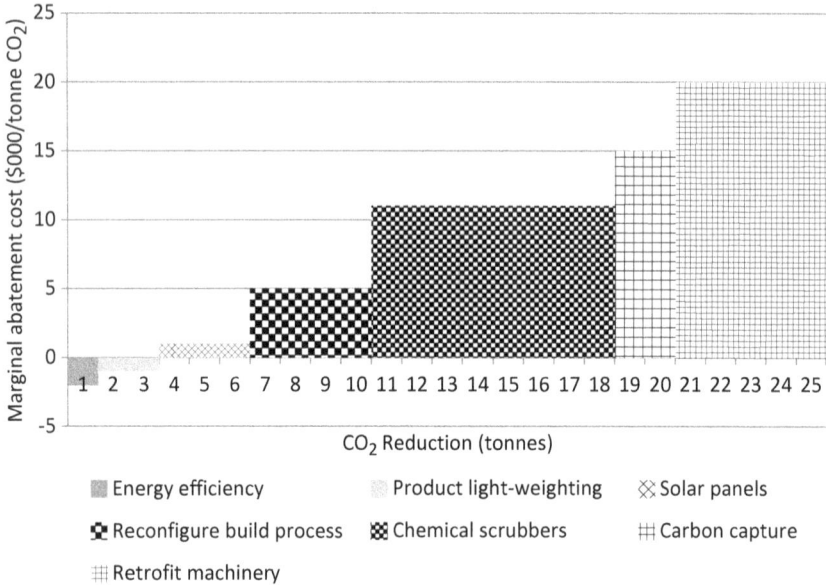

Fig. 4.4   A marginal abatement cost curve

energy efficiency to reconfiguring build process. This is because it would be less expensive to install these technologies than pay the $5000 per tonne CO_2 tax. However, it will pay a tax on the remaining 8 tonnes of CO_2 emitted, as paying the tax is less costly than installing carbon capture and retrofitting machinery.

The use of multiple MACCs allows the simulation of an emissions trading policy (see Corrigan 2011 and Ando and Harrington 2006 for good examples), which allows a demonstration of how the price of permits affects a firm's cost-effective response and how this policy instrument achieves regulatory requirements more cost-effectively than regulation. To teach these concepts the authors have developed a simulation of an industry comprising five firms, each with an equal market share. Each firm differs in terms of the type of product they manufacture, their capital vintage, and quantity of emissions. This means each firm has a different MACC (an example is given in Fig. 4.5), which represents a different business to the firms represented in Figs. 4.3 and 4.4.

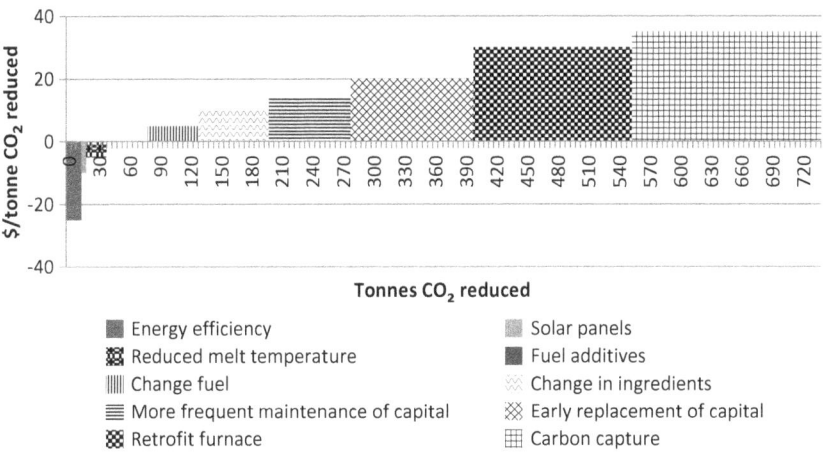

Energy efficiency   Solar panels
Reduced melt temperature   Fuel additives
Change fuel   Change in ingredients
More frequent maintenance of capital   Early replacement of capital
Retrofit furnace   Carbon capture

Fig. 4.5 Simulation—marginal abatement cost curve

The simulation begins when the facilitator (who acts as the government's environment protection agency) announces it will introduce regulation to achieve a reduction of CO_2 emissions across the industry. To ensure fairness, all companies are compelled to reduce their CO_2 emissions by the same quantity, which collectively meets the government's reference line, a total of 330 tonnes of CO_2 per company and 1650 tonnes in total.

The regulations take the form of a technology standard, similar to most environmental regulation applied worldwide. Technology standards specify the exact production processes, management procedures, or technology that must be used in an economic activity. These packages of measures are usually termed *Best Available Techniques (BAT)*. BAT is usually specified by environmental regulators on the basis that they will achieve the required environmental standard without excessive cost. When firms are certified as using a BAT they are then issued a permit to operate.

The simulation begins when students are divided into five teams, given their MACC and the facilitator provides each group with the list of BAT that all firms must apply (Table 4.2). Students are told that application of BAT will guarantee reduction of 330 tonnes of CO_2 in every firm and is

Table 4.2 Best available techniques

Energy efficiency (motion detecting lights, improve building insulation, etc.)
Install solar panels
Reduced glass melt temperature
Fuel additives
Change fuel type
Change glass ingredients
More frequent maintenance of capital

a legally binding requirement. BAT must be implemented to receive an environmental permit, without which the firm cannot legally operate. In this first part of the simulation the students must answer two questions: how much does the application of the BAT cost and by how much does it reduce emissions?

Comparing Fig. 4.5 and Table 4.2 this firm will over-comply when it deploys BAT (all techniques listed in Table 4.2). The regulation compels it to undertake more frequent maintenance of capital, which means that the firm will reduce close to 360 tonnes of CO_2. This will be similar for all firms. Capital items cannot be partially installed, which means that most firms will over-comply, highlighting the inflexibility of technology standards. At the conclusion of the round it is clear that the regulation is causing some firms to pay more than others, thus changing relative competitiveness. This allows an exploration of how regulation could change competitiveness and whether it is fair on those firms with higher costs, but also higher levels of pollution.

The next step of the simulation is to introduce an emissions trading scheme, where firms are allocated enough permits to cover all but 330 tonnes of their baseline emissions. The rules of the game are that there must be one permit submitted to the facilitator at the end of the game for each tonne of CO_2 emitted. The difference between this and regulation is that firms can now buy and sell surplus permits. Therefore, they must carefully consider their breakeven price at which it becomes cheaper to buy permits to satisfy regulatory requirements, or make the reduction internally.

Usually this process is stimulated by a facilitator calling out permit prices (much like an auction), which allows students to judge how different permit prices affect their decisions. There is one price that will clear the market for permits and meet the regulatory requirements. This can either be given to students at the beginning or students can be left to trade permits in a 'free market' scenario, which is more time consuming. Once they are given the optimal permit price students are asked to calculate their costs of compliance and emission reductions.

Following this process, it becomes clear that emissions trading gives firms the option to outsource compliance, where this is cheaper than doing it themselves. For several firms they over-comply, but make a profit from this, since they are able to sell their permits where the abatement costs are below the permit sale price. Others do not reduce their emissions to 330 tonnes because it is cheaper to buy permits. At the market clearing price emissions trading will achieve the required compliance at less cost than the regulation. This should allow a discussion of why economic instruments allow more flexibility and there should be recognition that those who are able to undertake abatement most cheaply achieve the bulk of emission reductions, but they are adequately compensated by the permit market.

Exploring MACCs is a useful exercise in that it allows students to understand what is required to comply cost-effectively with a range of regulatory instruments. It also has the benefits of showing some insight into the rationale of why economists promote the use of economic instruments over regulation and how this can affect firm profitability. In this way it focuses on the sustainability from a managerial perspective, rather than a societal perspective.

The main drawback of this approach is that it is a time-consuming exercise, needing at least two hours to complete. To complete this exercise in two hours there also needs to be some pre-session reading, which defines key concepts, such as abatement, and explains how MACCs are constructed and used. In practice this has also needed a lot of explanation and control from faculty members, particularly when class size goes above 50. This is often difficult to accommodate, given the already crammed nature of a microeconomics (business) course syllabus. The general feedback has been that the session is useful and interesting, but also challenging. This type of simulation may be best reserved for when exclusively focusing on sustainability in business economics, but as a part of a microeconomics course, there may not be enough time available to cover this topic.

Infusing Sustainability into Economics

The previous section discussed teaching how businesses comply with environmental regulation. This applies when business activity or excessive competition causes damage to the environment or society. Figure 4.2 showed that businesses could also use sustainable actions beyond the reference line to exploit markets, defend market share, or to achieve greater resource efficiency. These are important elements of many corporate strategies and so sustainability in business economics teaching could be mixed into other sessions, rather than being a distinct topic. Over time many companies have used sustainability as a critical element of their strategy (Epstein et al. 2015) and so there is a wealth of applied case study material.

Mixing sustainability into a microeconomics (business) course gives the content an immediate relevance to all students, regardless of the level of their interest in sustainability. It has the added advantage that it allows them to root economic theory into practical applications, which is helpful to those studying economics for the first time. The investigation and discussion of applied case studies allows students to debate and build each other's knowledge. This can be a powerful tool when teaching sustainability. It is an emotive subject for some and for others it is not. Bringing these two types of students together is useful to challenge the former and to stimulate the interest of the latter. The rest of this section discusses where we believe sustainability in business economics can provide useful examples or cases to illustrate key concepts.

From a broad strategic viewpoint sustainability can be used to think about demand, supply, and prices. Presenting students with broad trends provides material to support student thinking on how socio-economic trends affect markets. Figure 4.6 presents some major emerging trends that will shape future markets but also present some sustainability concerns. For instance, The United Nations (UN) projects that the global population will increase by approximately 14% to 9.8 billion people in

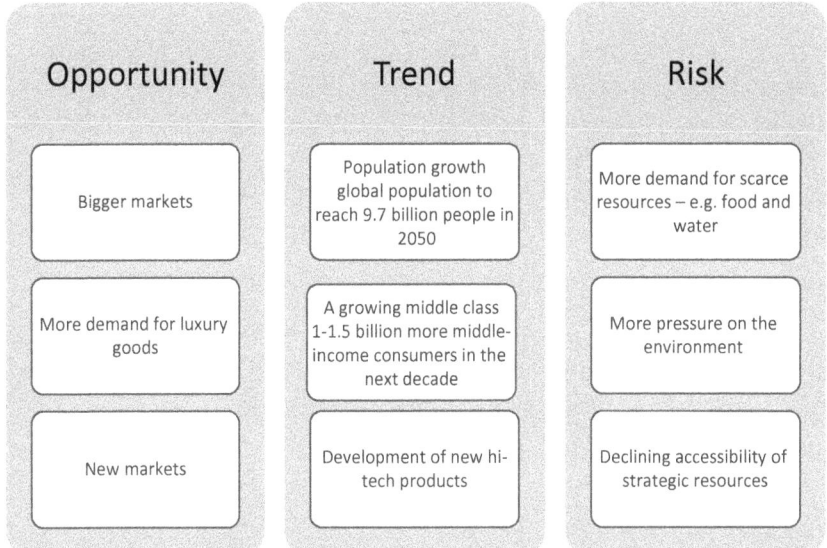

Fig. 4.6 Emerging opportunities, trends, and risks

2050 (UN 2017), raising questions as to what this will do to the demand for food and other commodities (FAO 2017). The Brookings Institute (2017) expects 1–1.5 billion people to join the middle class in the next decade, meaning they will have money to spend once they buy everything necessary for survival. Again this is likely to mean more demand for technology products, hi-tech entertainment, cars, air travel, and education. The innovation of new hi-tech products is accelerating and provides new markets.

In this type of exercise students can draw out demand and supply schedules to explore what these broad trends mean for demand, supply, and prices. They can then further reflect what happens if supplies of commodities are reduced or disrupted because of climate change or overuse of resources. This enables a thoughtful, purposeful use of demand and supply schedules to determine prices, but also a free scope to imagine future implications of these trends.

This should enable students to develop the link between broad demand and supply trends (Fig. 4.6) and market exploitation opportunities, where successful firms are innovating products and services that rely on fewer resources or increase productivity. The Organisation for Economic Co-operation and Development (OECD) defines this market development as 'green growth', investments and innovations that will underpin sustained growth and give rise to new economic opportunities. Current practice is replete with examples of green growth. For instance, the multinational conglomerate General Electric (GE), which has had well-publicised pollution issues (*The New York Times* 2016), has developed its Ecomagination wing, which aims to develop incrementally more efficient technologies. Fortune magazine (2016) reports that through the end of 2015, GE had invested $17 billion in clean tech R&D through Ecomagination while generating $232 billion in revenue from its products.

Many companies have embraced environmental markets as a new opportunity and there is scope to explore how environmental innovations can be used to bypass competition and exploit new markets. The environmental technology market was worth $1.05 trillion in 2015 (Select USA 2015). More and more governments have now raised their reference line for car emissions, banning the sale of petrol and diesel cars post 2040 to improve air quality. This has made innovation around electric engines critically important to car manufacturing (Boretti 2017). One example that has been particularly useful in generating classroom discussion is the urine powered mobile phone charging technology (Walter et al. 2017). On first consideration students find the idea frivolous and even a little unpleasant, but after further consideration they appreciate the value of taking an abundant, waste product and using it to replace other scarce resources like electricity. This is the essence of sustainable technology, taking waste and using it as a resource.

Beyond market trends, sustainability-based case studies can be used to illustrate concepts such as barriers to entry and product differentiation. For instance, regulation increases the cost of market participation because it requires firms to invest in capital items and have more sophisticated environmental and safety systems in place (Costantini and Mazzanti 2012; Rennings and Rammer 2011; Angerer et al. 2008). This has the effect of raising the cost of competing in a sector. For example, stricter waste regulations tend to have the effect of concentrating waste management markets, away from smaller operators. Environmental policy instruments, such as emissions trading, also can have the effect of ensuring the continuance of emission rights for incumbents, but more stringent laws for new entrants (Revesz and Kong 2011; Gurtoo and Antony 2007). Governments have frequently deployed environmental standards as a non-tariff barrier to entry for imports (Ederington and Minier 2003).

Hence, several sectors may actually lobby for tighter regulation, because they perceive that it limits competition in their sector (Taylor et al. 2015). In general, the more onerous environmental regulation is for new entrants, the less competition there is likely to be, thus protecting incumbents. However, once in the market firms can lobby for even stricter regulation: low-cost airlines, with newer fleets frequently call for more onerous air quality regulation, in the knowledge that it will hurt older fleets.

Sustainability can also be used as the basis for product differentiation in oligopoly or monopolistic competition market structures. For instance, Puma uses sustainability to differentiate its brand in the sports apparel market. While most sports brands have a sustainability strategy, Puma have made sustainability a central part of their ethos and competitive strategy (Gröschl et al. 2017; Cameron 2011), going as far as committing their strategic suppliers to sustainability reporting. While this is not necessarily a market acquiring strategy, as Nike dominates the sector but does not focus their strategy on sustainability, it is a way that Puma can appear different and appeal to sustainability-minded buyers. Similar examples exist in the cosmetics sector, with companies that have taken the lead in avoiding animal testing and in the coffee sector with fair trade products.

The resource efficiency element of sustainability can be used as an example to draw out the principles of *Cost-Benefit Analysis (CBA)* within a classroom session analysing the appraisal of capital items. Resource efficiency refers to reductions in material or energy inputs that lower overall costs of production, while maintaining or increasing output. This usually involves upfront investment in a relatively expensive capital item that allows for energy or resource savings over a longer timeframe. These characteristics make such investments a good case study of CBA.

The authors have used the example of solar panels as an applied example within teaching sessions. Most of the costs of installation are experienced in the installation phase, usually the project start-up year (year 0). Against this most of the benefits of solar panels flow across the lifetime of the project, which can be 20 years and beyond. These benefits comprise savings made by generating, rather than buying electricity and also payment for any surplus energy that is 'exported' to the grid. Hence there is a need to make all costs and benefits comparable across time for accurate comparison against a risk-free alternative. Given the long lifetime of the investment, the length of the payback period is also an important aspect of the appraisal.

There are several elements about a renewable energy investment that can be expanded to give a more nuanced treatment of CBA. The return on investment depends on the wholesale electricity price and assumptions regarding solar cell efficiency over the life of the investment. This provides opportunity to explore sensitivity analysis and how the analyst can use multiple scenarios to judge the reliability of the outcome of a CBA.

The use of CBA to determine resource savings is critical for demonstrating sustainability at the board level. Unless it is for compliance reasons, most action needs to be financially viable and outputs of a CBA will demonstrate this. There are lots of prominent examples of other input efficiency projects that could be developed into a case study. Coors Brewers Ltd. successively reduced the weight of its 300 ml Grolsch beer bottle, saving approximately 8000 tonnes of glass annually (WRAP 2007). However, usually financial appraisal is taught in other modules on a business course, so CBA in the sustainability context can often repeat previous material.

Corporate social responsibility is supported by the three pillars of social, economic, and environmental sustainability. Most focus to date has been on the environmental pillar, which has meant that the social pillar has received less attention. This is something that, by definition, has remained outside environmental economics. However, to be relevant to business teaching sustainability economics also needs to address how businesses improve their social performance.

Sustainability Teaching in Macroeconomics

Environmental economics has predominantly focused on issues related to microeconomics. However, this does not mean that the macroeconomic elements should be ignored. At the *2012 Rio+20 Conference* world leaders met to agree a range of measures that would ensure 'decent jobs, clean energy and a more sustainable and fair use of resources'. This discussion centred on the creation of a 'Green Economy': how the current 'business as usual' economy can be re-shaped to achieve better social outcomes (UNEP 2012).

This followed widespread recognition that the way in which society has approximated economic wellbeing may not accurately reflect social wellbeing (Pearce et al. 1989). For instance, gross domestic product (GDP) does not account for the depreciation of natural capital. Studies have shown a divergence between economic growth (as measured by GDP) and the *Index of Sustainable Economic Welfare (ISEW)* which includes environmental as well as other welfare indicators (Kubiszewski et al. 2013; Fleurbaey 2009). The rationale for using alternative measures is that GDP treats consumption as a positive economic activity. This is not always true. For example, deforestation, wetland drainage, and oil spills all cause an increase in economic activity in the short term, but are outweighed by longer term social and environmental costs.

Methods for green accounting such as the *UN System of Environmental and Economic Accounts* have been developed to put monetary values on environmental degradation so that they can be included in national income accounts. In this way a decline in the stock of natural capital is shown as a sign of unsustainable activity. There has also been widespread use of sustainability indicators, used to determine broad movements in national sustainability.

Incorporating elements of green accounting into a macroeconomics syllabus forms the basis of discussions around what constitutes the measurement of economic growth, how should we adjust our estimates of wellbeing to include environmental gains and losses, or in a way that more closely links to human wellbeing? This is particularly pertinent with the rise of concepts such as the *circular economy*, which conceptually is a model where end-of-life products are used as intermediate inputs for a new range of products, thus reducing waste and use of natural resources.

Final Reflections

In many ways teaching sustainability in business economics is similar to teaching quantitative methods. Students come to the classroom with varying amounts of knowledge, confidence, and interest. This makes it challenging, if not impossible, to deliver something that satisfies everyone in the classroom. For some students discussion about the basics of sustainability including the history, broad concepts, and policy implications can in itself be enlightening, while for others this may not extend their knowledge nor satisfy their enquiring minds and they can leave the classroom disappointed. Investigating compliance issues introduces complex managerial issues, but often there is a need to stress the strategic nature of compliance to those that see it as an otherwise operational issue. This way of teaching is time consuming, where sustainability is just one topic on a crowded syllabus. Infusing sustainability within the syllabus offers a way to make sustainability interesting to all, while providing highly relevant examples and case studies that support wider learning of economic concepts.

This is consistent with the direction of business practice. There are many examples of successful businesses that have put sustainability at the heart of their economic strategies and these can be utilised to build effective case studies or examples. Taught material should reflect this. There is a need to move from teaching sustainability as a distinct topic within economics and instead blend it into the syllabus. This also provides an opportunity to broaden the scope of sustainability. To date sustainability in business economics has focused on environmental economics from a social perspective, but sustainability includes elements of social responsibility and care for employees. Again there are many examples of companies that embrace this wider view of sustainability in their economic strategies that can be used as a basis of taught examples.

It is the hope of many sustainability professionals that sustainability becomes extinct as a separate subject and instead becomes an intrinsic part of business. This appears to be the direction of travel in teaching sustainability business economics. However, for those wanting to teach *Sustainability in Business Economics* as a distinct module, we briefly set out a short module outline. Naturally, this can be flexed to suit particular module lengths and target audiences.

- *Demand, supply, and price determination*: using projections of population growth and resource demand and creation of new markets for environmentally sustainable technology as stimulus material (see Fig. 4.5).
- *Competitive strategy*: analysing the use of sustainability as a means of product differentiation and new market creation.
- *Resource efficiency and CBA*: creating competitive advantage through the selection of efficient or renewable technology.
- *Government and business*: the use of MACCs and compliance with regulation.
- *Macroeconomics*: green accounting and alternatives to GDP.

References

Ando, Amy, and Donna Harrington. 2006. Tradable Discharge Permits: A Student Friendly Game. *Journal of Economic Education* 37: 187–201.

Ang, Frederic, and Steven Van Passel. 2012. Beyond the Environmentalist's Paradox and the Debate on Weak Versus Strong Sustainability. *BioScience* 62: 251–259.

Angerer, Gerhard, Ralf Nordbeck, and Christian Sartorius. 2008. Impacts on Industry of Europe's Emerging Chemicals Policy REACH. *Journal of Environmental Management* 86: 636–647.

Aslaksen, Iulie, Solveig Glomsrod, and Anne Myhr. 2013. Post-normal Science and Ecological Economics: Strategies for Precautionary Approaches for Sustainable Development. *International Journal of Sustainable Development* 16: 107–126.

Barbier, Edward. 2011. The Policy Challenges for Green Economy and Sustainable Economic Development. *Natural Resources Forum* 35: 233–245.

———. 2012. The Green Economy Post Rio+20. *Science* 338: 887–888.

Bordt, Michael. 2018. Discourses in Ecosystem Accounting: A Survey of the Expert Community. *Ecological Economics* 144: 82–99.

Boretti, Aleberto. 2017. The Future of the Internal Combustion Engine after "Diesel-Gate". Paper presented at SAE International Conference on Advances in Design, Materials, Manufacturing and Surface Engineering for Mobility, ADMMS 2017; Chennai; India; July 19, 2017.

Brookings Institute. 2017. The Unprecedented Expansion of the Global Middle Class. Accessed January 16, 2018. https://www.brookings.edu/research/the-unprecedented-expansion-of-the-global-middle-class-2/.

Burtraw, Dallas, and Matt Woerman. 2013. Economic Ideas for a Complex Climate Policy Regime. *Energy Economics* 40: S24–S31.

Cameron, Andrew. 2011. A Sustainable Workplace—We're All in It Together. *Strategic Direction* 28: 3–5.

Coase, Ronald. 1960. The Problem of Social Cost. *The Journal of Law and Economics* 3: 1–44.

Corrigan, Jay. 2011. The Pollution Game: A Classroom Game Demonstrating the Relative Effectiveness of Emissions Taxes and Tradable Permits. *Journal of Economic Education* 42: 70–78.

Costantini, Valeria, and Massimiliano Mazzanti. 2012. On the Green and Innovative Side of Trade Competitiveness? The Impact of Environmental Policies and Innovation on EU Exports. *Research Policy* 41: 132–153.

Daly, Herman. 1973. *Towards a Steady State Economy*. New York: W. H. Freeman & Co Ltd.

Daly, Herman, and John Cobb. 1989. *For the Common Good: Redirecting the Economy Toward Community, the Environment and a Sustainable Future*. Boston: Beacon Press.

Ederington, Josh, and Jenny Minier. 2003. Is Environmental Policy a Secondary Trade Barrier? An Empirical Analysis. *Canadian Journal of Economics* 36: 137–154.

Ekins, Paul, Sandrine Simon, Lisa Deutsch, Carl Folke, and Rudolf De Groot. 2003. A Framework for the Practical Application of the Concepts of Critical Natural Capital and 'Strong Sustainability. *Ecological Economics* 44: 165–185.

Epstein, Marc, Adriana Buhovac, and Kristi Yuthas. 2015. Managing Social, Environmental and Financial Performance Simultaneously. *Long Range Planning* 48: 35–45.

FAO. 2017. *The Future of Food and Agriculture: Trends and Challenges*. Accessed January 16, 2018. http://www.fao.org/3/a-i6583e.pdf.

Fleurbaey, Marc. 2009. Beyond GDP: The Quest for a Measure of Social Welfare. *Journal of Economic Literature* 47: 1029–1075.

Fortune Magazine. 2016. How GE Is Changing the World. Accessed January 16, 2018. http://fortune.com/2016/08/19/general-electric-change-world/.

Ghisellini, Patrizia, Catia Cialani, and Sergio Ulgiati. 2016. A Review on Circular Economy: The Expected Transition to a Balanced Interplay of Environmental and Economic Systems. *Journal of Cleaner Production* 114: 11–32.

Glen, John, and Joe Nellis. 2010. 'The Price You Pay': The Impact of State-Funded Secondary School Performance on Residential Property Values in England. *Panoeconomicus* 57: 405–428.

Gröschl, Stefan, Patricia Gabaldón, and Tobias Hahn. 2017. The Co-evolution of Leaders' Cognitive Complexity and Corporate Sustainability: The Case of the CEO of Puma. *Journal of Business Ethics*, 1–22.

Gurtoo, Anijula, and Simon Antony. 2007. Environmental Regulations: Indirect and Unintended Consequences on Economy and Business. *Management of Environmental Quality* 18: 626–642.

Hahn, Robert. 2000. The Impact of Economics on Environmental Policy. *Journal of Environmental Economics and Management* 39: 375–399.

Hanley, Nick, Jason Shogren, and Ben White. 2006. *Environmental Economics in Theory and Practice*. 2nd ed. Basingstoke: Palgrave.

Hartwick, John. 1977. Intergenerational Equity and the Investing of Rents from Exhaustible Resources. *American Economic Review* 67: 972–974.

Hodge, Ian. 1989. Compensation for Nature Conservation. *Environment & Planning A* 21: 1027–1036.

Hotelling, Harold. 1931. The Economics of Exhaustible Resources. *Journal of Political Economy* 39: 137–175.

Johansson, Per-Olov. 1991. *An Introduction to Modern Welfare Economics*. Cambridge: Cambridge University Press.

Jordan, Andrew, Rudiger Wurzel, and Anthony Zito. 2003. New' Instruments of Environmental Governance: Patterns and Pathways of Change. *Environmental Politics* 12: 1–26.

Kahneman, Daniel, and Jack Knetsch. 1992. Valuing Public Goods: The Purchase of Moral Satisfaction. *Journal of Environmental Economics and Management* 22: 57–70.

Kubiszewski, Ida, Robert Costanza, Carol Franco, Philip Lawn, John Talberth, Tim Jackson, and Camille Aylmer. 2013. Beyond GDP: Measuring and Achieving Global Genuine Progress. *Ecological Economics* 93: 57–68.

Liu, Jing-Yue, and Chao Feng. 2018. Marginal Abatement Costs of Carbon Dioxide Emissions and Its Influencing Factors: A Global Perspective. *Journal of Cleaner Production* 170: 14–33.

Malthus, Thomas. 1798. *Essay on the Principle of Population*. Oxford: Oxford University Press.

Morris, Joe, Rowbotham, Alex, Angus, Andrew, Mann, Michael, and Poll, Ian. 2009. A Framework for Estimating the Marginal Costs of Environmental Abatement for the Aviation Sector. *OMEGA Project 14*. Bedford: Cranfield University.

O'Niell, John. 1993. *Ecology, Policy and Politics: Human Well-being and the Natural World*. London: Routledge.

Parson, Edward., and Eric Kravitz. 2013. Market Instruments for the Sustainability Transition. *Annual Review of Environment and Resources* 38: 415–440.

Pearce, David, Anil Markandya, and Barbier Edward. 1989. *Blueprint for a Green Economy*. London: Earthscan Publications Ltd.

Perman, Robert, Yue Ma, Michael Common, David Maddison, and J. McGilvray. 2011. *Natural Resource and Environmental Economics*. 4th ed. London: Addison Wesley.

Rao, Pinninti. 2000. *Sustainable Development: Economics and Policy*. Padstow: Blackwell Publishers.

Rennings, Klaus, and Christian Rammer. 2011. The Impact of Regulation-Driven Environmental Innovation on Innovation Success and Firm Performance. *Industry and Innovation* 18: 255–283.

Revesz, Richard, and Allison Kong. 2011. Regulatory Change and Optimal Transition Relief. *North Western University Law Review* 106: 1582–1626.

Rivas Casado, Monica, Jan Serafini, John Glen, and Andrew Angus. 2017. Monetising the Impacts of Waste Incinerators Sited on Brownfield Land Using the Hedonic Pricing Method. *Waste Management* 61: 608–616.

Select USA. 2015. Environmental Technology Spotlight: The Environmental Technology Industry in the United States. Accessed January 16, 2018. https://www.selectusa.gov/environmental-technology-industry-united-states.

Solow, Robert. 1986. On the Intergenerational Allocation of Natural Resources. *Scandinavian Journal of Economics* 88: 141–149.

Taylor, Chris, Simon Pollard, Sophie Rocks, and Andrew Angus. 2012. Selecting Policy Instruments for Better Environmental Regulation: A Critique and Future Research Agenda. *Environmental Policy and Governance* 22: 268–292.

———. 2015. Better by Design: Business Preferences for Environmental Regulatory Reform. *Science of the Total Environment* 512–513: 287–295.

The New York Times. 2016. G.E. Spent Years Cleaning Up the Hudson. Was It Enough? Accessed January 16, 2018. https://www.nytimes.com/2016/09/09/nyregion/general-electric-pcbs-hudson-river.html.

UN. 2017. World Population Prospects 2017. Accessed January 16, 2018. https://esa.un.org/unpd/wpp/.

UNEP. 2012. A Guidebook to the Green Economy: Issue 1: Green Economy, Green Growth, and Low-Carbon Development—History, Definitions and a Guide to Recent Publications. Accessed January 16, 2018. https://sustainabledevelopment.un.org/content/documents/GE%20Guidebook.pdf.

Walter, Xavier, Andrew Stinchcombe, John Greenman, and Ioannis Ieropoulos. 2017. Urine Transduction to Usable Energy: A Modular MFC Approach for Smartphone and Remote System Charging. *Applied Energy* 192: 575–581.

World Commission on Environment and Development. 1987. *Our Common Future.* Oxford: Oxford University Press.

WRAP. 2007. Lightweight Glass Containers: Understanding Consumer Perceptions. Accessed January 16, 2018. http://www.wrap.org.uk/sites/files/wrap/14325%2003%20Consumer%20Perceptions%20CS%20for%20web%2027th%20March%2007.pdf.

Yin, Kwong, Adrian Ward, Paul Dargusch, and Anthony Halog. 2018. The Cost of Abatement Options to Reduce Carbon Emissions from Australian International Flights. *International Journal of Sustainable Transportation* 12: 165–178.

5

Thinking Globally, Teaching Sustainability: Embedding Sustainability in International Business Studies and Addressing Student Responses

George Ferns

Introduction

Globalization is pervasive—the twenty-first century is often regarded as the century of globalization (Stiglitz 2006; Giddens 2001). As Kofi Annan, the ex-Secretary-General of the United Nations (UN) once remarked: "arguing against globalization is like arguing against the laws of gravity" (Kofi Annan 2000). Globalization affects us all; everything seems to be connected to everything else, and everyone seems to be linked to everyone else. Relatedly, globalization is not a straightforward phenomenon, which makes it difficult to grasp, and therefore accurately define (Scholte 2005). Globalization is more of an ongoing, complex, and ever evolving process rather than an end state—it cannot therefore be conceptualized in a traditional, linear sense (Stromquist and Monkman 2014).

The growth of globalization has, without doubt, resulted in many benefits (Dunning 2006a). As the Director-General of the World Trade

G. Ferns (✉)
Cardiff University, Cardiff, UK
e-mail: fernsg@cardiff.ac.uk

© The Author(s) 2019
K. Amaeshi et al. (eds.), *Incorporating Sustainability in Management Education*,
https://doi.org/10.1007/978-3-319-98125-3_5

Organization (WTO), Pascal Lamy (2006) indicates: "globalization has led to the opening and the vanishing of many barriers and walls, and has the potential for expanding freedom, democracy, innovation, social and cultural exchanges while offering outstanding opportunities for dialog and understanding." Lower commodity prices have given us the ability to construct metropolitan cities from scratch, faster shipping times has allowed emerging economies to access global markets, and without globalization the digital revolution would probably not have happened (Crenshaw and Robison 2006). Therefore, globalization has resulted in much greater connectivity among people across the world (e.g., Tsagarousianou 2004). We have in a sense come together as a melting pot of cultures and communities: "[…] never before in the history of the world have so many people been able to learn about so many other people's lives, products and ideas" (Friedman 2002, iv).

However, globalization has also brought with it many challenges. As the World Bank for example argues, "while globalization is a catalyst for and a consequence of human progress, it is also a messy process that requires adjustment and creates significant challenges and problems." For example, globalization has significantly impacted natural systems given the relentless extraction of natural resources, especially in the global south (Bakker 2007). This exposes another central critique relating to globalization—some nations benefit more than others (Klein 2010; Nissanke and Thorbecke 2006). Those that have benefited the most are usually western, developed nations in contrast to non-industrialized countries, which often lose out on globalization's overpromised benefits (Pieterse 2015; Jensen and Sandström 2011; Banerjee and Linstead 2001).

Globalization also suffers from precisely that which defines it—interconnectedness. As Diamond (2005, 2), in his book *Collapse: How societies choose to fail or succeed*, suggests: "globalization makes it impossible for modern societies to collapse in isolation." In other words, because of this global entanglement, situations occur where no single nation is either willing or capable to address what Ulrich Beck (1995) famously framed as 'global problems of risk.' These include, amongst others, the current migrant 'crisis' in Europe, major ecological crises such as global climate change or the recent financial crisis (see also Giddens 2013). Undoubtedly, these events were shaped or, in some cases, even caused by globalization. In relation to the recent financial crisis, an OECD (2013, 128) for instance report warns: "the crisis seriously calls into question [...] globalisation, which to a certain extent amplified risks linked to banking activities and financial markets and brought about financial imbalances among leading economic powers."

Both the above-mentioned benefits and challenges have, to varying degrees, been stimulated by international business (IB) activity. Despite minor setbacks due to events such as Brexit and Trump's protectionist policies (Khan 2017), business increasingly invests outside their national boundaries and thereby facilitate globalization (UNCTAD 2016). After all, there are good reasons to do so, including, amongst others: producing at lower costs, tapping into new consumer segments, accessing novel technologies, and sourcing skilled workers. Globalization has also resulted in multinational companies (MNCs) becoming more productive and efficient in delivering products and services (Dunning 2000). Famously, the two most populous countries—India and China—have seen major improvements relating to jobs, technology, and infrastructure due to the process of globalization (Sharma 2009; Scholte 2005).

Given the above-mentioned developments, it should not be surprising that globalization has significantly affected business schools. This not only includes the impact of globalization on the diversity of the student population, but globalization becoming a core part of business school curricula (Stromquist 2007). Indeed, whether on an MBA, doing a Master's in human relations, or studying finance, economics, or accounting—theories and concepts relating to globalization are a guaranteed part of the curriculum. Furthermore, there is an increasing need for business schools to train future managers to be able to work in international environments and across cultures (Cornuel 2007). However, business schools have been criticized for failing to educate future leaders about sustainability. For example, business schools are often 'blamed' for propagating unethical behaviour of future managers (Ghoshal 2005), producing future corporate psychopaths (Bergman et al. 2014), and indoctrinating students with a free-market ideology (Pfeffer and Fong 2004), amongst others. This sentiment is reflected in a significant body of research that has amounted in the past decade addressing barriers to implementing sustainability into higher education (Delgado-Ceballos et al. 2012; Dyllick 2015). The underlying consensus is that, despite the need for sustainability in business practice, business schools are not producing the sort of managers capable of filling this gap. Instead, graduates remain focused too narrowly on generating financial returns through short-term actions; the current mind-set is one of '*either* profits *or* sustainability' rather than '*both* profits *and* sustainability' (Shrivastava 2010; Aragon-Correa et al. 2017).

Considering these shortcomings, how can we re-orientate business and management studies to embrace a sustainability perspective on globalization? In the sections that follow, I address this question by drawing on my experience teaching IB at three business schools in the United Kingdom. There are of course other areas of business and management studies that have similarly been affected by globalization—for instance organizational behaviour (Morgan 2017), strategic management (Doh 2005), and entrepreneurship (Knight 2000). However, IB is particularly a useful case for the purpose of this chapter given that it is almost entirely constituted by globalization. This chapter is structured in two parts. First, I discuss the main pillars of IB curricula, highlighting shortcomings with the mainstream approach and proposing a sustainability perspective that addresses these shortcomings. Second, I discuss four student types, each with their own challenge that hinders productive engagement with the sustainability agenda. I also include certain strategies that educators can employ to help students overcome these pedagogical blockages.

Shifting IB from the Mainstream to a Sustainability Perspective

Below I discuss two key foundational pillars of a typical IB course. It is important to mention that these two pillars by no means constitute *all* aspects of an IB programme. Rather, these foci seem to define most IB programmes. This does not mean that ethics or sustainability do not at all feature in typical IB programmes; in fact, it is rather likely that they do. However, a sustainability perspective is usually (if not always) an add-on. This section is structured by (a) first discussing each pillar, (b) then highlighting its key shortcoming, (c) followed by a solution to this shortcoming in the form of a sustainability element.

Pillar 1: Defining the MNC

The start of almost any IB course involves defining what we mean by IB and globalization and how these are related. Typically, globalization is defined as a process that integrates and interconnects social, economic, and political systems (Luthans and Doh 2012). Lecture content is usually centred around a narrow discussion of what a MNC is. This may involve using the United Nations Conference on Trade and Development's (UNCTAD) World Investment Report, which indicates how much foreign assets a company has under its control. In addition, course content draws from popular press lists and rankings that indicate MNC presence around the world, and the biggest companies globally—for example, Fortune 500. At the end of an introductory lecture, students' impression of IB and globalization usually involves grand conceptions of MNCs and their operations—it is all about big, successful, and flashy businesses with their head offices in Europe or the United States making billions of dollars through their operations non-industrialized parts of the world. The 'critical' element normally centres around questioning whether globalization is overexaggerated or a myth. Here, Alan Rugman's (2012) *The End of Globalization* is commonly used as a counterpoint for hyper-globalization (see also Friedman 2005; Ohmae 1999).

A key shortcoming with this approach regarding sustainability is that the power effects of MNCs are largely neglected. In other words, curricula usually stop at the point of defining MNCs and globalization, thereby neglecting the impact of MNC activity on marginalized groups, the natural environment, and society at large (Rondinelli and Berry 2000). In cases where impacts are acknowledged, these are commonly restricted to economic consequences such as job creation and positive 'spill overs' of private sector interest (Meyer 2004). However, both negative and positive roles of MNCs are important as "firms are increasingly called upon to play a positive role, and thus contribute to a more sustainable development" (Kolk and van Tulder 2010, 119).

Power related to MNC activity can of course be conceptualized in various ways (Morgan 2017), which should be recognized in IB curricula. This ranges from MNCs visibly influencing the political sphere through lobbying, to the invisible power of MNC pressuring local governments in developing countries to act in favour MNCs (Ramamurti 2001). Without emphasizing such influences students are not exposed to, for instance, the possibility of a dominant transnational capitalist class (Sklair 2001), or the prevalence of interlocking directorships (Dreiling and Darves 2016). In addition, it is important to emphasize that MNCs are especially impactful regarding development goals. For example, MNCs play a significant role in poverty alleviation (and poverty creation) (Dunning 2006b). Yet, irrespective of these power effects, the role of MNC is frequently framed narrowly to encompass mostly the economic purpose of business (Banerjee 2003). Students are therefore exposed to a particularly constricted conceptualization of globalization that is almost always in the interests of MNCs.

A sustainability perspective on globalization seeks to expose power effects—especially those that relate to unsustainable practices resulting from globalization. In this regard, a sustainability perspective contains explicit recognition that MNC activity is intertwined not only with economic systems, but with ecological and social systems as well. Therefore, the impacts of MNCs is best taught not solely as the outcome of market-based processes, but, importantly as politically motivated. For example, issues such as inequality and environmental degradation are not conceptualized—as is common with mainstream approaches—as an externality resulting from business decisions alone, but issues that are shaped by non-market forces. These include other power sources, vested interests, and worldviews that may also be responsible for producing social and environmental issues. Students should be made aware that these power sources can be utilized for positive effects—inequality and environmental degradation can be reversed by utilizing the power of MNCs (Annan 2002).

Pillar 2: Internationalization

The second important pillar regards the holy grail of IB—internationalization. This central area of any IB programme concerns strategies for 'going global' such as exporting, foreign direct investment, licencing, and so on. Emphasis here is predominantly placed on balancing issues such as control and risk when doing business abroad. Commonly, material draws from classical cases such as MacDonald versus Coca Cola, which relate to the debate between standardization and adaptation (Doh 2005). To answer the question of *why* firms internationalize a wide range of theories are utilized, famously including the work of Vernon (1966) regarding the life cycle of firms, Dunning's (2000) eclectic theory of multinationals and Bartlett and Ghoshal's (2002) models of organization. The main point regarding internationalization is that students are able to identify which strategy an MNC should adopt given certain economic and cultural conditions. Therefore, students are normally tasked with putting themselves in the position of a manager, or, alternately, think of themselves as consultants pitching to investors looking to internationalize.

The main issue with IB's emphasis on internationalization is the assumption of managers as rational decision makers, and that globalization functions in a linear way. This is problematic in light of sustainability because social and environmental systems are complex (Whiteman et al. 2013; Levy and Lichtenstein 2011; Rotmans and Loorbach 2009). Hence, students are taught that markets, individuals, and organizations operate on a set of controllable processes. When decisions have unintended outcomes, the mainstream approach suggests that this is merely a flaw of poor decision making and faulty information. However, both globalization and sustainability do not operate in such an oversimplified manner. For example, global economic, ecological, and social systems function based on an intricate system of interconnected cause and effect arrangements. If this sort of networked approach is not incorporated into curricula, an over deterministic view of organizational life is reproduced (Jackson 2004, 177). MNCs play an important role here; however, their role forms part of a complex web of other roles. To teach students that firms' internationalization strategies operate outside this web where managers are framed as hyper muscular enforcers of globalization is, from my experience, somewhat counterproductive.

To address these issues, a sustainability perspective foregrounds complexity. The course content I usually present always contains explicit recognition that we are never able to 'paint the whole picture.' A sustainability perspective also rejects the traditional top-down hierarchical conceptualization of MNC activity—that is, the MNC's top management team makes decisions that ultimately trickle down throughout their operations globally. In addition, engaging students with the basics of, for instance, complexity theory (e.g., Levy and Lichtenstein 2011), humbles students in terms of their relationship with marginalized discourses—for example, 'nature' (Hajer and Fischer 1999), or the developing world (Meadowcroft 2000). By this I mean that focusing on complexity instead of linearity re-allocates the student from a privileged position at the top the hierarchy, to a more equal position. Therefore, while mainstream approaches reproduce the idea that western managers enforce their decisions 'from the top,' a sustainability perspective emphasizes how decisions are made 'among stakeholders.' In so doing, the MNC is re-defined in a much broader sense—its activity encompasses a whole variety of organizations, including non-governmental organizations (NGOs), other civil society organizations, local governments, and so on (Ferns and Amaeshi 2017). Hence, teaching about the role of MNCs within the globalization context involves embedding MNCs within a wider network of localities, as opposed to the traditional hierarchical, linear approach. As Morgan (2017, 768) suggests, this approach "dissects the rational model of the multinational, revealing how groups are struggling inside the organization to make a difference to how they live and how their localities are affected by these processes of globalization."

To sum up, adopting a sustainability approach may encourage students to develop a more holistic approach to studying IB. They therefore become more sensitive to the complex interconnectedness that is so inherent to globalization. This reflexivity of global systems is useful for sustainability as IB students begin to appreciate how contemporary grand challenges are politically intricate, and that these challenges require an alternative understanding of the role of business in a globalized world. Students therefore develop a sort of 'global consciousness' as they start to feel that they belong to this global system (Suàrez-Orozco 2007). Importantly, advancing a sustainability perspective within IB curricula does not happen effortlessly. As discussed next, students' preconceptions and worldviews often hinder their ability to fully reap pedagogical benefits.

Student Responses to a Sustainability Perspective (and What to Do About Them)

A sustainability perspective on globalization can engender several different responses from students. Below I present *some* of these responses; indeed, there may be many other types, for instance in other higher education contexts outside the United Kingdom. Nevertheless, the student types I illustrate below seem to capture the most salient examples from my own experience. Depending on the extent to which either of the two IB pillars (discussed above) is stressed, students may enact different responses. The main idea is that when confronted with a particular response, we, as educators, should identify which elements of a sustainability perspective could be modified to improve students' learning experience.

Radicals

These students are well exposed to social and environmental issues. They embody the typical 'activist' student and are preoccupied with exposing all sorts of injustices relating to race, gender, and the environment. The sustainability aspect of my class is therefore very much appreciated as radicals enthusiastically support the underlying 'critical' tone of lectures. These students do not shy away from sharing their thoughts and opinions during class, a practice that usually involves identifying a hegemonic structure—for example, capitalism—and critiquing it. Radicals claim to never to shop at H&M or ware Nike shoes as they are all too familiar with the classic case studies, Guardian newspaper articles, and YouTube documentaries that shame companies for their corporate irresponsibility (e.g., McVeigh 2017). Radicals propagate an anti-globalization worldview and argue that the positive effects of globalization far outweigh the benefits. In doing so, these students confess a preference for local businesses, as opposed to mega chains. During class, these anti-corporate crusaders make it their mission to find wrong with practically everything that has to do with big business, money, or capitalism.

The modus operandi of radicals poses particular challenges not only in terms of furthering the sustainability agenda during lectures, but for their own development as students. The main concern is bias. Radicals have the tendency to praise sustainability without much reflection, which results in a 'green halo effect' (Smith et al. 2010). The opposite occurs with capitalism, which radicals consider the antithesis of sustainability. While these arguments may have *some* validity, taking an extreme view that the relation between sustainability and capitalism is always a zero-sum game is, at least for students' intellectual development, rather unproductive. Hence, radicals' basic assumptions, passion, and fanaticism often hinder their ability to think critically and 'see' the whole picture. They are for instance often oblivious to geopolitical realities and cultural complexity, both of which need to be taken into consideration when learning about globalization and sustainability. But instead of considering such sensitives, radicals respond with aggressive rhetoric, the effects of which can negatively affect other students.

One particular instance comes to mind. Discussing the social and environmental impacts of MNCs I utilized a case of mining company's operations in the Democratic Republic of the Congo, focusing in particular on how the mining company was able to extort local government agencies to secure contracts. A radical rose occasion to and passionately remarked: "you see! This is exactly what we are fighting against. These companies need to be completely abolished." Another student, who is from a mining town in South Africa disagreed, calmly mentioning that "where I am from, the same company has built schools, roads, and a hospital. It is may be too extreme to just abolish them." The radical was furious, now with a raised voice insisted: "WHAT?! How can you possibly support companies that profit from the destruction of our planet? You obviously don't care about climate change and the poor people that it will affect the most!" The whole class, including myself, was visibly shaken by the outburst. The radical's eyes had become red and teary, he looked at me and said "don't you agree? I mean people just don't get it! Globalization is ruining our lives!" I was now in a bit of a predicament. Swiftly, I responded: "well, we need to take a balanced view as well. Everyone experiences globalization differently." It was clear that I had taken the easy way out, and the class noticed that I did not wish to side with the radical's emphatic views. Strangely, I felt somewhat disillusioned in the sense that I, to a certain degree, agreed with the radical, but did not want to seem extreme to the other students who are, after all, entitled to their own opinion and views.

Because radicals sit at the extreme end of the spectrum, managing their responses is rather difficult. However, from my experience, radicals can become more reflexive and open to learning about globalization and IB by emphasizing non-traditional business models, and alternative modes of capitalism. This includes, for example, engaging with concepts such as the circular economy or micro-finance loans, which, to varying degrees, incorporate sustainability thinking with business success. Importantly, to win over radicals these concepts must be framed around notions of justice, equality, peace, and so on. For example, teaching about the importance of micro-finance in relation to globalization must be linked to how micro-finance creates more gender equal societies in developing countries as women become empowered financially. This opens up room for discussion regarding the overlap between globalization, business, and social impacts. The main idea here is not to resist the ideas of radicals (these will not change during a semester studying IB) but to 'play their game' and use examples where they see overlap with their own ideals.

The Traditionalists

Traditionalists contrast shapely with radicals in the sense that they completely reject the sustainability element of my class. These students may agree that globalization is happening and that it is causing profound change in terms of social and economic systems, but they refuse to accept the negative consequences of globalization. Thereby, traditionalists frequently argue that the negative impacts of globalization are exaggerated. For these students, the status quo is completely acceptable. From my experience, traditionalists are usually from privileged backgrounds. However, rarely do these students admit their privilege. Traditionalists also reject the whole discussion regarding power of MNCs or other institutions, instead, commonly arguing that they are somehow unaffected by social structures or power regimes. Traditionalists would rather learn about globalization through orthodox theories; they are interested in simple answers to complex questions. However, a sustainability perspective suggests that there is no simple answer and that globalization is a multifaceted phenomenon, both of which the traditionalist finds frustrating.

Traditionalists are hindered by their unwillingness to forgo past ideas that contradict a sustainability perspective. In this regard, traditionalists feel attacked by an alternative worldview. After all, why should they believe me, their lecturer, that globalization has a 'dark side' that must be taken seriously? The student is ultimately faced with a choice: either to confront a sustainability perspective as a challenging alternative reality to what they are comfortable with or to reject this realization and respond with animosity. The traditionalist chooses the latter. In so doing, concepts ranging from sustainable development to anarchism are all mocked rather than given a fair, intellectually informed evaluation.

A particularly salient example involved a student launching a complaint that her professor (this was a colleague of mine on the same course) was purporting a communist ideology during class. This stemmed from the professor using Marxist theory to speak about the 'treadmill of production' and the global ecological crisis (e.g., Pulver 2007). Because this was a formal complaint, the matter was investigated by the head of our department. The student claimed that she was personally offended by, what she referred to as, the professor's "leftist propaganda, which does not belong in a business school." My colleague (who, somewhat ironically, is everything *but* a leftist) mentioned to her that the material was not intended to be ideological; rather, it was purely an academic exercise. The student however was not satisfied with the explanation and demanded an official apology. Of course, the professor agreed, but under one condition: the student should write her term essay, which counted for 70% of her final grade, on the topic of why Marx does not belong in IB studies. She happily agreed and took up the challenge. Her essay was surprisingly reflexive and she received a high mark.

As the above example illustrates, in contrast to radicals, traditionalists may respond more constructively to being challenged. Traditionalists can be enticed to engage with the sustainability agenda by using examples where MNCs benefit financially from sustainability. Cases should therefore be framed around 'win-win' situations. This is especially effective when focusing on the threat that social and environmental issues pose. When traditionalists are challenged to solve these threats, they usually seem rather motivated to engage with the subject in a more productive way. Climate change is a case in point. I have often encountered situations where traditionalists denounce sustainability as getting in the way of MNCs' financial objectives. However, when climate change is framed as a challenge that will, if addressed, produce higher financial returns in the long run, and when this challenge is assigned to the student personally (as in the lecturer says, 'I have a challenge for you'), traditionalists are the first to respond with all sorts of 'solutions.'

The Deer in the Headlights

These students (hereafter, 'the deer') are so overcome by the sustainability aspect of the class that they withdraw completely. The state of the world ecologically, the power of multinationals, their political influence, global inequality—these issues all seemed so distant until they arrived at university. Now, the intellectual cocoon that provided them with a sense of comfort throughout high school is shattered. The deer shut down and do not know how their miniscule influence on 'wicked problems' (Lazarus 2009) or 'grand challenges' (George et al. 2016) can ever have an effect. Importantly, in contrast to the traditionalists, the deer completely accept the serious impacts of globalization and MNC power. In this respect, they are similar to radicals; however, they differ in the sense that deer are overwhelmed having to live with this newly acquired knowledge. This of course leads to a state of inertia. The response is not only a state of shock, but confusion:

> *How is it possible that for so long I have cherished buying Fairtrade products, but now I've been told it may have reverse effect on farmers, but what should I do? I can buy the supermarket's normal brand of coffee, but then I'm only perpetuating consumerism and supporting big business. Maybe I can try to just buy my coffee locally, but again, the poor farmers will lose out? What about Starbucks, they're ethical aren't they ... no wait, they're involved with a tax scandal. What should I do? I just want some coffee!*

As the course goes on, the deer stare deeper into my eyes with a dazed look of bewilderment and fear. There is also usually a sort of embarrassment that these students exhibit—that is, "how could I never have realized this?" Such embarrassment is not productive in the sense that the deer rarely engage during class because they may feel as if their knowledge is far inferior to what is being taught in class. In many ways, the deer simply sit in the middle of the road, waiting for the impending crisis to hit them. Because they personalize and internalize their new-found knowledge, their self-absorption leads to tunnel vision. They cannot see the bigger picture and fail to grasp that sustainability is a systemic issue that does not revolve around them.

So, the question here is how to get the deer to stop staring at the headlights? A useful strategy here is not to be defeatist. This is something I only learned recently after initially not realizing the prevalence of deer in my class. Of course, the dire state of the Earth system cannot be understated, nor can we ignore the seriousness of social issues. However, when students are left with no answers at the end of class, there is a significant risk that they lose faith in their own ability to address these challenges. Therefore, it is important to highlight potential ways to transcend social and environmental crises; using illustrative examples that range from standard approaches—for example, solar energy being a realistic alternative energy because of Chinese production—to the more radical ideas—for example, de-growth as a potential way to become more sustainable. For deer, these suggestions, albeit with their own shortcomings, provide a useful escape hatch that they can use to separate themselves from the issue at hand, and reflect on a more realistic basis about their agency.

The Highbrows

Highbrow students are those who find everything about the intersection between sustainability and globalization fascinating. They are very keen students who are passionate scholars; highbrows read all the course material, request extra reading, and frequently score high marks on their assignments and exams. The sustainability element, in particular, presents a much-wanted intellectual challenge for highbrows. There a certain controversy surrounding sustainability that attracts them. Importantly, although they are engaged with the subject on an academic level, highbrows are not bothered to take any action. Instead, they leave activism to radicals. Being largely detached from the issue this way, results in highbrows not changing aspects of their daily life due to the course. From my experience, highbrows enjoy debate surrounding sustainability issues with classmates. Highbrows do not speak about sustainability arrogantly—this is below them. They are purely interested in the higher-order pursuit of studying globalization and sustainability for the sake of their own education. However, much of their information gathering is fact finding, which is problematic because it can drain students' creativity. This, in turn, results in a situation where they believe that their arguments are good, but as their lecturer I know that they are merely repeating arguments made by others. Hence, they often engage with the study of sustainability and globalization in terms of quantity, instead of quality.

John is a typical highbrow. Having graduated from an elite university for his undergraduate studies, I had the pleasure of having John as a master's student. He took my IB course as an elective because of, according to him, "a passion for understanding different cultures." Indeed, John never seemed interested in the business side of the course; he was especially keen to learn about how globalization was changing the world. On the first day of class he immediately approached me and asked whether he could come speak to me after class about his group assignment, which was only due in 10 weeks! Somewhat reluctantly, I agreed (I was hesitant because I had not yet fully prepared their assignment task). As soon as the lecture was over, John followed me back to my office. We sat down and as I started my computer John was already busy elaborating on all the reading he has done for the class. He spoke confidently about his theoretical knowledge, ranging from Foucault to Stiglitz, asking me questions such as "I was thinking of basing my essay on the writings of Heidegger's Being and Time, but I don't quite agree with the accuracy of the translated version we have in the library, can I use my own translation from the German original? I have a copy at home." While questions like this made for interesting discussion, we hardly spoke about sustainability or globalization. Instead, the conversation was driven heavily by theory. Worryingly, when I asked John what he will do for the group assignment, he smirked, "don't worry, usually everyone just follows my lead, because, well, you know. … I know a bit more than they do!"

Admittedly, I am sometimes reluctant to interfere with the way high-brows engage with a sustainability perspective on globalization. This mainly because highbrows seem sort of harmless—their grades are good and they truly enjoy learning about the topic. I might also be prejudiced here because I see myself somewhat as falling into this camp (I suppose may sustainability academics do). Therefore, I am well-aware of the draw-backs of becoming too involved with sustainability issues from a purely intellectual standpoint; one quickly loses oversight of the seriousness of sustainability issues, and that they affect the daily lives of both humans and the natural world. Nevertheless, facilitating highbrows to engage on a deeper level with sustainability can be achieved. From my own experience, engaging with highbrows through their own personal experiences helps build a connection between their intellectual pursuit and sustainability issues. In other words, when speaking about MNCs and human rights for example, enquiring about their own personal experiences, for instance when their rights were abused, creates moments where the student realizes that, in fact, they *should* consider sustainability for more than just intellectual stimulation.

Conclusion

This chapter sought to address some of the challenges that arise when attempting to further a sustainability agenda in higher education. I focused on incorporating a sustainably perspective in my teaching of globalization. Here, I found significant gaps between what we teach, and the realities of a modern (unsustainable) world. Since commencing my career as an aca-demic, I remain rather shocked at how little sustainability features in most subjects in UK higher education, despite so many universities claiming to follow, for example, the UN Principles for Responsible Management Education. This remains surprising given, as Aragon-Correa et al. (2017, 470) argue: "the tension between changing the world for the better and improving company financial performance is inextricably tied to the teach-ing of sustainability and the teaching tools that exist for this purpose."

If the direction to teach more about sustainability does not come from the 'top-down,' then we as sustainability scholars must further the sustainability agenda from the 'bottom up.' This involves infusing our course content with concern for environmental and social injustices that are spurred on my irresponsible business practices. I have, in this chapter, shared my experience attempting to do so. I reflected on the two main pillars of IB and highlighted how these are problematic in terms of sustainability. I have also proposed an alternative perspective that both makes explicit reference to power effects of MNCs and appreciates the complexity of globalization and sustainability. This, I argued, would engender more holistic student engagement with the sustainability agenda. However, as most of us in higher education will be familiar with, sustainability does not come without resistance. I drew here on my experience, illustrating four student types, each with their own unproductive responses regarding sustainability. I also provided some strategies that would help students become more open to studying sustainability in relation to globalization.

There are two main implications of what I have proposed earlier. First, in terms of *what* we teach, sustainability is about including content that reflects the complexity of social and natural systems. We must accordingly introduce more theory that embraces complexity (see Williams et al. 2017 for overview), rather than relying on concepts that reproduce linear ways of thinking. The second implication regards *how* we teach. By reflecting on typical student responses to a sustainability perspective, we must be more adaptive in our delivery of course content; changing how we frame sustainability issues depending on our audiences. Only in doing so, can we overcome instances whereby certain students respond to sustainability topics in unproductive ways.

Overall, I hope other colleagues can utilize the reflections discussed in this chapter to improve the way they teach at their respective institutions. It is arguably through our teaching that we make biggest impact. This should be taken seriously, despite the significant challenges we face. I opened this chapter with a quote from Kofi Annan about the hegemonic character of globalization. I will now close by again quoting the former Secretary-General of the UN again: "Knowledge is power. Information is liberating. Education is the premise of progress, in every society, in every family."

References

Annan, Kofi. 2000. Globalization Tops 3-Day U.N. Agenda For World Leaders. New York, NY. http://www.nytimes.com/2000/09/03/world/globalization-tops-3-day-un-agenda-for-world-leaders.html.

Annan, K. 2002. *Both Business and Society Benefit from Working Together*. New York, NY: BASD http://basd.free.fr/docs/speeches/20020901_annan.html.

Aragon-Correa, J. Alberto, Alfred A. Marcus, Jorge E. Rivera, and Amy L. Kenworthy. 2017. Sustainability Management Teaching Resources and the Challenge of Balancing Planet, People, and Profits. *Academy of Management Learning and Education* 16 (3): 469–483. https://doi.org/10.5465/amle.2017.0180.

Bakker, Karen. 2007. The 'Commons' Versus the 'Commodity': Alter-globalization, Anti-privatization and the Human Right to Water in the Global South. *Antipode* 39 (3): 430–455. Wiley Online Library.

Banerjee, S.B. 2003. Who Sustains Whose Development? Sustainable Development and the Reinvention of Nature. *Organization Studies* 24 (1): 143–180.

Banerjee, S.B., and Stephen Linstead. 2001. Globalization, Multiculturalism and Other Fictions: Colonialism for the New Millennium? *Organization* 8 (4): 683–722. Thousand Oaks, CA: Sage Publications.

Bartlett, Christopher A., and Sumantra Ghoshal. 2002. *Managing across Borders: The Transnational Solution*. Cambridge, MA: Harvard Business Press.

Beck, U. 1995. *Ecological Politics in an Age of Risk*. Cambridge: Polity Press.

Bergman, J.Z., J.W. Westerman, S.M. Bergman, J. Westerman, and J.P. Daly. 2014. Narcissism, Materialism, and Environmental Ethics in Business Students. *Journal of Management Education* 38 (4): 489–510. https://doi.org/10.1177/1052562913488108.

Cornuel, Eric. 2007. Challenges Facing Business Schools in the Future. *Journal of Management Development* 26 (1): 87–92. Emerald Group Publishing Limited.

Crenshaw, Edward M., and Kristopher K. Robison. 2006. Globalization and the Digital Divide: The Roles of Structural Conduciveness and Global Connection in Internet Diffusion. *Social Science Quarterly* 87 (1): 190–207. Wiley Online Library.

Delgado-Ceballos, Javier, Juan Alberto Aragón-Correa, Natalia Ortiz-de-Mandojana, and Antonio Rueda-Manzanares. 2012. The Effect of Internal

Barriers on the Connection Between Stakeholder Integration and Proactive Environmental Strategies. *Journal of Business Ethics* 107 (3): 281–293. https://doi.org/10.1007/s10551-011-1039-y.

Diamond, Jared M. 2005. *Collapse: How Societies Choose to Fail or Succeed*. London: Penguin Books.

Doh, Jonathan P. 2005. Offshore Outsourcing: Implications for International Business and Strategic Management Theory and Practice. *Journal of Management Studies* 42 (3): 695–704. Wiley Online Library.

Dreiling, M.C., and D. Darves. 2016. *Agents of Neoliberal Globalization: Corporate Networks, State Structures, and Trade Policy*. Cambridge: Cambridge University Press.

Dunning, J.H. 2000. The Eclectic Paradigm as an Envelope for Economic and Business Theories of MNE Activity. *International Business Review* 9 (2): 163–190. Elsevier.

———. 2006a. Comment on Dragon Multinationals: New Players in 21 St Century Globalization. *Asia Pacific Journal of Management* 23 (2): 139–141. Springer.

———. 2006b. Upgrading the Quality of Global Capitalism: The Moral Dimension. In *Multinational Corporations and Global Poverty Reduction*, ed. S.C. Jain and S. Vachani, 346–379. Cheltenham: Edward Elgar Publishing.

Dyllick, Thomas. 2015. Responsible Management Education for a Sustainable World: The Challenges for Business Schools. *Journal of Management Development* 34 (1): 16–33.

Ferns, George, and Kenneth Amaeshi. 2017. Struggles at the Summits: Discourse Coalitions, Field Boundaries, and the Shifting Role of Business in Sustainable Development. *Business & Society*. https://doi.org/10.1177/0007650317701884.

Friedman, T.L. 2002. *Globalization—The Hopes and the Fears*. Warwick, NY: Awake!.

———. 2005. *The World Is Flat: A Brief History of the Twenty-First Century*. New York, NY: Penguin Books.

George, G., J. Howard-Grenville, A. Joshi, and L. Tihanyi. 2016. Understanding and Tackling Societal Grand Challenges through Management Research. *Academy of Management Journal* 59 (6): 1880–1895. https://doi.org/10.5465/amj.2016.4007.

Ghoshal, Sumantra. 2005. Bad Management Theories Are Destroying Good Management Practices. *Academy of Management Learning & Education* 4 (1): 75–91.

Giddens, Anthony. 2001. *The Global Third Way Debate*. London: Polity Press.

———. 2013. *The Politics of Climate Change*. Hoboken, NJ: John Wiley & Sons.

Hajer, M., and F. Fischer. 1999. Beyond Global Discourse: The Rediscovery of Culture in Environmental Politics. In *Living with Nature: Environmental Politics as Cultural Discourse*, ed. M. Hajer and F. Fischer, 1–20. Oxford, UK: Oxford University Press.

Jackson, Terence. 2004. *Management and Change in Africa: A Cross-Cultural Perspective*. London: Routledge.

Jensen, Tommy, and Johan Sandström. 2011. Stakeholder Theory and Globalization: The Challenges of Power and Responsibility. *Organization Studies* 32 (4): 473–488. London, UK: Sage Publications.

Khan, Mehreen. 2017. Trump's Protectionist Policies Threaten Rising Foreign Investment, Warns UN. *Financial Times*. https://www.ft.com/content/b5b6a84c-9cbf-3a12-94a4-bdb77aa7e46e.

Klein, Naomi. 2010. *The Shock Doctrine*. London, UK: Penguin.

Knight, Gary. 2000. Entrepreneurship and Marketing Strategy: The SME under Globalization. *Journal of International Marketing* 8 (2): 12–32. American Marketing Association.

Kolk, A., and R. van Tulder. 2010. International Business, Corporate Social Responsibility and Sustainable Development. *International Business Review* 19 (1): 119–125. https://doi.org/10.1177/1745691612459060.

Lamy, P. 2006. Humanising Globalization. Santiago de Chile, 30 January.

Lazarus, Richard J. 2009. Super Wicked Problems and Climate Change: Restraining the Present to Liberate the Future. *Cornell Law Review* 94 (5): 1153–1233. https://doi.org/10.2139/ssrn.1302623.

Levy, David, and B. Lichtenstein. 2011. Approaching Business and the Environment with Complexity Theory. In *The Oxford Handbook of Business and the Natural Environment*, ed. A.J. Hoffman and P. Bansal, 591–608. Oxford, UK: Oxford University Press http://works.bepress.com/david_levy/10/.

Luthans, F., and J.P. Doh. 2012. *International Management: Culture, Strategy, and Behavior*. New York, NY: McGraw-Hill.

McVeigh, Karen. 2017. Cambodian Female Workers in Nike, Asics and Puma Factories Suffer Mass Faintings. *Guardian*, June 25. https://www.theguardian.com/business/2017/jun/25/female-cambodian-garment-workers-mass-fainting.

Meadowcroft, J. 2000. Sustainable Development: A New(ish) Idea for a New Century? *Political Studies* 48: 370–387.

Meyer, K.E. 2004. Perspectives on Multinational Enterprises in Emerging Economies. *Journal of International Business Studies* 35 (4): 259–276.

Morgan, G. 2017. Globalization and Organizations. In *Introducing Organizational Behaviour and Management*, ed. David Knights and Hugh Willmott, 3rd ed., 490–534. Boston, MA: Cengage.

Nissanke, Machiko, and Erik Thorbecke. 2006. Channels and Policy Debate in the Globalization–inequality–poverty Nexus. *World Development* 34 (8): 1338–1360. Elsevier.

OECD. 2013. *The 2008 Financial Crisis—A Crisis of Globalisation?* Paris.

Ohmae, K. 1999. *The Borderless World: Power and Strategy in the Interlinked Economy*. New York, NY: HarperCollins.

Pfeffer, J., and C.T. Fong. 2004. The End of Business Schools? Less Success than Meets the Eye. *Academy of Management Learning and Education* 1 (1): 78–95.

Pieterse, Jan Nederveen. 2015. *Globalization and Culture: Global Mélange*. Lanham, MD: Rowman & Littlefield.

Pulver, S. 2007. Making Sense of Corporate Environmentalism: An Environmental Contestation Approach to Analyzing the Causes and Consequences of the Climate Change Policy Split in the Oil Industry. *Organization & Environment* 20 (1): 44–83. https://doi.org/10.1177/1086026607300246.

Ramamurti, Ravi. 2001. The Obsolescing 'Bargaining Model'? MNC-Host Developing Country Relations Revisited. *Journal of International Business Studies* 32 (1): 23–39. JSTOR.

Rondinelli, Dennis A., and Michael A. Berry. 2000. Environmental Citizenship in Multinational Corporations: Social Responsibility and Sustainable Development. *European Management Journal* 18 (1): 70–84. Elsevier.

Rotmans, Jan, and Derk Loorbach. 2009. Complexity and Transition Management. *Journal of Industrial Ecology* 13 (2): 184–196. https://doi.org/10.1111/j.1530-9290.2009.00116.x.

Rugman, Alan. 2012. *The End of Globalization*. London: Random House.

Scholte, Jan Aart. 2005. *Globalization: A Critical Introduction*. Basingstoke: Palgrave Macmillan.

Sharma, Shalendra D. 2009. *China and India in the Age of Globalization*. Cambridge: Cambridge University Press.

Shrivastava, Paul. 2010. Pedagogy of Passion for Sustainability. *Academy of Management Learning and Education* 9 (3): 443–455. https://doi.org/10.5465/AMLE.2010.53791826.

Sklair, L. 2001. *The Transnational Capitalist Class*. Oxford: Blackwell.

Smith, N.C., D. Read, and S. López-Rodríguez. 2010. Consumer Perceptions of Corporate Social Responsibility: The CSR Halo Effect. 2010/16/

INSEAD. Fontainebleau. https://papers.ssrn.com/sol3/papers.cfm?abstract_id=1577000.

Stiglitz, Joseph E. 2006. *Making Globalization Work*. New York, NY: W.W. Norton & Company.

Stromquist, Nelly P. 2007. Internationalization as a Response to Globalization: Radical Shifts in University Environments. *Higher Education* 53 (1): 81–105. Springer.

Stromquist, Nelly P., and Karen Monkman. 2014. *Globalization and Education: Integration and Contestation across Cultures*. Vol. 1. Lanham, MD: Rowman & Littlefield Education.

Suàrez-Orozco, M. 2007. Learning in the Global Era: International Perspectives on Globalization and Education. *The Review of Higher Education* 32 (4): 317. https://doi.org/10.1017/CBO9781107415324.004.

Tsagarousianou, Roza. 2004. Rethinking the Concept of Diaspora: Mobility, Connectivity and Communication in a Globalised World. *Westminster Papers in Communication and Culture*. London: University of Westminster Press.

UNCTAD. 2016. World Investment Report. Geneva.

Vernon, Raymond. 1966. International Investment and International Trade in the Product Cycle. *The Quarterly Journal of Economics* 80 (2): 190–207. JSTOR.

Whiteman, Gail, Brian Walker, and Paolo Perego. 2013. Planetary Boundaries: Ecological Foundations for Corporate Sustainability. *Journal of Management Studies* 50 (2): 307–336. https://doi.org/10.1111/j.1467-6486.2012.01073.x.

Williams, Amanda, Steve Kennedy, Felix Philipp, and Gail Whiteman. 2017. Systems Thinking: A Review of Sustainability Management Research. *Journal of Cleaner Production* 148: 866–881. Elsevier Ltd. https://doi.org/10.1016/j.jclepro.2017.02.002.

6

Sustainability in Marketing

Teresa Heath and Sally McKechnie

Introduction

Marketing is predicated on creating "value for customers and build[ing] strong customer relationships in order to capture value from customers in return" (Kotler et al. 2017, 5) or as the most recent American Marketing Association (2008) definition states on "creating, communicating, delivering, and exchanging offerings that have value for customers, clients, partners, and society at large". While such representations endow marketing with an important social and economic function in society, they overlook sustainability concerns, as they rely on prevalent notions of value, which tend to neglect the "intrinsic value" (O'Neill 1993, 8) of the natural world, the notion of value linked to sustainability (see McDonagh and Prothero 2014), as well as other forms of non-materialistic value such as the value of justice or equity.

T. Heath (✉) • S. McKechnie
Nottingham University Business School, Nottingham, UK
e-mail: teresa.pereiraheath@nottingham.ac.uk; sally.mckechnie@nottingham.ac.uk

© The Author(s) 2019
K. Amaeshi et al. (eds.), *Incorporating Sustainability in Management Education*,
https://doi.org/10.1007/978-3-319-98125-3_6

Businesses (and marketing in particular) impact on the physical environment through *what they take* (the natural resources they use such as oil and water), *what they make* (the products derived from those resources), and *what they waste* (industrial waste causing pollution and destruction of natural systems) (Hawken 1993, 12; Fuller 1999). These effects are considerable and are driven by a "high consumption way of life", which is "utterly unsustainable" (Assadourian 2010, 186). News stories remind us daily of the severity of problems that threaten sustainability (e.g. global warming, plastics in oceans, poverty and growing income, and wealth inequalities). According to a recent study by the Intergovernmental Science-Policy Platform on Biodiversity and Ecosystem Services (IPBES), biodiversity continues to decline, endangering the world's capacity to provide food, water, and security to billions of people (Watts 2018). Beyond the negative implications for humans and their well-being, this is worrying for the sake of the "intrinsic worth" (Pepper 1997) of nature.

While many companies and consumers have reinvented practices and patterns of producing and consuming more attendants to the environment, the net effect of such effort remains insufficient given the scale of the environmental problems. At the same time, the rhetoric of marketing scholarship, reflected in the hegemony of the normative managerial marketing approach espoused in many marketing textbooks, tends to portray marketing as a benign force (Hackley 2003, 2009; Brown 1995), distant from ecological and other adverse effects. This is despite marketing arguably being the primary tool used by businesses to create and maintain consumer cultures (Assadourian 2010). As a result, sustainability remains largely overlooked within academic conversations about recent trends in the marketing discipline (McDonagh and Prothero 2014).

To engage meaningfully with sustainability we need, as marketing scholars, to contextualise discussions of the construct within the marketing curriculum and not relegate them to a sub-topic of an introductory or revision lecture in our courses. The aim of this chapter is to share our views on the urgency of making sustainability a fundamental topic of our teaching, as well as our experiences of how we have been embedding sustainability within our teaching. We will cover pedagogy, design, and content, as well as the challenges that underscore our efforts. However, before doing so, it is important that we provide some brief context to recent initiatives to develop sustainability within the curriculum at university level and school level that have impacted our attempts to embed sustainability within marketing education.

Background

The Stockholm Declaration of the United Nations Conference on the Human Environment of 1972 was the first to allude (even if indirectly) to the importance of sustainability in higher education (Wright 2002). Principle 19 of the Declaration states that "*Education in environmental matters, for the younger generation as well as adults, giving due consideration to the underprivileged, is essential in order to broaden the basis for an enlightened opinion and responsible conduct by individuals, enterprises and communities in protecting and improving the environment in its full human dimension*" (United Nations 1972). Since then, around the world, various national and international bodies have lent support to developing educational resources to incorporate sustainability in order to help to create a more sustainable future by aligning with the United Nations initiative of the Decade of Education for Sustainable Development (DESD) between 2005 and 2014 (UNESCO 2005). The British Government set out its vision for a more sustainable environmental, social, and economic future in its report: "Securing the Future: Delivering the UK Sustainable Development Strategy" (HM Government 2005). This report highlights the key role of compulsory education for young people to raise awareness of sustainable development and provide them with skills to put sustainable development into practice in later life. At the same time, it acknowledges the need to increase "sustainability literacy" elsewhere in colleges, universities, and professional development. Next, the Higher Education Funding Council for England (HEFCE) launched a *Sustainable Development in Higher Education* policy document to underpin the government's goal of sustainable development within the higher education sector in England (HEFCE 2005), in which it articulated the following vision: "*Within the next 10 years, the higher education sector in this country will be recognised as a major contributor to society's efforts to achieve sustainability—through the skills and knowledge that its graduates learn and put into practice, and through its own strategies and operations.*" The accompanying ten-year action plan has undergone regular review, cumulating in the recent publication of HEFCE's policy development and framework for future work in this area (HEFCE 2014). An examination of the latest vision statement indicates some minor amendments to broaden the scope by including the role of research, knowledge transfer, and community engagement in promoting sustainable development: "*HEFCE's vision is that universities and colleges are widely recognised as leaders in society's efforts to achieve sustainability—through the understanding, skills and attitudes that students gain and put into practice, through research and knowledge exchange, and through community involvement, as well as through their strategies and operations that bring all these together*" (HEFCE 2014).

Against this backdrop of higher education responding to the sustainability agenda, our university (the University of Nottingham) was one of seven pilot institutions that participated in the Higher Education Academy's (HEA) Green Academy programme launched in 2011 to develop and embed sustainable development within the curriculum (HEA n.d.). Naturally, the Nottingham University Business School's engagement with this organisational change programme to promote the sustainability agenda at school level has been accompanied by various collaborations with other stakeholders. For example, the School is a Champion School for the United Nations Principles for Responsible Management Education (PRME) in the 2018–2019 cycle and an active member of a business-led community outreach organisation, Business in the Community. At the same time, the School is subject to monitoring and review by the Quality Assurance Agency for Higher Education (QAA), which is responsible for raising the academic standards and quality of UK higher education. This means that it has to conform to QAA processes for quality assurance and curriculum management, which involves defining and assessing subject-specific learning outcomes for undergraduate and postgraduate degree programmes in terms of key areas of knowledge and understanding (which include the importance of sustainability issues) and skills (i.e. intellectual, professional, and transferable ones). Finally, increasingly stringent demands are being placed on the School by three key international business-education accreditation bodies (i.e. EFMD Quality Improvement System (EQUIS), Association of MBAs (AMBA), and Association to Advance Collegiate Schools of

Business (AACSB)) to demonstrate how sustainable (or sustainability) thinking is reflected in curricula, policies, and practice. The School's mission, which emphasises a strong commitment to delivering excellence, innovation, impact, responsibility, and sustainability, influences its teaching and learning strategy to ensure that these key areas are appropriately embedded into its programmes at undergraduate and postgraduate levels. Let us now consider how we have approached this task in marketing education.

Marketing Education for Sustainability

Raised public awareness of the urgency of environmental issues has been reflected in the growth of programmes and courses in business higher education dealing with sustainability and social responsibility (Moon and Orlitzky 2011); nevertheless, little is known about how marketing faculty integrate sustainability education into their courses (Nicholls et al. 2013). How we have approached this task has been influenced by our shared philosophical assumptions that reality is multiple, socially constructed within social, cultural, and historical contexts; and that knowledge generation is idiographic, time-bound and context-dependent (Hudson and Ozanne 1988). These assumptions require us to notice and challenge deeply ingrained beliefs and ways of thinking that constitute the Dominant Social Paradigm of Western, industrialised societies (Kilbourne et al. 1997; Kilbourne and Carlson 2008). These include the prevailing anthropocentric approach, which holds that the existence of the human species is "the central of most important fact in the universe" (Cambridge Dictionary 2018) and treats non-human species as important only for their instrumental value to humans (O'Neill 1993), as well as a materialistic view of progress and quality of life (Kilbourne et al. 1997). These ideologies are important for they condition views about how society relates to nature and colour arguments about environmental issues (Pepper 1997). It is argued that marketing serves as an engine for this paradigm because marketing relies on the promotion of a consumer-oriented vision of life and happiness (see, e.g. Alvesson 1994; Shankar et al. 2006; Varey 2010; Heath and Chatzidakis 2012). Marketing has, therefore, an "inherent drive toward unsustainability" (van Dam and

under the auspices of the QAA Business and Management Subject Benchmark Statements for undergraduate and postgraduate levels. Thus, since we are embedding sustainability in course content, it was necessary to demonstrate that each course satisfied the appropriate curriculum content items of the QAA subject benchmark statements for Business and Management. This is what happened in a compulsory course in "Consumers and Markets" for first-year undergraduate students, which was launched in 2014/2015, following the restructuring of the BSc Management degree.

This first-year course is important to signal to students that sustainability is a foundational matter within marketing. Its aim is to develop an understanding of the contexts in which markets develop, and marketing and consumption are practised, in order to enable students to develop a personal and critical perspective prior to studying the technical aspects of marketing management in the second and third years of their degree programme. Thus, for sustainability-oriented learning objectives and outcomes, the course was designed to develop a knowledge and understanding of "*The importance of sustainability issues, including an understanding of the challenges and opportunities arising from the activities of people and organisations on the economic, social and environmental conditions of the future*" and develop key intellectual skills (e.g. critical thinking), professional practical skills (e.g. self-awareness, openness and sensitivity to diversity issues), and transferable skills (e.g. communication) to enhance the employability of the students. Following the publication of the latest QAA subject benchmark statements in 2015, the course content was reviewed to meet the corresponding updated learning objectives and outcomes (i.e. to develop a knowledge and understanding of "*The need for individuals and organisations to manage responsibly and sustainably and behave ethically in relation to social, cultural, economic and environmental issues*") and develop key intellectual skills (e.g. conceptual and critical thinking), professional practical skills (e.g. self-analysis and awareness/ sensitivity to diversity issues), and transferable skills (e.g. emotional intelligence and empathy)). Next, we will illustrate how we incorporated the concept of sustainability as an underlying theme in this course.

Pedagogy and Teaching Methods

We consider ourselves to be facilitators of learning and therefore, in keeping with the features of suitable pedagogy to support education for sustainability (Littledyke and Manolas 2010), our pedagogical approach is student centred, concentrates on real-world contexts for critically examining sustainability issues relating to marketing and consumption, and focuses on shared learning experiences and active, constructivist methods to accommodate, extend, or challenge common beliefs. On the whole, we have employed the traditional educational methods of large-group lectures and small-group tutorials, which are supported by online material (e.g. news announcements, forum, and audio-visual materials) on our virtual learning environment (Moodle). The following account highlights content we cover, as well as practices and learning activities we employ to facilitate students' learning and critical engagement.

Setting the Context: Making the Case for Sustainability

Although the natural environment is pervasive in public discourse and there are opportunities for environmental education across the National Curriculum for primary and secondary state schools in England (National Association for Environmental Education 2018), we often find that students come to the classroom with little understanding of sustainability. Thus, to begin a discussion about the relationship between the business (and marketing) field and the planet, it is important to clarify to students the concept of sustainability and the interlinked nature of the economic, social, and environmental considerations that broad understandings of the concept entail (Crane and Matten 2016). This also serves to appease those less ecologically minded students, who may question the usefulness of sustainable considerations when these can hinder financial results.

While the "win-win-win" discourse that underlines the triple bottom-line principle of ecological, economic, and sociocultural sustainability (Elkington 1998) is very useful to present an attractive case for sustainability, caution is warranted in alerting students to the dangers of a rhetoric which may marginalise concern for ecology and reinforce business-as-usual approaches, thus contributing to unsustainability (see Milne and Gray 2013). Therefore, to acquaint marketing students with the sustainability agenda and raise their awareness of the importance of the topic, we find it helpful to provide a brief portrait of problems of the planet with regard to ecology and social issues, such as inequality and poverty; to this effect, we draw on a variety of contemporary evidence from press articles (e.g. *The Guardian*'s Climate Change section), academic articles, environmental reports, and publicly available videos and images with graphic representations of, and impactful content about, the severity of the environmental and social problems we face. Asking students in the classroom to calculate their carbon footprint using the World Wide Fund for Nature (WWF) environmental footprint calculator (see http://footprint.wwf.org.uk/) reinforces the idea that there are limits on the ability of the planet to sustain our consumption levels and facilitates a thoughtful discussion of actions they might take to reduce their impact on the planet. Students can then appreciate that sustainability is a "megatrend" and that materialism and overconsumption encouraged by market systems constitute "one set of barriers to sustainable living" (Scott, Martin and Schouten 2014, 282).

From then, we can ask students to consider "Why should we care about the good of future generations and non-humans?" (O'Neill 1993). As well as arousing guilt (and perhaps perplexity) about humans' impact on the Earth, these considerations are designed to engage students with the moral imperative of respecting the limits of the planet for future generations (O'Neill 1993; Reid 1996), a principle put forward earlier in Rawls' (1971) well-known *Theory of Justice* (see also Heath and Chatzidakis 2012). We have found that not all students will agree that there is a moral requirement to attend to the needs of future generations, which opens up differing positions to be taken in ensuing lively and reflective debates.

Instructors can then contextualise marketing discourse and practice within the sustainability agenda and probe students to consider whether and how marketing has progressed to "meet the needs of the present without compromising the ability of future generations to meet their own needs" (WCED 1987). Taking a critical perspective, instructors may wish to problematise the Brundtland Report's widely accepted definition of sustainable development by challenging the vague notion of needs (see Reid 1996). They may also draw on critical marketing to discuss claims that "false" needs (e.g. "the tendency to give priority to economic over ecological goals") and a misconstruction of wants as needs are commonly used by marketers to influence demand (Alvesson 1994, 303).

Next, a study of the history of environmental matters in marketing helps students to grasp the challenges and complexity of discussing sustainability within marketing. Such an account is also useful for students to be able to ground environmental discussions of marketing within the temporal and contextual frameworks in which they emerge.

A Brief Historical Review of Marketing's Relation to Sustainability

Kilbourne and Beckmann (1998), Leonidou and Leonidou (2011), and McDonagh and Prothero (2014) all offer comprehensive reviews, on which we shall draw to provide a brief discussion of the topic. Our account is far from exhaustive, and only purports to highlight streams of thought, ideas, and concepts that have marked this field of the discipline.

Following the seminal works of Rachel Carson's (1962) *Silent Spring*, the Club of Rome's report *The Limits to Growth* (Meadows et al. 1972), and the concomitant growing awareness of worsening natural-environmental problems and the human (and corporate) responsibility therefor, several marketing scholars took an interest in the environmental agenda (Peattie 2001; Kilbourne and Beckmann 1998; Belz and Peattie 2009). The growing environmental regulations and stakeholders' concerns about pollution also contributed to this interest (Leonidou and Leonidou 2011). Thus, in the 1970s, a first stream of studies (as identified by Kilbourne and Beckmann 1998), attempted to identify (and measure) who *socially conscious* (Anderson and Cunningham 1972; Webster 1975), *ecologically concerned* (Kinnear et al. 1974), or *environmentally concerned* consumers were (Murphy et al. 1978). Although the need for this understanding was often justified with reference to its managerial relevance (e.g. Anderson and Cunningham 1972), intrinsic ecological concerns for the impact of rising consumption on the planet were already put forward by Fisk (1973), who proposed a set of criteria for a theory of *responsible consumption*. Some of these studies were quite narrowly focused (Peattie 2001) on consumers' attitudes and/or behaviour in relation to specific products, such as gasoline (Kassarjian 1971) or detergents (Henion 1972; Kinnear and Taylor 1973). In the 1980s, literature in the field turned towards energy conservation and efficiency (e.g. Allen 1982; Anderson and Claxton 1982) and attitudes towards environmental regulations, which marked the second stream of research (Kilbourne and Beckmann 1998). A few studies further looked at how some consumers were choosing to embrace a lifestyle of voluntary simplicity, characterised by ecological awareness, and efforts to reduce personal levels of consumption (Leonard-Barton 1981). At the same time, efforts proceeded to understand the unclear relationship between environmental attitudes and behaviour (e.g. Balderjahn 1988).

During the 1980s and 1990s, amidst media attention to several environmental disasters and growing problems, public concern about the environment rose (Peattie 2001; Belz and Peattie 2009). As companies discovered that "green" sells, environment friendliness became a competitive factor (Belz and Peattie 2009) or a marketing tool (van Dam and Apeldoorn 1996). Accordingly, the late 1980s and 1990s saw the proliferation of "green marketing" initiatives (Ennew and McKechnie 1992; Ottman 1993), whereby businesses attempted to produce and market "greener" products to attract those consumers who were concerned about the environment and willing to pay a premium for the sake of it (see Kilbourne 1998; Peattie 1999; Belz and Peattie 2009).

Green marketing would be later described as "activities which attempt to reduce the negative social and environmental impacts of existing products and production systems, and which promote less damaging products and services" (Peattie 2001, 129). Unsurprisingly, there was a continued interest in the environment within academic marketing studies, many of which sought to characterise environmentally concerned consumers (e.g. Brown and Wahlers 1998) and examine the relationship between environmental attitudes and behavioural intentions or behaviour (e.g.

Schwepker and Cornwell 1991). Efforts were concomitantly dedicated to informing the development of marketing strategies (e.g. Menon and Menon 1997; Brown and Wahlers 1998), including advertising decisions (e.g. Davis 1994; Obermiller 1995) attendant upon the environmental agenda.

In spite of the apparent enthusiasm with which businesses embraced the green agenda, their strategies involved, to a great extent, only superficial changes or changes which were insufficient given the magnitude of transformation required for addressing the needs of the planet (Kilbourne 2010). Green marketing activities were "primarily managerial strategies to increase sales and only secondarily green" (Kilbourne 1998, 642). That represented, as van Dam and Apeldoorn (1996, 51) articulated, a "micro solution for a macro problem", which fell short of what a truly green approach to marketing necessitated (Kilbourne 1998; van Dam and Apeldoorn 1996). To make matters worse, green marketing was somehow decried amidst the realisation that some companies were merely engaging in "green washing" or "green selling", simply adjusting promotional campaigns or public relations efforts, but otherwise behaving *as usual* (Peattie and Crane 2005; Peattie 1999; Gordon et al. 2011). The MTV 2008 Switch campaign was a global youth-focused campaign to promote environmentally friendly lifestyle choices. Playing "The Green Song" from this campaign (YouTube 2018) can vividly illustrate to students the concept of green washing and open up discussion in the classroom.

From around the mid-1990s on, a new stream of studies emerged, which recognised the limitations of a managerial, green agenda and pushed for the inclusion of macromarketing considerations (Kilbourne et al. 1997; Kilbourne and Beckmann 1998; Peattie 1999). This research stream also offered a greater critical outlook of marketing vis-à-vis sustainability than mainstream studies did hitherto, which challenged marketing's assumptions and its effects on the environment and framed the environmental problem and marketing's discussions therein within the cultural context of Western, developed societies (van Dam and Apeldoorn 1996; Kilbourne et al. 1997; Kilbourne and Beckmann 1998). This evolution is supported by developments in the area of critical marketing, which question marketing's role in fostering a consumer-oriented vision of life (e.g. Alvesson 1994; see also McDonagh and Prothero 2014). Since then, many studies have devoted attention to explain the Dominant Social Paradigm of Western, industrialised societies and the ways in which the values and beliefs embedded therein (e.g. limitless economic growth, the association of happiness with consumption, a belief that technology will find solutions to the environmental problems, and anthropocentrism) affect our attitudes and behaviour in ways that are damaging to sustainability (e.g. Kilbourne et al. 1997; Kilbourne 1998; Kilbourne and Carlson 2008; Varey 2010; Heath and Chatzidakis 2012; McDonagh and Prothero 2014).

Such broader reflections paved the way for ecologically minded scholars to question current levels of consumption (e.g. Kilbourne et al. 1997; Buchholz 1998) and call for limits to growth (e.g. Varey 2010). As Kilbourne and Carlson (2008) noted, "green products and green consumers are first and foremost products and consumers. While green products are slightly less resource intensive, they still require resources. If consumers consume more of them, no net gain is realized" (p. 107). These concerns are accompanied by a shift in some scholars' discourses from green marketing (which has often too managerialist a focus) to sustainable marketing (which evinces broader and future-oriented concerns). A truly sustainable approach to marketing is an appeal, amongst others, to "accept the limitations of marketing philosophy", "value continuity over profit", accept the need for regulations to the market system and move beyond replacing products to rethinking levels of consumption (van Dam and Apeldoorn 1996, 53; Belz and Peattie 2009).

However, despite many business attempts, the overall outlook on sustainability did not improve; in the 1990s, the degree to which businesses "moved closer to real sustainability" was deemed "minimal" (Peattie 1999, 131), and more recent assessments remain, sadly, far from optimistic. The observations that "overall consumption growth has offset most incremental eco-efficiency improvements" (Peattie and Peattie 2009, 262) and that "[t]he past 20 years of debate and business initiatives linked to marketing and the environment have clearly failed to deliver significant change or substantive progress towards sustainability" (Peattie and Peattie 2009, 262) shed a grim light on our planet's prospects and the effectiveness of the overall green/sustainable initiatives. As a consequence, in the last decade, and amid growing sustainability concerns, including

Apeldoorn 1996, 45; see also Kilbourne et al. 1997), which bestows marketing educators with an added responsibility to engage with this topic.

To be meaningful, such an engagement needs to be predicated on a deep understanding of (un)sustainability and a genuine commitment to address the implications this poses to our discipline. A sustainability approach to marketing needs to take the notion of "environment friendliness" as more than a "marketing tool" to sell more "green products" (see van Dam and Apeldoorn 1996, 52). Likewise, we believe that educators in marketing (and other fields) should not reduce the incorporation of sustainability into curricula to a mere requirement to satisfy the demands of external or internal stakeholders; rather, they need to embrace it as a fundamental topic ("*the* pressing issue", McDonagh and Prothero 2014, 1200) within their curricula. This should vest the sustainability agenda with a strengthened sense of urgency. In marketing education, in particular, this necessitates a macro approach, which conceives marketing discipline and practice beyond the constrained set of beliefs and ways of thinking within the Dominant Social Paradigm (see Kilbourne and Carlson 2008; Gordon et al. 2011) that often work against sustainability. Thus, either through developing new programmes and courses that specifically address sustainability matters pertaining to the discipline and practice of marketing, or via systematically integrating these concerns into the curricula of existing courses, we seek to challenge an uncritical approach to looking at the discipline (see also Catterall et al. 2002) that tends to remove marketing systems and practices from their consequences on the planet.

Planning for and Designing Sustainability Education in Marketing

As is normal for higher education programmes and courses, there are policies and procedures in place for curriculum design and management in keeping with the institution's requirements. At our Business School, curriculum design should be relevant to degree title, the School's mission and vision, and faculty's teaching and research interests. It is managed marketing practice. Martin and Schouten (2014) draw on the AMA's (2008) most recent definition of marketing to articulate sustainable marketing as marketing that does not damage, and may even improve human and environmental conditions: "the process of creating, communicating and delivering value to customers in such a way that both natural and human capital are preserved or enhanced throughout" (p. 18). A similar understanding that marketing can preserve or enhance the planet for the future is popular in marketing textbooks, such as Kotler et al.'s (2017), who model their definition of sustainable marketing on the WCED's (1987) definition of sustainable development: "Socially and environmentally responsible marketing that meets the present needs of consumers and businesses, while also preserving or enhancing the ability of future generations to meet their needs" (p. 593). This kind of rhetoric, however, risks downplaying the urgency of sustainability by suggesting that marketing is about enhancing consumers' lives, including those of future generations. Perhaps, the broadest and most sustainability-oriented understanding of marketing, which they term sustainability marketing, is found in Belz and Peattie (2009, 18): "it delivers solutions to our needs that are:

- *Ecologically oriented*, taking account of the ecological limits of the planet and seeking to satisfy our needs without compromising the health of ecosystems and their ability to continue delivering ecosystem services.
- *Viable*, from technical feasibility and economic competitiveness perspectives.
- *Ethical*, in promoting greater social justice and equity, or at the very least in terms of avoiding making any existing patterns of injustice worse.
- *Relationship-based*, which move away from viewing marketing in terms of economic exchanges, towards viewing it as the management of relationships between businesses and their customers and other key stakeholders."

While comprehensive, this conceptualisation may be seen as too long to be practically used, which could limit its adoption. However, in their book, Belz and Peattie (2009) do offer a shorter articulation of the concept that retains its broad focus.

Embedding Sustainability Throughout the Marketing Curriculum

Along with having dedicated sessions to address sustainability in marketing, we integrate the topic throughout the different parts of curriculum. Thus, for example, we derive implications for sustainability when we analyse the various elements of the marketing environment (e.g. How does sustainability and the natural environment impact on the technological environment?; How may sustainability-related concerns such as employers' working conditions or respect for the natural environment affect suppliers' choices?), as well as when discussing reasons and strategies for new product development. In particular, we look at meanings of consumption and brands, consumer culture, and consumers' behaviour through the lens of sustainability, exposing how consumption-oriented lifestyles significantly impact the planet. We explain to students that the responsibility for fostering sustainable development does not lie entirely on the business side; individual consumers have an equally important role therein (Heath and Chatzidakis 2012; Gordon et al. 2011), as widely recognised in marketing literature (e.g. Connolly and Prothero 2003); we also discuss how more environmentally oriented, or "mindful" ways of consumption (Sheth et al. 2011), "collaborative consumption" and "sharing" (Belk 2014) and "anti-consumption" practices (e.g. Cherrier et al. 2011) can help to move sustainability forward. Monbiot's (2012) insightful opinion article "The Gift of Death" highlights the impact and futility of excessive consumption in the industrialised world and should facilitate an interesting conversation in the classroom about the impact on sustainability of excessive consumption; "Bake them a cake, write them a poem, give them a kiss, tell them a joke, but for god's sake stop trashing the planet to tell someone you care. All it shows is that you don't." (Monbiot 2012).

In addition, sustainability matters can be usefully entrenched in discussions of the marketing mix, so that students appreciate that companies' operational choices can (and should) be attendant to society and the environment. As Kotler (2011) outlines in a short article celebrating the 75th anniversary of the *Journal of Marketing*, these considerations may focus on issues in relation to each of the four P's such as: production and packaging of items in ways (and using materials) that are more sustainable and reduce waste (product); pricing options that reflect products' environmental friendliness (price); channel organisation decisions attendant to the social and environmental impact of a company's production and distribution facilities (place); decisions about where and how to communicate companies' offerings so as to minimise their environmental impact (e.g. reducing promotional print campaigns in favour of digital campaigns) and promote the company's commitment to sustainability (promotion) (see also Fuller 1999). A more comprehensive discussion of what the "greening" of the marketing mix may involve is provided by Simintiras et al. (1997), whilst the effects of such green marketing practices on companies' performances are addressed by Leonidou et al. (2013).

Finally, throughout the different sections and subjects covered, we always endeavour to share with students examples of companies' and brands' (e.g. Fair Trade, Ben & Jerry's) best practices in sustainability to inspire them in their future careers. We show them that while many companies have been successfully reinventing their marketing mixes to respond to these growing environmental concerns (Leonidou et al. 2013), a few have been especially ingenious (e.g. IKEA's plans for using the Ecovative's mushroom-based packaging, Borhuaer 2017) in joining critical voices that advocate limits for consumption and waste. That is the case of Patagonia's well reported 2011 campaign "Don't buy this jacket"; this campaign raised consumers' awareness of the environmental impacts of the clothing industry (and specifically of producing and transporting a particular jacket), whilst garnering considerable publicity for the company. Intercalating discussion with these and other examples (e.g. advertising campaigns by environmental pressure groups, such as Greenpeace and WWF) can be inspiring for students to derive implications for sustainable development.

Pedagogical Challenges and Assessment

Increasing student diversity (including cultural diversity) poses an important challenge to instructors. Students vary not only in terms of their sociocultural background but also in their academic background. For example, some may have already studied business-related subjects in compulsory education, while others may not; and some may already be oriented towards adopting a deep approach to learning, while others lean towards a surface approach. From the outset, we recognise that not every student will be equally interested in learning (or be prepared to learn) about sustainability issues and developing a personal and critical perspective of marketing. We also acknowledge that a growing number of our students come from emerging economies where sustainability issues are not necessarily of a major concern. Nevertheless, we try to encourage our students to engage with such issues through the various classroom interventions we have described earlier.

Another challenge is the impact of cohort size on the design and planning of students' learning activities. We have found that the increasing size of the cohort (from just under 300 students in 2014/2015 to more than 400 students in 2017/2018) limits the opportunities for our preferred learning activities (e.g. small-group discussions, debates, and students' presentation of essays) and assessment methods that would befit the sustainability-related topics we cover. Notwithstanding this problem, we try to engage students in the classroom via frequently inviting their participation in class discussions and activities over a period of 11 weeks and use two sessions of small-group tutorials (groups of about 20 students) to explore selected areas covered in the large-group lectures in more detail. Throughout the course we encourage students to adopt a deep approach to their learning and routinely give formative feedback in the classroom to support learning. For pragmatic reasons, we have opted for summative assessment by one 1.5-hour examination, which takes the form of a choice of two essay questions out of five. We provide practice exam questions on our virtual learning environment.

A third challenge is that there are still only a relatively small number of textbooks and little other pedagogical material dedicated to sustainability and marketing for educators wishing to engage students with these conversations. This is especially the case for those of us who wish to address these matters in macro and critical ways throughout the whole marketing curriculum. We find that combining pedagogical material from mainstream marketing textbooks (e.g. Kotler et al. 2017), readings from specialised books on sustainability and marketing (e.g. Belz and Peattie 2009) and selected journal articles, can help to overcome such deficiency in balanced and useful ways.

Thus far, our efforts seem to have been recognised in students' evaluation of teaching and the course, as well as in their own performance, which have been very encouraging. Overall, students have been able to articulate social and ecological concerns in their interventions in the classroom (especially in tutorial sessions), with some being especially keen to learn more about these matters in the context of marketing. Some have also formally (and informally) commented on how they enjoyed this course and the teaching approaches employed. Results of students' examination performance have also been positive and in line with the results obtained in other courses in their degree. Equally, the course seems to help students as they progress in their studies. For example, by the time many of students from the first cohort had taken an elective course in "Consumer Behaviour" in their final year in 2016/2017, one of the authors observed a more informed and deeper level of student engagement with sustainable consumption issues.

Final Thoughts

We believe that the social, environmental, and economic problems we face globally and the perils they represent for the sustainability of the planet (both for humans and other species) require us, as educators in higher education (and especially in marketing), to treat sustainability as an integral part of our curriculum. This urges us to move beyond superficial discussions of the topic and contextualise sustainability within the historical and ideological framework (Pepper 1997) that underscores social assumptions about markets and marketing. Our ability to convince students of the urgency of sustainability lies largely in the "power of stories" we tell and the ways in which they fit students' prior beliefs (see Fisher 1989; Heath and Heath 2016, 812). Students may fail, at first, to appreciate both the intrinsic importance, and the business implications, of the sustainability agenda. They may view these concerns as overly pessimistic (in our experience, students sometimes do express such views). Up-to-date information and evidence from multiple sources, and real-life case studies and examples from practice and the press, guided by reflective discussion of relevant scholarly work, help to build the case for sustainable development.

We note that our scholarly efforts are somewhat thwarted by the limited and mostly managerially oriented work published in mainstream marketing journals, which gives the impression that sustainability is still mostly taken as a micro and managerial issue, and of a relatively minor importance (McDonagh and Prothero 2014). This problem is evinced in, and exacerbated by, a significant proportion of the journals that have engaged with the sustainability agenda in marketing still only being rated two stars in the Chartered Association of Business Schools' most recent Academic Journal Guide 2018 (e.g. *Journal of Macromarketing*, *Journal of Marketing Management*, *International Journal of Consumer Studies*). Such ratings and their impact on scholars' opportunities for progression may discourage many of us from researching sustainability, which, together with a preference for research-based teaching in many institutions, make it less likely that this subject will feature centrally in curricula.

Education is a core site in which "inroads into environmental value formation can be made" (O'Brien 1995, 168). Changing ingrained ways of thinking, however, necessitates consistent messages and integrated efforts at institutional, personal, political, and economic levels (O'Brien 1995). As Gordon et al. (2011) remind us, the need for dramatic action on climate change and other sustainable-related issues is still a live political issue about which people need to be convinced. Many, including crucially the current President of the United States, have cast doubt on the very idea of climate change, while others, as discussed by Monbiot (2018), are overly eager to adopt the most optimistic possible prediction in environmental matters.

Marketing is the means by which organisations enable and shape consumption of goods and services. This means that it will inevitably play a central role in the task of trying to establish sustainable practices for production and consumption, if not as a tool for good then as an obstacle to be overcome. Thus, it is vitally important that our students, as future marketers or campaigners for sustainability, are exposed to a broad and contextualised view of marketing, which is attendant to its effects. For these reasons, shunting sustainability to the margins of marketing curricula should no longer be an option.

References

Allen, Chris T. 1982. Self-perception Based Strategies for Stimulating Energy Conservation. *Journal of Consumer Research* 8 (4): 381–390.

Alvesson, Mats. 1994. Critical Theory and Consumer Marketing. *Scandinavian Journal Management* 10 (3): 291–313.

AMA. 2008. Press Release: The American Marketing Association Releases New Definition for Marketing. Accessed February 1, 2018. https://archive.ama. org/archive/AboutAMA/Documents/American%20Marketing%20 Association%20Releases%20New%20Definition%20for%20Marketing. pdf.

Anderson, C. Dennis, and John D. Claxton. 1982. Barriers to Consumer Choice of Energy Efficient Products. *Journal of Consumer Research* 9 (2): 163–170.

Anderson, W. Thomas, and William H. Cunningham. 1972. The Socially Conscious Consumer. *Journal of Marketing* 36 (3): 23–31.

Assadourian, Erik. 2010. Transforming Cultures: From Consumerism to Sustainability. *Journal of Macromarketing* 30 (2): 186–191.

Balderjahn, Ingo. 1988. Personality Variables and Environmental Attitudes as Predictors of Ecologically Responsible Consumption Patterns. *Journal of Business Research* 17 (1): 51–56.

Belk, Russell. 2014. You Are What You Can Access: Sharing and Collaborative Consumption Online. *Journal of Business Research* 67 (8): 1595–1600.

Belz, Frank-Martin, and Ken Peattie. 2009. *Sustainability Marketing: A Global Perspective*. Chichester: Wiley.

Borhuaer, Scott. 2017. IKEA Unveils Its Plans for Mushroom-Based Packaging. Accessed March 16, 2018. https://minipakr.com/2017/02/22/ikea-unveils-its-plans-for-mushroom-based-packaging/.

Brown, Stephen. 1995. *Postmodern Marketing*. London: ITPB.

Brown, Joseph D., and Russell G. Wahlers. 1998. The Environmentally Concerned Consumer: An Exploratory Study. *Journal of Marketing Theory and Practice* 6 (2): 39–47.

Buchholz, Rogene A. 1998. The Ethics of Consumption Activities: A Future Paradigm? *Journal of Business Ethics* 17 (8): 871–882.

Cambridge University Press. 2018. Cambridge Online Dictionary, Cambridge Dictionary Online. Accessed March 15, 2018. https://dictionary.cambridge.org/dictionary/english/anthropocentric.

Carson, Rachel. 1962. *Silent Spring*. Boston: Houghton Mifflin Company.

Catterall, Miriam, Pauline Maclaran, and Lorna Stevens. 2002. Critical Reflection in the Marketing Curriculum. *Journal of Marketing Education* 24 (3): 184–192.

Cherrier, Helene, Iain R. Black, and Mike Lee. 2011. Intentional Non-consumption for Sustainability: Consumer Resistance and/or Anti-consumption? *European Journal of Marketing* 45 (11/12): 1757–1767.

Connolly, John, and Andrea Prothero. 2003. Sustainable Consumption: Consumption, Consumers and the Commodity Discourse. *Consumption, Markets and Culture* 6 (4): 275–291.

Crane, Andrew, and Dirk Matten. 2016. *Business Ethics*. 4th ed. Oxford: Oxford University Press.

Davis, Joel J. 1994. Consumer Response to Corporate Environmental Advertising. *Journal of Consumer Marketing* 11 (2): 25–37.

Elkington, John. 1998. Partnerships from Cannibals with Forks: The Triple Bottom Line of 21st Century Business. *Environmental Quality Management* 8 (1): 37–51.

Ennew, Christine, and Sally McKechnie. 1992. Green Marketing: Can the Banks Respond? *International Journal of Bank Marketing* 10 (7): 8–9.

Fisher, Walter R. 1989. *Human Communication as Narration: Towards a Philosophy of Reason, Value and Action*. Columbia, NY: University of South Caroline Press.

Fisk, George. 1973. Criteria for a Theory of Responsible Consumption. *Journal of Marketing* 37 (2): 24–31.

Fuller, Donald A. 1999. *Sustainable Marketing: Managerial-Ecological Issues*. Thousand Oaks, CA: SAGE Publications, Inc.

Gordon, Ross, Marylyn Carrigan, and Gerard Hastings. 2011. A Framework for Sustainable Marketing. *Marketing Theory* 11 (2): 143–163.

Hackley, Chris. 2003. 'We Are All Customers Now…' Rhetorical Strategy and Ideological Control in Marketing Management Texts. *Journal of Management Strategy* 40 (5): 1325–1352.

———. 2009. *Marketing: A Critical Introduction*. London: Sage.

Hawken, Paul. 1993. *The Ecology of Commerce: A Declaration of Sustainability*. New York: HarperCollins.

HEA. n.d. Education for Sustainable Development in Higher Education. Available at: Education for Sustainable Development in Higher Education. Accessed March 16, 2018.

Heath, Teresa, and Andreas Chatzidakis. 2012. 'Blame It on Marketing': Consumers' Views on Unsustainable Consumption. *International Journal of Consumer Studies* 36 (6): 656–667.

Heath, Teresa, and Matthew Heath. 2016. 'Once Upon a Time There Was a Consumer…': Stories of Magic and the Magic of Stories. *Journal of Marketing Management* 32 (9–10): 811–826.

HEFCE. 2005. Sustainable Development in Higher Education. Accessed March 16, 2018. http://webarchive.nationalarchives.gov.uk/20100303151747/, http://www.hefce.ac.uk/pubs/hefce/2005/05_28/.

———. 2014. Sustainable Development in Higher Education: HEFCE's Role to Date and a Framework for Its Future Actions. Accessed March 16, 2018. http://www.hefce.ac.uk/media/hefce/content/pubs/2014/201430/ HEFCE2014_30.pdf.

Henion, Karl E. 1972. The Effect of Ecologically Relevant Information on Detergent Sales. *Journal of Marketing Research* 9 (1): 10–14.

HM Government. 2005. Securing the Future: Delivering UK Sustainable Development Strategy. TSO (The Stationery Office).

Hudson, Laurel Anderson, and Julie L. Ozanne. 1988. Alternative Ways of Seeking Knowledge in Consumer Research. *Journal of Consumer Research* 14 (4): 508–521.

Kassarjian, Harold H. 1971. Incorporating Ecology into Marketing Strategy: The Case of Air Pollution. *The Journal of Marketing* 35 (3): 61–65.

Kilbourne, William E. 1998. Green Marketing: A Theoretical Perspective. *Journal of Marketing Management* 14 (6): 641–655.

———. 2010. Facing the Challenge of Sustainability in a Changing World: An Introduction to the Special Issue. *Journal of Macromarketing* 30 (2): 109–111.

Kilbourne, William E., and Suzanne C. Beckmann. 1998. Review and Critical Assessment of Research on Marketing and the Environment. *Journal of Marketing Management* 14 (6): 513–532.

Kilbourne, William E., and Les Carlson. 2008. The Dominant Social Paradigm, Consumption and Environmental Attitudes: Can Macromarketing Education Help? *Journal of Macromarketing* 28 (2): 106–121.

Kilbourne, William E., Pierre McDonagh, and Andrea Prothero. 1997. Sustainable Consumption and the Quality of Life: A Macromarketing Challenge to the Dominant Social Paradigm. *Journal of Macromarketing* 17 (1): 4–24.

Kinnear, Thomas C., and James R. Taylor. 1973. The Effect of Ecological Concern on Brand Perceptions. *Journal of Marketing Research* 10 (2): 191–197.

Kinnear, Thomas C., James R. Taylor, and Ahmed A. Sadrudin. 1974. Ecologically Concerned Consumers: Who Are They? *Journal of Marketing* 38 (2): 20–24.

Kotler, Philip. 2011. Reinventing Marketing to Manage the Environmental Imperative. *Journal of Marketing* 75 (4): 132–135.

Kotler, Philip, Gary Armstrong, Lloyd C. Harris, and Nigel Piercy. 2017. *Principles of Marketing*. 7th European ed. Harlow: Pearson Education Limited.

Leonard-Barton, Dorothy. 1981. Voluntary Simplicity Scale and Energy Conservation. *Journal of Consumer Research* 8 (Dec.): 243–252.

Leonidou, Constantinos N., Constantine S. Katsikeas, and Neil A. Morgan. 2013. 'Greening' the Marketing Mix: Do Firms Do It and Does It Pay Off? *Journal of the Academy of Marketing Science* 41 (2): 151–170.

Leonidou, Constantinos N., and Leonidas C. Leonidou. 2011. Research into Environmental Marketing/Management: A Bibliographic Analysis. *European Journal of Marketing* 45 (1/2): 68–103.

Littledyke, Michael, and Evangelos Manolas. 2010. Ideology, Epistemology and Pedagogy: Barriers and Drivers to Education for Sustainability in Science Education. *Journal of Baltic Science Education* 9 (4): 285–301.

Martin, Diane, and John Schouten. 2014. *Sustainable Marketing*. Harlow: Pearson.

McDonagh, Pierre, and Andrea Prothero. 2014. Sustainability Marketing Research: Past, Present and Future. *Journal of Marketing Management* 30 (11–12): 1186–1219.

Meadows, Donella H., Dennis L. Meadows, Jørgen Rangers, and William W. Behrens III. 1972. *The Limits to Growth*. Washington: Potomac Associates.

Menon, Ajay, and Anil Menon. 1997. Enviropreneurial Marketing Strategy: The Emergence of Corporate Environmentalism as Market Strategy. *The Journal of Marketing* 61 (1): 51–67.

Milne, Markus J., and Rob Gray. 2013. W(h)ither Ecology? The Triple Bottom Line, the Global Reporting Initiative, and Corporate Sustainability Reporting. *Journal of Business Ethics* 118 (1): 13–29.

Monbiot, George. 2012. The Gift of Death. *The Guardian*. Accessed December, 11, 2017. http://www.monbiot.com/2012/12/10/the-gift-of-death/.

———. 2018. You Can Deny the Environmental Calamity—Until You Check the Facts. *The Guardian*. Accessed March 23, 2018. https://www.theguardian.com/commentisfree/2018/mar/07/environmental-calamity-facts-steven-pinker.

Moon, Jeremy, and Mark Orlitzky. 2011. Corporate Social Responsibility and Sustainability Education: A Trans-Atlantic Comparison. *Journal of Management & Organization* 17 (5): 583–603.

MTV Switch. 2008. *The Green Song*. Accessed March 22, 2018.

Murphy, Patrick E., Norman Kangun, and William B. Locander. 1978. Environmentally Concerned Consumers—Racial Variations. *Journal of Marketing* 42 (4): 61–66.

National Association for Environmental Education (NAEE). 2018. UK National Association for Environmental Education: *Supporting Education for Sustainable Development*. Accessed March 22, 2018. http://naee.org.uk/curriculum-resources/.

Nicholls, Jeananne, Joseph F. Hair Jr., Charles B. Ragland, and Kurt E. Schimmel. 2013. Ethics, Corporate Social Responsibility, and Sustainability Education in AACSB Undergraduate and Graduate Marketing Curricula: A Benchmark Study. *Journal of Marketing Education* 35 (2): 129–140.

O'Brien, Martin. 1995. Changing Environmental Values—Introduction. In *Values and the Environment*, ed. Y. Guerrier, N. Alexander, J. Chase, and M. O'Brien, 167–170. West Sussex: John Wiley & Sons Ltd.

O'Neill, John. 1993. *Ecology, Policy and Politics: Human Well-Being and the Natural World*. London and New York: Routledge.

Obermiller, Carl. 1995. The Baby Is Sick/the Baby Is Well: A Test of Environmental Communication Appeals. *Journal of Advertising* 24 (2): 55–70.

Ottman, Jacquelyn. 1993. *Challenges and Opportunities for the New Marketing Age*. Lincolnwood, IL: NTC Business Books.

Peattie, Ken. 1999. Trapping Versus Substance in the Greening of Marketing Planning. *Journal of Strategic Marketing* 7 (2): 141–148.

———. 2001. Towards Sustainability: The Third Age of Green Marketing. *The Marketing Review* 2: 129–146.

Peattie, Ken, and Andrew Crane. 2005. Green Marketing: Legend, Myth, Farce or Prophesy? *Qualitative Market Research: An International Journal* 8 (4): 357–370.

Peattie, Ken, and Sue Peattie. 2009. Social Marketing: A Pathway to Consumption Reduction. *Journal of Business Research* 62 (2): 260–268.

Pepper, David. 1997. *Modern Environmentalism—An Introduction*. London: Routledge.

Rawls, John. 1971. *A Theory of Justice*. Cambridge: The Belknap Press of Harvard University Press.

Reid, David. 1996. *Sustainable Development—An Introductory Guide*. London: Earthscan.

Schwepker, Charles H., and T. Bettina Cornwell. 1991. An Examination of Ecologically Concerned Consumers and Their Intention to Purchase Ecologically Packaged Products. *Journal of Public Policy & Marketing* 10 (2): 77–101.

Scott, Kristin, Diane M. Martin, and John W. Schouten. 2014. Marketing and the New Materialism. *Journal of Macromarketing* 34 (3): 282–290.

Shankar, Avi, Julie Whittaker, and James A. Fitchett. 2006. Heaven Knows I'm Miserable Now. *Marketing Theory* 6 (4): 485–505.

Sheth, Jagdish N., and Rajendra S. Sisodia. 2005. Does Marketing Need Reform? *Journal of Marketing* 69 (4): 10–12.

Sheth, Jagdish N., Nirmal K. Sethia, and Shanti Srinivas. 2011. Mindful Consumption: A Customer-Centric Approach to Sustainability. *Journal of the Academy of Marketing Science* 39 (1): 21–39.

Simintiras, A.C., B.B. Schlegelmilch, and A. Diamantopolous. 1997. 'Greening' the Marketing Mix: A Review of the Literature and an Agenda for Future Research. In *Green Management—A Reader*, ed. P. McDonagh and A. Prothero, 413–434. London: The Dryden Press.

UNESCO. 2005. *United Nations Decade of Education for Sustainable Development (2005–2014): International Implementation Scheme*. Paris: UNESCO.

United Nations. 1972. *Report of the United Nations Conference on the Human Environment*. Accessed March 22, 2017. http://www.un-documents.net/unchedec.htm.

van Dam, Ynte, and Paul A.C. Apeldoorn. 1996. Sustainable Marketing. *Journal of Macromarketing* 16 (2): 45–66.

Varey, Richard J. 2010. Marketing Means and Ends for a Sustainable Society: A Welfare Agenda for Transformative Change. *Journal of Macromarketing* 30 (2): 112–126.

Watts, Jonathan. 2018. Destruction of Nature as Dangerous as Climate Change, Scientists Warn. *The Guardian*, March 23. Accessed March 23, 2018. https://www.theguardian.com/environment/2018/mar/23/destruction-of-nature-as-dangerous-as-climate-change-scientists-warn.

WCED, World Commission on Environment and Development. 1987. *Our Common Future*. Oxford: Oxford University Press.

Webster, Frederick E., Jr. 1975. Determining the Characteristics of the Socially Conscious Consumer. *Journal of Consumer Research* 2 (3): 188–196.

Wilkinson, Richard, and Kate Pickett. 2009. *The Spirit Level: Why More Equal Societies Almost Always Do Better*. London: Penguin Books.

Wright, Tarah S.A. 2002. Definitions and Frameworks for Environmental Sustainability in Higher Education. *Higher Education Policy* 15: 105–120.

YouTube. 2018. MTV Switch 2008: The Green Song. Accessed March 15, 2018. https://www.youtube.com/watch?v=Bg0QminAPMM.

7

Sustainable Finance in Education

Will Oulton

Introduction

There is a question that I often get asked from the many people that I meet in the normal course of my work and it usually goes along the lines of "what academic courses would you recommend for someone wanting to move into a career in sustainability and sustainable finance?"

Although I have been involved in teaching modules on such courses for well over 15 years, it is still a challenging question to easily answer, particularly in the area of sustainable finance where it is still difficult to find discrete courses on this increasingly important topic.

This chapter seeks to explain the history of sustainable investment and finance, highlight some of the reasons as to why the skill set is still difficult to find in the financial services sector and the implications of this in future. It will also seek to anticipate how a generational change may influence the demand for such competencies and help drive greater capital flows into long-term sustainable and responsible investments (RIs)

W. Oulton (✉)
First State Investments, London, UK
e-mail: Will.Oulton@firststate.co.uk

© The Author(s) 2019
K. Amaeshi et al. (eds.), *Incorporating Sustainability in Management Education*,
https://doi.org/10.1007/978-3-319-98125-3_7

those of climate change, loss of biodiversity, and world inequalities (Wilkinson and Pickett 2009; Belz and Peattie 2009; Watts 2018), and a loss of trust in marketing (e.g. Sheth and Sisodia 2005), we have observed a growing number of marketing scholars advocating radical, substantive, or dramatic changes (e.g. Varey 2010; Kilbourne 2010; Scott et al. 2014) in our ways of thinking about, and engaging with, marketing and consumption.

This historical account, supported with debates and discussions of relevant case studies (e.g. "Unilever—a prototype for tomorrow's company?" in Kotler et al. 2017, 618–620) and other examples of business practices and principles (M&S's "Plan A", Lush's "Our Green Policy", The Body Shop's "Enrich Not Exploit Commitment"), should highlight to students the plurality of "sustainability" discourses that have populated the marketing discipline and practice since at least the 1970s. It also challenges them to appreciate both the complexity of, and urgency for, marketing engaging creatively and meaningfully with the sustainability agenda.

Defining Sustainable Marketing

To reflect changes in the discipline and practice of marketing in face of the ecological imperative, several conceptualisations of what a sustainable marketing orientation entails have been produced. Discussing with students some of these definitions helps to highlight the strong managerial focus that understanding of the phenomenon tends to maintain (see also McDonagh and Prothero 2014), which may lessen the perceived urgency of the environmental and social matters at stake. Thus, for example, Fuller (1999) defines sustainable marketing as: "the process of planning, implementing, and controlling the development, pricing, promotion, and distribution of products in a manner that satisfies the following three criteria: (1) customer needs are met, (2) organisational goals are attained, and (3) the process is compatible with ecosystems" (p. 4). Fuller (1999) argues that this definition is a "logical extension of contemporary marketing's managerial orientation, not a radical departure from it" (p. 4); it treats sustainability as an additional variable to consider to the which will benefit investors, the environment, and the wider society and is creating increasing career opportunities for suitably qualified and experienced people.

Sustainable Finance: A Long and Winding Road

Investors in increasing numbers across the world today believe that Environmental, Social, and Corporate Governance (ESG) factors constitute sources of long-term investment risk and return. There has also been a growth in academic and other research, which is providing the evidence to support and underpin that belief and as a consequence, global investors including the world's major asset owners and other stewards of capital have developed investment approaches where ESG factors are identified, evaluated, and considered in their analysis, monitoring, and decision-making processes.

For many investors, how a company identifies and manages its operational and reputational risks and the economic and commercial opportunities from ESG issues is a key indicator of the quality of its board, its executive management, and the overall business. The best investors seamlessly integrate both an assessment of financial quality with ESG quality to form a holistic view of an enterprises risk and the potential to deliver long-term earnings growth and therefore value. To support this, investment professionals today also have access to a range of ever-improving ESG data and analysis from a growing number of commercial sources.

There have been numerous studies (Clark et al. 2015) which have identified that using such ESG data and selecting the highest-ranking ESG quality companies, those companies tend to deliver superior long-term performance on a range of key business indicators as compared to their peers. In times of market stress, studies have also shown that higher-quality ESG companies can withstand such pressures with a greater degree of resilience than their weaker ESG peers. This was partly highlighted in a compelling research report published by McKinsey Global Institute titled "Measuring the Economic Impact of Short Termism"

(Barton et al. 2017), which used a matrix of indicators to identify companies that had a long-term strategic outlook. However, evidence that short-termism genuinely detracts from corporate performance and economic growth has remained scarce, partly because of difficulties in measuring the phenomenon, which does not correspond to any single quantifiable metric and is a confluence of many complex factors. McKinsey used a data set of 615 large- and mid-cap US publicly listed companies over the period 2001–2015 and created a five-factor Corporate Horizon Index. It is based on patterns of investment, growth, earnings quality, and earnings management. This enabled the separation of "long-term" companies from others and compared their relative performance, after controlling for industry characteristics and company size.

McKinsey's findings showed that companies classified as "long term" outperformed their shorter-term peers on a range of key economic and financial metrics. For example, in the industry groups that delivered above-average shareholder returns during this 14-year period, long-term companies captured an even greater share of the total returns (47%) while representing an even smaller percentage of the sample (26%). Even in the industries with below-average shareholder returns, long-term companies captured a greater percentage of the total returns than would be expected.

ESG and sustainability issues are considered as significant long-term factors and are subject to increasing amounts of study identifying them as drivers of long-term corporate and investment performance. This has encouraged financial advisors, consultants, rating agencies, and investment platform providers to develop various tools and processes to identify asset managers with the competency and skill sets to identify such factors and companies and therefore take advantage of this increasingly apparent market inefficiency.

Although there have been major advances in the past decade on the understanding of how ESG factors may impact performance as both corporate reporting and data availability have increased, the practice of assessing and making investment choices and decisions based upon such information goes back much further, over a century and beyond.

A Brief History of Sustainable Investment

The origins of what is today known as sustainable investment can argu-ably be traced back to the late 1700s to the Quaker movement, in the first example of socially motivated investment. The Quakers (Quaker 2018), who formed a century before, were inspired to support many of the issues central to the sustainability agenda of today including human rights, animal rights, environmental protection, and the careful use of the earth's natural resources. This translated into a refusal to invest their money in business activities which were against many of these values such as tobacco and alcohol production and gambling. This is an early exam-ple of a "do no harm" ethical or value-based screening approach that is still seen in many socially RI portfolios, also known as SRI funds, today.

The perception underlying this was that a strong value-based approach was a positive virtue and therefore any approach of avoidance of compa-nies involved in "bad" practices was the way to invest. This was high-lighted in the 1920s when the US-based Pioneer Group launched an investment fund which included the screening out of what became known as "sin" stocks from their portfolio by using a "sin screen." It was at this time that the term SRI became widely used.

The following three decades saw relatively slow progress in the take-up of SRIs. However in the mid-1960s, with the outbreak of the Vietnam War and the US government's involvement in the conflict, the issues relating to the human and environmental impacts of some of the chemi-cal products used in the conflict hit the headlines via the extensive TV coverage of the conflict. The public outrage was on the use of chemicals such as "Agent Orange" (History.com 2018), an extensively used herbi-cide and defoliant which included one of the most toxic of all the dioxins known as tetrachlorodibenzo-p-dioxin (TCDD), which has since been classified as a human carcinogen. Agent Orange was sprayed on almost 20% of Vietnam's forest and crop land, destroying some 20,000 Km^2 of foliage and causing severe and persistent environmental and human damage. The use of chemicals, along with the highly visible impact of the flammable compound known as Napalm, caused a public reaction that was a catalyst for the emergence of "ethical" investment; again, it was a screening-out process in this case of the corporations involved in the manufacture of these weaponised chemical compounds.

A decade later in the 1970s, once again political motivations caused the investment, civil society, and political worlds to clash in the form of the apartheid regime in South Africa. There was a high-profile boycott of Western companies operating in South Africa and a subsequent wave of divestment of companies which were seen to be supporting or profiting from the South African government's policies. The drivers were students who were campaigning to have their universities divest from such companies. This is very similar to the fossil fuel divestment campaigns we have seen in recent years which have emanated from the campus grounds of many higher education establishments across the world and the USA in particular.

In the 1980s, the term "ethical investment" became widely adopted in the UK driven by faith-based investors with tobacco and a range of other ethics-based screens becoming standard criteria used for the selection of companies in ethical investment funds. The 1980s also witnessed a number of high-profile corporate disasters creating profound and significant environmental and social consequences and these catapulted attention on poor corporate governance and health and safety practices. There were two major incidents during this period which attracted worldwide attention. The first was the 1984 Bhopal Disaster (Hays 2008) at the Union Carbide plant in India, which claimed thousands of lives and left nearly half a million injured. The second was the 1989 Exxon Valdez (Gannon 2014) disaster, at its time the worst environmental disaster in US history. On 24 March 1989, the tanker Exxon Valdez (owned by the Exxon Shipping Company) grounded on Bligh Reef in Alaska's Prince William Sound, rupturing its hull and spilling nearly 11 million gallons of Prudhoe Bay crude oil into a remote, scenic, and biologically productive body of water. The leak of crude oil covered 1300 miles of coastline and 11,000 square miles of ocean, killing thousands of marine birds, fish, and mammals and causing billions of dollars in costs. Both of these events have had long-lasting impacts, which are still evident today decades after the incidents.

The year before the Exxon Valdez disaster in 1988, the critically important climate forum, the Intergovernmental Panel on Climate Change

(IPCC), was formed to collate and assess scientific evidence on climate change. It has been, since its formation, an extremely influential and highly regarded group that has added immense value and data to the climate debate. The regular updates from the IPCC have been closely followed by the many global investor groups focused on ESG issues, particularly climate related.

Throughout the 1980s and 1990s, the interest in and attention given to ESG issues continued to grow and took a step change with the emergence of two financial indices from index giants FTSE (FTSE4Good Indices) (FTSE 2018) and Dow Jones (Dow Jones Sustainability Indices) (Sustainability-indices 2018). These benchmarks enabled low-cost index funds to emerge and add to the range of investment options available to investors. They also allowed for the first time a way to easily follow and compare the financial performance of the world's most responsible and sustainable companies compared to the broad market. However it was in 2006, with the formation and launch of the United Nation Principles for Responsible Investment (UNPRI) (UNPRI 2018) by then Secretary General Kofi Annan, that "mainstream" financial institutions, hitherto largely absent from this debate, started to seriously and systematically integrate ESG issues into and alongside their standard financial analysis and wider investment processes.

In 2014, at a press conference in London, when the Executive Director of the United Nations Environment Programme (UNEP) announced plans to create a set of neutral, global, UN-endorsed principles—supported by action plans—to define best practice RI by institutional investors. This marked the first time the UN had directly engaged with the world's institutional investors and was seen as an important step towards fulfilling the Millennium Development Goals and commitments of the World Summit for Sustainable Development. With a budget of US $320,000, a task force of forward-looking individuals, with the mandate of taking a leadership role "at odds with sector norms, if necessary" was convened to develop the principles (UNPRI 2018).

Leading institutions from 16 countries, representing more than US $2 trillion of invested capital, officially signed the principles at a launch event held at the New York Stock Exchange. The six principles were drafted by a group of institutional investors in a year-long process, supported by a 70-person group of experts from intergovernmental and governmental organisations, civil society, and academia.

This process was co-ordinated by investment consultancy Mercer (Mercer 2018) and the PRI's UN partners, the United Nations Environment Programme Finance Initiative (UNEP FI) and the UN Global Compact.

The adoption of the principles by financial institutions got off to a slow start from the original small number of signatories, but started to pick up following the global financial crisis in 2008. The negative comments aimed at the excessive risk-taking practices and short-term-focused behaviours in the financial services sector from policy makers, regulators, the media, and civil society coincided with this pickup in support for the PRI.

As at the end of 2017 almost 1800 entities, representing some US $60 trillion of invested capital, had become signatories being guided by the six principles. This makes the PRI the leading global investment association bringing together asset owners, advisers, service providers, and asset managers from all over the world to demonstrate their commitment to RI. By a combination of engagement, sharing of best practices, and learning, the PRI seeks to support its signatories in understanding the implications of sustainability for investment and promoting the incorporating of ESG factors within investment processes. A decade after its establishment, the PRI is today widely recognised for its leadership role in creating awareness globally about RI and helping progress RI within the core processes of investors around the world.

Notwithstanding the highly laudable efforts of the PRI and other ESG-related trade groups and organisations, RI has still to be mainstreamed in the financial services industry. Despite hugely increased awareness, implementation still lacks depth across many financial institutions. The major challenge is that mainstreaming RI effectively involves a system change—a paradigm shift that, amongst other things, will require a corresponding culture change within the world of institutional investors and with it a higher degree of knowledge skills and expertise. This is no easy task: at a fundamental level, it is proving difficult to change or redirect the financial services sector. Even following the global financial crisis, it would appear that, rather than change, the failing system has, in broad terms, merely been repaired with largely the same people doing similar things as before, albeit in a tighter and less permissive regulatory environment.

Genuine global industry ESG integration and adoption of RI will require additional efforts and a greater diversity and depth of knowledge, skills, and understanding from employee's entering or wishing to flourish in the sector. It is in this aspect that business schools and other higher education facilities can play a leading and hugely significant role to address some of the current gaps.

Sustainable Finance: Nature Scope and Demand

There are differing views on what the term sustainability means, and therefore there is no global consensus on a definition. The name sustainability is derived from the Latin *sustinere* (to hold; put up with; sustain). Sustain can mean "maintain," "support," or "endure," so we can think of this in terms of activities contributing to the health of the ecosystem, avoiding environmental degradation and resource scarcity, and promoting social equality health and cohesion. Put even more simply, "do no harm."

In its "Action Plan for Financing Sustainable Growth" (Financial Stability, Financial Services and Capital Markets Union 2018) published in March 2018, the European Commission identified the lack of a common taxonomy and labels for identifying what constitutes sustainability and sustainable businesses as a barrier to meeting the EU's goals of embedding sustainability into the European capital market system. To address this the EU is to create a Technical Committee of industry experts to work on solving this issue.

One of the many issues the Commission is seeking to resolve is that of providing better information to the citizen savers of Europe as to how sustainable their financial products actually are. The rationale being that if more users of financial products question and challenge their suppliers on the "do no harm" or the sustainability credentials, we should see faster market-driven progress to a fairer and socially connected capital market system, one that can benefit investors, provide economic growth, job creation, and the environment. However the commission also recognises that some policy interventions will be required to encourage and stimulate such market forces and that the market cannot be relied upon to solve some of the most pressing issues such as climate change alone.

Policymakers are aware that since the 1940s, economic data has superseded all other market data, with profit margins and short-term stock prices often driving corporate strategies and with national policies dominated by the influence of gross domestic product (GDP) growth forecasts. However, as was once again proven by the last financial crisis, profit margins or GDP do not tell decision-makers anything about the health of a workforce, the environment, or a nation and provides few clues as to the dependencies on environmental and human capital and emerging trends and opportunities. It is these factors that sustainable investment professionals place a great deal of emphasis on, to not only identify companies that are adapting to market and evolving consumer preferences but are also best placed to profit from them in the long term. In response, many companies are spending considerable resources on promoting their own sustainability credentials, for example, Marks & Spencer's *Plan A* (M&S Plan A 2025 Commitments 2018) programme, so called because as they say, there is no Plan B for the planet. Sustainability is becoming big business and is increasingly being identified as a driver of long-term corporate and investment performance.

For cxample, of academic studies (Clark et al. 2015):

- 80% show that stock price performance of companies is positively influenced by good sustainability practices
- 88% showed a positive correlation between sustainability and operational performance
- 90% find a relationship which points to superior sustainability practices reducing a firms cost of capital
- After reporting environmentally positive events, stocks show an average outperformance of 0.84%. Conversely, after negative events, stocks underperform by 0.65%

And

- Morgan Stanley found that investing in sustainability has usually met, and often exceeded, the performance of comparable traditional investments on both an absolute and a risk-adjusted bases, across asset classes and over time

A key driver of interest in sustainability and sustainable investment is also generational. Millennials (those born in the 1980s and 1990s) are much more attuned to sustainability and social justice than any generation before due in part to the emergence of social media and that sustainability has been for some time taught in primary and secondary schools. By 2025, it is estimated that Millennials will constitute 25% of the US population (Fisher and Zirin 2015).

There are many potential business and investment implications to this including:

- Perceived unsustainable or socially controversial businesses will have difficulty attracting and retaining talent
- More investment schemes will undergo greater scrutiny of their actual investments by their clients and beneficiaries
- Social media technology will enable a greater degree of peer-to-peer investment activity, putting pressure on the increased disclosure of environmental and social impacts
- Millennials will want investment advice on the same terms as they get from other businesses—digitally delivered, socially/environmentally conscious, cheap, and networking oriented

The values and beliefs of Millennials will therefore create a desire to understand the social and environmental impacts of their investments. This will shape their investment choices, so a rise in interest in investments with positive impacts, where the impacts and societal benefits are quantified, will appeal over and above those where such impacts are at best unclear. Although competitive financial returns are and will remain important, evidence shows that there is a desire to align such returns with a positive impact, reflecting the individual's own interests and values.

The Emergence of the Sustainable Finance Professional: Niche to Mainstream

In 2015, when the UN launched its Sustainable Development Goals (SDGs) with the ultimate aim to "end poverty, protect the planet and ensure prosperity for all," many questions arose as to how the capital markets and the asset management industry can play a role in meeting these goals. Asset managers have a dual role—one being the deployment of capital to companies that can deliver the goods and services that will allow the goals to be achieved, and a second, and highly influential, role is as corporate owners, that is, by using the shareholdings to hold companies to account for their actions and behaviours that may prevent the goals from being met and using that influence to change practices, often in collaboration with other shareholders.

The interest in the SDGs from the financial sector has been growing with a number of asset owners committing to deploy a proportion of their capital to SDG investments and with asset managers across the world developing financial products with the specific purpose of investing in companies that have a clear contribution to make to the SDGs. These products will require investors to look beyond short-term, benchmark-relative investment returns and more to the impact of companies' activities and operations on the real economy. This will require a new set of analytical tools and skills that the majority of investment analysts in the industry have yet to engage with and develop.

An example of how some investors are attempting to plug this gap can be found in the UK's Cambridge University's Centre for Sustainability Leaderships' Investment Leaders Group (ILG). The ILG's mission is to influence the investment chain to take greater account of sustainability.

At the time the ILG was formed in 2013, the financial industry was still in the process of digesting the findings of the UK-government-commissioned "Kay Review" (Gov.UK 2014) authored by renowned economist Professor John Kay on the impact of short-termism on UK equity markets, and the global economy was still feeling the impacts of the effects of the global financial crisis. The ILG members identified short-termism in financial markets as a cause of underinvestment, economic inefficiency, and poor decision-making by corporations, which was undermining long-term value creation. This was also a moment in time when there was an emerging consensus that short-termism had not served the economy well, but in particular it had not served the end users of capital markets well, the citizen savers and investors of the world.

It was also clear that there was yet to emerge an industry consensus on what to do about the issues and little if any work had been done regarding the question of actually "how, in practice" can a long-term, patient-investment approach be implemented which was not driven by short-term incentives or behaviours. The ILG's work had, in response, been focusing on how investment mandates can support long-term investment, and developed a toolkit, published in a report titled "Taking the Long View: A Toolkit for Long-Term, Sustainable Investment Mandates" (CISL 2018), which identifies a set of ten elements to help investors design or assess investment mandates and strategies that can make a particularly strong contribution to long-term, responsible, and sustainable investment as these issues are not addressed in the professional financial qualification syllabuses.

An insightful and interesting research programme run by the main professional financial training organisation, the CFA Institute and State Street (CFA Institute 2018), released a report titled "Discovering PHI, Motivation as the Hidden Variable of Performance" that provided some sobering data on the state of thinking from finance industry professionals (7000 investment professionals were surveyed from 20 countries). PHI refers to purpose, habits, and incentives.

Some of the key findings were:

- The majority believe they would be fired after 18 months of relative underperformance
- Only 28% remain in the industry to help clients meet financial goals
- Higher PHI scores are more likely to deliver superior long-term investment performance (only 17% have this)
- Money is a de-motivator—pressure to meet short-term incentives = higher stress and less motivation to work in clients' interests

• Millennials have higher PHI than older colleagues, but there is a tipping point at age 51.

The "habits" part of the PHI equation can be taught. Habits are a consequence of a process and can be informed and influenced by educational and high-quality teaching, however the sort of academic courses available to support a client and societal sensitive centric investment philosophy are still hard to find in today's education system and are required by the investment professional of tomorrow to move out of the "nice" and very much into the "mainstream."

The Changing Skill Sets Required for Sustainable Finance Professionals

Although the PRI principles and various best practice guidelines provide a useful framework for those starting out down a RI track, it is not in anyone's interests to have a "one size fits all" approach. The approach to RI should be unique to each investor organisation's philosophy, culture, and general investment approach.

A report from Inflexion Point Capital Management commissioned by the Norwegian Ministry of Finance as part of its four-yearly review of Norges Bank's management of the Government Pension Fund Global titled "Mapping of Global Responsible Investment Best Practices" (Lie and Kieman 2017) identifies ten common "building blocks" that enhance an institution's chances of hardwiring RI successfully into robust asset management operations that have a long-term and responsible outlook. These include:

1. Leadership from the top;
2. Recognition of long investment horizon;
3. Belief that RI brings net positive benefits;
4. Integration of RI into investment beliefs;
5. Strengthening risk management;
6. Total portfolio approach reflecting organisation circumstances;

7. Building partnerships with peer investors;
8. Commitment to engagement;
9. Intermediary alignment; and
10. Commitment to continuous improvement and innovation.

Across the 15 institutions interviewed for the report, there were some distinct trends found, which included the role of the RI professional and the analytical skills required and exhibited.

The report notes, "*Often, institutions regard new resources dedicated to RI as an investment in becoming a more effective manager, rather than a cost. Despite difficulties of quantifying RI's impact on portfolio performance, institutions believe RI has strengthened the level of trust among their stakeholders as well as enhancing the organization's reputation and international profile.*"

"*There was a strong consensus among institutions that a balanced RI programme should embrace both active and passive investment approaches. While active management is not an absolute prerequisite for an effective RI strategy, it is typically more narrowly focused and company-specific and does provide a greater opportunity to deploy the full range of RI tools than do passive approaches. Across both investment styles, **RI exposes risk factors which may not be picked up by traditional financial analysis, yet could have a material bearing on portfolio performance.***"

The report emphasised that for those investors interviewed and who have a strong conviction and belief that ESG issues can affect the long-term risk/return dynamic, they require and need to ensure that investment analysts have the training tools and skills to identify them.

Is Traditional Financial Training and Curricula Fit for Purpose?

For financial professionals working in the industry, there are a small number of qualifications that are accepted and recognised as displaying a minimum level of professional competency and skill.

The best known is the Chartered Financial Analyst (CFA) qualification (CFA Institute 2018) run by the CFA Institute. The CFA Institute describe this as "*a program that provides a strong foundation of advanced investment analysis and real-world portfolio management skills that will give you a career advantage.*" It also states that "*Completing the CFA Program shows employers and clients you have mastered a broad range of practical portfolio management and advanced investment analysis skills.*"

Historically there has been relatively little coverage of sustainability and ESG issues in the CFA curriculum. Since the 2008 financial crisis however and under pressure from some of the membership, they have been looking at how they can improve their content to include sustainability and ESG issues. The curriculum that students are currently undergoing still relies on standard financial theory and models of financial analysis that have been shown in the past to be wanting. There is a similar tale for the syllabus and content of other financial services trade organisations' training and accreditation courses.

A number of commentators have noted that these training mechanisms produce financial analysts who think the same way, believe in and trust the same theories, and use the same financial and risk models and as a consequence find it difficult to develop their own thinking as to how to evaluate risk based upon the array of ethical, governance, environmental, and social issues and risks that companies face and that certain corporate behaviours can expose them to.

There are some notable exceptions to the training courses provided by the professional bodies which have emerged from outside the standard finance curricula. For example, the Sustainability Accounting Standards Board (SASB) has developed a range of training modules which are well regarded including the Fundamentals of Sustainability Accounting (FSA) course and credential drawing from the principles of accounting.

The FSA Credential is designed to inform students of the link between material sustainability information and a company's financial performance. The majority of test takers are professionals in investment analysis (who would also be undertaking the CFA and similar training), consulting, and sustainability. SASB claims that this is the only credential that teaches students "*How sustainability information can be financially material; and, what you can do with that information.*" The former question is one that the majority of financial analysts consistently struggle with.

The FSA curriculum is broken into three core parts:

- *Part I*: The Need for Sustainability Accounting Standards
  - Provides the historical, legal, and investing context for understanding how materiality is understood in the capital markets and why this is relevant for sustainability accounting
- *Part II*: Understanding SASB Sustainability Accounting Standards
  - Describes why an industry-specific approach to identifying the sustainability information that is most likely to be financially material helps you focus on the business case for sustainability
- *Part III*: Using SASB Standards
  - Explores implications of material sustainability information and outlines considerations for using SASB standards, whether you are an investment analyst, consultant, or employee at a company reporting sustainability information

The FSA is examined at two levels; the first level "Level I" covers:

- How sustainability factors impact financial performance
- The legal context for material sustainability information
- A common language to describe the materiality of sustainability information to finance, legal, and accounting professional

The second level "Level II" is aimed at teaching

- How industry-specific sustainability information can inform corporate strategies or investor recommendations
- The skills needed to evaluate corporate performance on sustainability factors

This course is presented for people looking to enhance their knowledge of integrating sustainability into both investment and strategic business thinking. It will be interesting to see how the take-up of the SASB Credential develops and grows over the coming years.

Another well-respected course is run by the PRI's Academy. This course was originally created by an RI industry trade association, the Responsible

Investment Association of Australia (RIAA), which had developed it with the support of a grant awarded by the Australian government.

The PRI Academy was developed as a separate business unit within the PRI to *"provide industry leading training for financial services, corporate and other professionals with the goal of helping individuals to understand how environmental, social and governance issues are impacting company performance, shareholder value and investment decision making."*

The Academy has a global curriculum with the objective of upskilling teams and professionals across all investment and capital markets. PRI Academy courses have been designed to include content from leading international experts, real life and hypothetical case studies, and financial modelling. It is also designed to help students maximise the practical application of key ESG concepts in the shortest possible time frame.

The PRI Academy offers three web-based courses:

- *RI Fundamentals*—a short two-hour introduction to the basic principles that underlie and define RI
- *RI Essentials*—a comprehensive examination of RI from theory to practice
- *Enhanced Financial Analysis*—the Academy's advanced course, which takes an in-depth look in to the use of sustainability data in fundamental investment analysis

Responsible Investment Fundamentals is a short training course designed to provide an introduction to RI. The course covers the business case for RI and explores the key principles of RI, uses real-life case studies to illustrate the materiality of ESG issues in business, introduces strategies for identifying and managing new approaches to ESG, and identifies sustainability data in financial modelling.

The Responsible Investment Essentials course is marketed by the PRI as the "international Gold standard for ESG training." It was developed as the PRI Academy's foundational course, focusing on the identification and implementation of ESG factors in investment decision-making. This course takes 12–14 hours to complete and builds on the Fundamentals course by also identifying methods for integrating sustainability data into financial modelling.

The Enhanced Financial Analysis course is an advanced course that explores and examines the use of sustainability data in fundamental investment analysis and stock valuation, which is an essential skill for analysts working in active investment teams (as opposed to index-tracking passive investment teams). This course takes 6–8 hours to complete and works through a series of topics that help identify the critical ESG issues relevant to sustainability performance, key value drivers, and overall financial outcomes.

Academic Opinion on Sustainability Teaching

The global financial crisis once again shone a bright light on the limitations of financial and economic teaching, models, theories, and disciplines in being able to predict risk. Even long-held theories such as diversification did not help as everything dramatically declined in value.

The fourth SDG has a specific target of "quality education" in supporting and delivering the aims of the goals. This means that an interdisciplinary approach to sustainability and sustainable finance education is required. What has become clear is that investment and business professionals must be able to understand and integrate concepts from different areas and disciplines including human rights, climate change, biodiversity, ethical theory, and stakeholder management and relations according to Annan-Diab and Molinari in their 2017 paper published in the *International Journal of Management Education* titled "Interdisciplinarity: Practical Approach to Advancing Education for Sustainability and for the Sustainable Development Goals" (Annan-Diab and Molinari 2017).

They highlight that knowledge is fragmented into disciplines in both academic and business environments, which means that understanding and managing issues that are complex and involve many different problems becomes extremely challenging.

Finance and economics have a fairly well-established set of topics abased on various theories and market-related modelling and statistical techniques. Sustainability and sustainable development has a footprint in several disciplines such as biology, nutrition, agriculture, environment, geography, physics, law sociology, history, economics, and political science to name a few. This leads one to conclude that sustainable finance also needs to blend the traditional financial agenda with a range of other disciplines to fully understand the contribution of finance to sustainability and sustainable development.

This might lead to a conclusion that highlights today's thinking that education for both finance and sustainability is lacking in an important aspect—that the blending of both disciplines is critical. For finance industry stakeholders who feel a sense of frustration with today's finance practitioners, (those people who have trodden the path of gaining well-established (and sustainability/ESG free) professional qualifications), the words of Albert Einstein, who is credited with the much-quoted "Insanity is doing the same thing over and over again and expecting different results" might well ring true!

Should Responsible and Sustainable Finance Replace the Way Finance Is Currently Taught?

The reader of this chapter should now have an appreciation of how the interest in identifying and evaluating environmental and social factors has grown rapidly and has become a common feature in the financial services sector in many mainstream financial institutions. However, it appears that the teaching of finance, certainly at undergraduate level, has not yet recognised and mirrored this trend. Where some sustainable finance content is included, it is usually a result of those academic institutions having individuals and pockets of expertise and interest in the topic. Sustainability being included in the teachings of finance and accountancy is the exception and certainly not the norm.

The current UK Quality Assurance Agency (QAA) subject benchmark statements for undergraduate accounting degrees and finance degrees provide a useful proxy for course content and it is obvious that there is little, if any, coverage of how to assess and account for the sustainability practices and activities of enterprises in the teaching modules. In fact, searching for the word sustainability gave one result in the accounting statement in a list of examples and absolutely none in the finance statement. Sustainable was mentioned once in the finance benchmark but in the context of a need for awareness of ethical and social issues, but not mentioned in the accounting benchmark. Translating sustainability and specific environmental and social issues as "ethical" matters is a debate the finance industry had over a decade ago and came through with a broad industry agreement of the distinction between the issues.

It could be argued that the current teaching of finance and accountancy in general has significant gaps in terms of integrating the increased knowledge and information we have today on the financial impacts of sustainability and on a range of key business indicators. The question would be how to address this as the new financiers and accountants of the future will emerge, much more aware of sustainability than previous generations and into a much more sustainability-sensitive world.

The work being done outside of academia by entities such as SASB and the PRI is a useful start; however, the key trade and member groups in the finance and accountancy world need to engage and act. An example of this is the UK-based but internationally networked Institute of Accountants England & Wales (ICAEW) that have identified this as an issue and are looking to do something about it. Similarly the Accounting for Sustainability (A4S) group, one of His Royal Highness (HRH) the Prince of Wales' charity groups, is bringing together Chief Financial Officers (CFOs), the finance sector, and academia in trying to address this weakness.

Success will only come if academia engages and works with the finance industry and their associated groups to modernise finance and accountancy teaching to reflect the emergence of sustainability and sustainable finance. It is suboptimal to have a cohort of individuals who, as is the case today, have to reassess some of their taught knowledge to account for sustainability in their analysis and evaluation of enterprises.

Those organisations that have been developing this subject matter should be actively engaging with academia to impress the need for such teaching to be integrated into the traditional finance and accountancy curricula. This is what the financier and accountant of the future will no doubt need and indeed, demand.

Summary

The challenge for academics and those providing higher education on the topic of sustainability and sustainable investment is maintaining relevance in what is a fast-evolving investment discipline. To put this in context, and as covered in this chapter, financial markets have operated for well over a century in more or less the same way; however, it is only since the late 1990s that ESG data has started to become more embedded into the analysis of companies and not until a decade later that mainstream investors were going about systematically integrating these factors into their decision-making processes. This results in best practice being constantly evolved with a few appropriate case studies and even less in terms of the long-term financial impact on investment portfolios.

This makes for a challenging agenda for academic institutions to effectively engage on, even though there is increasing demand for education and training on the subject. A greater level of strategic engagement by academic institutions with the financial service sector and greater support for academic institutions by financial players has to be the model for the way forward. Such relationships exist, for example, at Cambridge University's successful ILG; however, they are not as common as they could and should be. Having such a relationship would help financial institutions increase their access to and ability to retain a wider diversity of talent. Currently the vast majority of professional investors in the sector globally are subject to the same educational process and content having come through the same training programme offered by the CFA Institute and similar; very few also complete the sustainability and ESG-centric trade group or academic administered courses.

It is time for educators to embrace the practitioners and for practitioners to value the development of new ways of thinking beyond the straightjacket of the CFA Institute's view of finance, which pays little regard to the impact of finance in the real world. This perceived problem has not gone unnoticed, for example, by a major supra national body in the form of the European Commission.

It is time for finance professionals to associate rather than disassociate their work with the real world they actually live in, which is very different from the narrow world of benchmarks, basis points, and bonuses.

Academia can step up and play a key role in this welcome enlightenment!

Appendix

Curricula of the main non-finance professional education and training courses.

The PRI Academy

1. RI Fundamentals

Covers: Defining RI; recognising ESG issues, trends, and themes; and identifying the relationship between ESG analysis and investment decision-making
Includes:

Introduction to RI

- Identifying traditional analysis versus ESG analysis
- Understanding the materiality of ESG issues

ESG in Financial Analysis

- Defining environmental issues
- Understanding investment taxonomy
- Integrate environmental issues in financial modelling

Environmental Factors in RI

* Recognise social factors in financial analysis
* Understand the risk of ignoring social issues in investment decisions

Social Factors in RI

* Understand the key material impacts of corporate governance
* Recognise corporate governance factors in financial modelling

Governance Factors in RI

* Defining engagement in practice
* Recognising the different types of engagement
* Identifying the outcomes of engagement

2. RI Essentials

Covers: Defining RI and E, S, and G issues; recognising how ESG issues are related to sustainability trends and themes; demonstrating how ESG issues create both risks and opportunities for investors; and identifying a process for incorporating analysis of ESG issues into investment decisions
Includes:

Introduction to RI

* Understand how ESG information complements traditional financial analysis
* Identify different types of ESG information relevant to financial analysis
* Understand elements of ESG analysis
* Recognise the role of "materiality" when analysing ESG factors
* Apply techniques for qualification and quantification of ESG factors
* Integrate ESG data into basic financial models

RI and Financial Analysis

- Define key environmental issues
- Understand the relationship between business activities and ecosystem services
- Identify key environmental "megatrends"
- Identify approaches to environmental analysis at a country, sector, and company level
- Understand how to incorporate environmental issues into financial models and ratio work

RI and the Environment, RI and Society

- Identify key societal issues
- Outline the relationship between social issues, companies, and investors
- Assess the investment implications of societal issues
- Understand how to apply techniques to incorporate social issues into financial models and ratio work

RI and Corporate Governance

- Describe corporate governance
- Understand why corporate governance is important to investors
- Understand the role of people, tools, and processes that constitute corporate governance
- Recognise best practice in corporate governance
- Understand how to incorporate corporate governance issues into financial models and ratio work

Implementing an RI Programme

- Develop a plan for implementing a RI programme that meets the requirements of the PRI within your organisation
- Identify the key people, processes, and tools related to RI

- Identify the key areas and elements that could be considered when implementing RI
- Identify the information you need for internal and external reporting on your RI activities

RI and Engagement

- Design an engagement plan
- Explain how to combine engagement with other RI strategies
- Understand how to track and measure engagement activity
- Set out the typical steps taken for engaging with a company
- Understand the use of benchmarking to evaluate

3. Enhanced Financial Analysis

Covers: Understanding ESG information uses and identifying the role of intangible value drivers in investment decision-making

Introduction

- Define integrated analysis
- Identify the relationship between ESG data and materiality
- Understand the basic concepts needed to identify factors most material financial value

The Case Study

- Identify ESG factors in traditional sector analysis
- Outline key environmental, social, and business indicators that can impact financial value
- Identify global trends and regulations and their impact on financial analysis
- Map ESG factors in to hypothetical case studies
- Measure the extent to which ESG issues will impact key financial metrics

Step 1: Identify

- Assess the degree to which ESG factors affect industry and company performance
- Identify the guiding principles for assessing ESG issues
- Assess ESG issues using risk mapping methodologies
- Evaluate revenue, profit margins, and operations using ESG data
- Assess and rank companies according to key ESG factors

Step 2: Assess and Analyse

- Understand the guiding principles of ESG integration
- Examine a Discounted Cash Flow (DCF) model with an ESG overlay
- Identify the entry points for ESG analysis in an EP model
- Rank and score company performance
- Recognise varying options of ESG analysis and integration

Step 3: Model and Integrate

- Identify the many uses for sustainability data
- The role of ESG data in direct financial modelling

Using ESG Information

- Identify the range of ESG data available
- Understand how to use multiple forms of ESG data
- Recognise the challenges faced in collecting ESG data
- Identify global initiatives, regulations, and tools that support ESG integration
- Understand the role of reporting

Sourcing ESG Information

- Recognise and apply the key principles of ESG analysis

Sustainability Accounting Standards Board (SASB)

FSA Credential has two levels. Level I:

- sets the context for sustainability accounting, describing the current market landscape and explaining the relevant legal considerations;
- outlines how SASB standards are designed to fit within that context; and
- covers the implications of sustainability accounting for both companies and investors

Level II moves beyond the principles-based curriculum of Level I to teach a practices-based curriculum. It will help readers learn how to apply sustainability accounting to their own work for the benefit of their organisation, the capital markets, and the economy at large.

FSA Credential Level I Syllabus

Part I: The Need for Sustainability Accounting Standards
Introduction

A Growing Demand

- Changing Valuations
- Sustainability Issues Are Business Issues
- Existing, Evolving, and Emerging Regulation
- Increasing Investor Interest

Historical and Legal Basis

- The Aftermath of the Stock Market Crash of 1929
- Disclosure as the Basis of the Securities Acts
- The Securities and Exchanges Commission (SEC) and Its Work

The Role of Accounting

- Early Statements on Generally Accepted Accounting Principles
- Historical Cost Accounting and the Rise of the Accounting Principles Board (APB)
- Decision-Usefulness Enters the Lexicon
- The Founding of the Financial Accounting Standards Board (FASB)
- The FASB's Conceptual Framework Project

Materiality: The Guiding Principle of Disclosure

- Foundational Cases: TSC v. Northway and Basic v Levinson
- The SEC's and FASB's Views of Materiality
- The National Resources Defence Council's (NRDC) Rule-Making Petition

SEC Disclosure Requirements

- Periodic Filing Requirements
- Regulation S-K Requirements for Form 10-K
- MD&A Section Disclosure
- The SEC's Climate Change Guidance
- Consequences of Inadequate Disclosure
- The Sarbanes-Oxley Act and Controls
- The SEC's Disclosure Effectiveness Initiative

Sustainability Accounting

- Pointing the Way Forward: the American Institute of Certified Public Accountants (AICPA), the FASB, and the Chartered Financial Analysts (CFA) Institute
- Sustainability Accounting and the Accounting Profession
- External Reporting
- Internal Decision-Making
- Current Initiatives

The State of Sustainability Disclosure

- Voluntary Sustainability Reporting
- Disclosure Overload
- Securities Law, Not Semantics
- Sustainability Ratings
- Benefits of Improved Sustainability Disclosure
  Part II: Understanding SASB Standards

The Importance of Standards

- Financial and Non-financial Accounting
- State of Sustainability Disclosure in SEC Filings

Introduction to SASB Standards

- US Capital Markets
- Likely to Be Material
- Decision-Useful
- Cost-Effective
- Industry-Specific

Identifying Industry-Level Disclosure Topics

- The Reasonable Investor Revisited
- Evidence-Based Research
- Stakeholder Consensus
- Evolving with the Marketplace

Components of a Standard

- Disclosure Guidance
- Disclosure Topics and Accounting Metrics
- Technical Bulletins and Interpretations

Emerging Themes Climate Change: Ubiquitous but Differentiated

- It's Not Climate Change Alone
- Unique Sector Sustainability Profiles
  Part III: Using SASB Standards

Corporate Use

- Considerations for Corporate Use
- Collecting Data
- Managing
- Reporting

Investor Use

- Overview
- Portfolio Construction
- Industry Analysis
- Company-Level Analysis
- Active Ownership

FSA Credential Level II Syllabus

Part I. Identifying the Material Financial Impacts of Sustainability Factors

- Evaluating How a Company's Circumstances Influence Material Sustainability Factors
- The Influences of Operations (Internal Factors) on Material Sustainability Factors
- The Influences of the Operating Environment (External Factors) on Material Sustainability Factors

* Assessing Sustainability Topics
* Applying the Five Factors
* Making Use of the Findings

Part II. Evaluating the Comparability of Sustainability Information

* Normalising Data for More Effective Comparisons
* Selecting Appropriate Measures for Use in Normalisation
* Normalising to Gain Insight into Performance Over Time
* Normalising to Improve Peer Comparisons
* Analysing the Spread of Industry Performance
* Recognising Data Types
* Looking at the Distribution of Data
* Summarising the Data
* Analysing Data Dispersion
* Dealing with Outliers and Non-normal Distributions
* Considering Company-specific Context in the Analysis
* Considering a Company's Operating Context
* Considering a Company's Performance Context

Part III. The Connection between Sustainability Performance and Valuation

* Assessing the Timing, Duration, and Intensity of Impacts
* Key Characteristics of Impacts
* Acute and Progressive Impacts
* Risks and Opportunities
* Accounting for the Interrelatedness of Impacts
* Using Material Sustainability Data in Financial Valuation
* Interrelated Impacts and Contextual Considerations
* Channels of Impact
* Integrating Sustainability into Valuation Models

References

Annan-Diab, Fatima, and Carolina Molinari. 2017. Interdisciplinarity: Practical Approach to advancing education for sustainability and for the Sustainable Development Goals, July 2017.

Barton, Dominic, James Manyika, Timothy Koller, Robert Palter, Jonathan Godsall, and Joshua Zoffer. 2017. *Measuring The Economic Impact of Short-Termism*. McKinsey Global Institute.

CFA Institute. 2018. CFA Institute Privacy Policy. Last modified May 25. Accessed July 31, 2018. https://www.cfainstitute.org/en/about/governance/policies/privacy-policy.

CISL. 2018. CISL Privacy Policy. Last modified April 2018. Accessed July 31, 2018. https://www.cisl.cam.ac.uk/privacy-and-cookie-policies.

Clark, Gordon L., Andreas Feiner, and Michael Viehs. 2015. From the Stockholder to the Stakeholder. How Sustainability Can Drive Financial Outperformance. Accessed July 31, 2018. https://arabesque.com/research/From_the_stockholder_to_the_stakeholder_web.pdf.

Financial Stability, Financial Services and Capital Markets Union. 2018. Action Plan for Financing Sustainable Growth. Accessed July 31, 2018. https://eur-lex.europa.eu/legal-content/EN/TXT/?uri=CELEX:52018DC0097.

Fisher, Andrea, and Jeremy Zirin. 2015. The Rising Millennials—UBS Wealth Management. Accessed July 31, 2018. https://www.ubs.com/content/dam/WealthManagementAmericas/documents/us-equities-the-rising-millennials-2015-06-23.pdf.

FTSE. 2018. FTSE Privacy Policy. Last modified February 28. Accessed July 31, 2018. https://www.ftserussell.com/legal/privacy-and-cookie-policy.

Gannon, Megan. 2014. Exxon Valdez 25th Anniversary: 5 Facts About the Historic Spill. *Livescience*, March 24.

Gov.UK. 2014, October 27. Kay Review of UK Equity Markets and Long-term Decision Making: Implementation Progress Report.

Hays, Jeffrey. 2008. Bhopal Disaster. Accessed July 31, 2018. http://factsanddetails.com/india/Nature_Science_Animals/sub7_9c/entry-4268.html.

History.com. 2018. A+E Networks Privacy Policy. Last modified 21 May. Accessed July 31, 2018. https://www.history.com/topics/vietnam-war/agent-orange.

Lie, Valborg, and Matthew Kiernan. 2017. Mapping of Global Responsible Investment Best Practices. Accessed July 31, 2018 http://inflectionpointcm.com/sites/default/files/document/norwaymof050118rs1404c.pdf.

Mercer. 2018. Mercer Privacy Policy. Last modified May 17. Accessed July 31, 2018. https://www.uk.mercer.com/privacy.html.

M&S Plan A 2025 Commitments. 2018.

PRI's Academy. https://priacademy.org/courses/.

Quaker. 2018. Quaker Privacy Policy. Last modified May 18. Accessed July 31, 2018. http://www.quaker.org.uk/privacypolicy.

SASB. https://fsa.sasb.org/.

Sustainability-indices. 2018. Sustainability-indices Privacy Policy. Accessed July 31, 2018. http://www.sustainability-indices.com/important-legal-information.jsp.

UNPRI. 2018. UNPRI Privacy Policy. Accessed July 31, 2018. https://www.unpri.org/privacy-policy.

8

Sustainability in Supply and Value Chain Management

Fred A. Yamoah

Introduction

Unlike other business and management disciplines, supply and value chain management has long been related to sustainability discourse because of its direct impact on sustainable development. Overall, stakeholders agree that incorporating sustainability principles into supply and value chain management curriculum through education and business sector partnerships could transform supply and value chain processes (Walker and Brammer 2009). An emerging viewpoint within supply and value chain sector is that 'a company is no more sustainable than its supply and value chains' (Krause et al. 2009). But there are many practical sustainability integration challenges.

Some researchers have highlighted the negative effects of supply and value chain operations on ecological footprint (King and Lenox 2001; Melnyk et al. 2003) and social equity (Carter and Jennings 2002). Many

F. A. Yamoah (✉)
Department of Management, Birkbeck, University of London, London, UK
e-mail: f.yamoah@bbk.ac.uk

© The Author(s) 2019
K. Amaeshi et al. (eds.), *Incorporating Sustainability in Management Education*,
https://doi.org/10.1007/978-3-319-98125-3_8

media reports have also canvassed for change and improvement (Vachon and Klassen 2006). Several businesses have responded to these negative reports by adopting systems that pay attention to reduce waste and greenhouse gas emissions, use less non-renewables, and avoid pollution (Pullman et al. 2009). However, there is no doubt that a lot more needs to be done for further improvement in supply and value chain management systems.

Efforts at embedding sustainability suffer from limited sustainability knowledge and skills (Figueiró and Raufflet 2015). It is part of the reason why some corporate executives still do not place sustainability at the centre of their business strategy for fear of becoming less competitive in the twenty-first century. Thus, one would agree with Lans et al. (2014) that, to ensure optimum opportunity for sustainable development organisations require a pull of human resource that can envisage integrating sustainability as a cardinal business resource to foster 'strategic renewal, innovation and venturing'.

The lack of sustainability expertise requires an ambitious effort to improve sustainability knowledge and skills among supply and value chain practitioners through higher education curriculum. Hence, the focus on higher education supply and value chain management provision to expose students to sustainability challenges so that they can cope creatively and successfully in their professional capacities (Rowe 2007). Undoubtedly, higher education is known for its transformational solutions that are channelled through curriculum design, teaching, and learning to resolve societal problems. Existing evidence shows that some higher education institutions (HEIs) are actively finding solutions to address sustainability challenges posed by supply and value chain systems (Blanco-Portela et al. 2017). Despite these creditable attempts, Grindsted (2011) points to a limited success in integrating sustainability into higher education curriculum.

Continuous collaboration between academic institutions and business sector partners to co-create sustainability knowledge is not only important because of the need to address increasing environmental and social challenges but also being mindful of the fact that sustainable supply and value chain management is an important determinant of the future success of a business (Accenture 2010). Although the challenge is big, teaching and learning provision on supply and value chain management is yet to be fully embedded with sustainability principles and practices in higher education curriculum.

Integrating sustainability into higher education supply and value chain provision in terms of programme design, teaching, and learning is at best, at the periphery, where some selected sustainability topics are covered in a couple of sessions of the existing supply and value chain management course modules. Supply and value chain management like other business management disciplines treats teaching and learning materials on sustainability as a supplementary topic that requires coverage to bring the course content in line with current momentum around education for sustainable education (Etse and Ingley 2016).

Whilst supply and value chain has consistently been related to ecological and social issues, the attention given to embedding sustainability into supply and value chain education has not adequately reflected the critical importance of curriculum to sustainable supply and value chain educational development and delivery process. AASHE (2014) pointed out that traditional higher education curriculum is not receptive to education for sustainability in general. Some of the efforts made so far to embed sustainability include real-world learning-based models that configure supply and value chain management curriculum with sustainability in a replicable stepwise process to facilitate sustainability knowledge transfer. To engender progressive engagement with sustainability, it beholds on us as supply and value chain scholars to adopt an interdisciplinary orientation to enable us to develop novel teaching materials and learning techniques that fully capture the essence of sustainable supply and value chain management. Regarding sustainability as a bolted-on matter to make supply and value chain management curriculum content aesthetically appealing will not deliver education for sustainability goals.

This chapter aims to re-echo the call for full integration of sustainability principles into supply and value chain management provision at higher education level as an urgent matter. It seeks to share with the community of practice personal experiences of attempts to integrate sustainability in supply and value chain modules at both undergraduate and postgraduate levels. It will ground a critical discussion on the integration process including pedagogical practices on the extant literature to reveals prospects and challenges to scaling up of sustainable supply and value chain management education. The next section provides background that draws on UNESCO's Global Action Programme (GAP) on Education for Sustainable Development (ESD) among other declarations as context.

Background

Negative ecological and social effects of business practices over many decades have been a major driver behind various declarations by international and national institutions to embed sustainability into educational curriculum. These calls for sustainability integration within the context of supply and value chain management can be described as a classic case of practice informing educational curriculum innovation. This is because the total effect of unsustainable supply and value chain systems and networks over decades is serving as the catalyst informing and questioning educational curriculum rational, content and delivery at present. Hence, negative environmental and social impact of corporate practices is driving the necessity to adapt existing educational curriculum which was not designed to promote education for sustainability; see AASHE (2010).

Brundtland report of 1987 and the proceedings from the United Nations Rio conference on sustainable development expressed concerns about existing educational provisions on sustainability for the lack of synergy between teaching and learning process and the need of society. Therefore, reforming and realigning the existing curriculum to fully integrate sustainability is an important task for educational institutions and academics. A number of declarations and initiatives of the United Nations have served as building blocks for the integration of sustainability knowledge and skills into curricula for future graduates. These declarations have in diverse ways also spurred support from stakeholders to promote collaborations and resources mobilisation towards fostering ESD (Shrivastava 2010).

In summary, these declarations and initiatives seek to signal formal as well as informal education to be able to play a pivotal role in promoting curriculum that will help resolve sustainability challenges in the short, medium, and long term. Scholarship on achievement so far is mixed. For example, Shephard (2008) commended efforts made at higher education level to resolve sustainability challenges through curriculum development and enrichment in the last three decades. On the contrary, Grindsted (2011) was sceptical about higher education's commitment to incorporating sustainability principles beyond its receptiveness to signing declarations.

The UK government's March 2013 report on ESD UK sets out its position on UNESCO's Decade of Education for Sustainable Development as follows: 'The UK Government and a wide range of national agencies believe that we need to foster, through education, the values, behaviour and lifestyles required for a sustainable future' (UK National Commission for UNESCO 2013). The report makes key recommendations that acknowledge work done at the national level but points out that there was more work to be done in terms of educational policy and support systems to ensure that ESD succeed.

Policies and programmes of the United Nations and the UK government provide justification for developing supply and value chain management curriculum underpinned by sustainability principles and delivered with innovative pedagogy to train students. HEIs in the UK have responded in diverse ways to these declarations. Of special interest to this background section is how HEIs have reacted to the ESD declaration. Majority of HEIs in the UK have signed declarations or published statements of commitments to embed sustainability into their existing provisions (Karatzoglou 2013; Ramos et al. 2015). To give meaning to these commitments, several HEIs have begun incorporating sustainability in their curricula (Wals 2014; Ramos et al. 2015). Many follow-up studies however found these efforts were limited in scope and form (Lozano et al. 2013; Mulà et al. 2017). Fiselier et al. (2018) for example, confirmed earlier assertions by Grindsted (2011) that many HEIs make limited or no effort to influence curriculum change or redesign.

Drawing on the above background, a personal reflection and commentary on the subject will be presented in the proceeding sections of this chapter. As a sustainability and supply and value chain management scholar with over a decade of higher education experience in the UK, I have been engaged with various processes including module leadership, curriculum development on sustainability-related modules in four (4) UK universities. Therefore, it envisaged that these reflections and contribution to the discourse on integrating sustainability in higher education supply and value chain curriculum are not only timely but will meaningfully engage with readers.

Supply and Value Chain Management and Sustainability in Retrospect

Supply and value chain management activities do not only play a vital role in achieving business objectives but they also have the potential in addressing sustainability issues. The strategic role of supply and value chain management and its potential to contribute significantly to sustainable development is evident through the lenses of academic scholars who have published on the subject mostly from the 1990s to 2018 (see Touboulic and Walker 2015; Dubey et al. 2017; Roy et al. 2018). This section maps the evolutionary pathway to sustainable supply and value chain management by drawing on comprehensive reviews of Roy et al. (2018); Dubey et al. (2017); Touboulic and Walker (2015); Carter and Easton (2011) and Seuring and Gold (2012) to espouse the historical trajectory of the relationship; the ensemble of theories and concepts embraced along the pathway and the future of supply and value chain management within the emerging sustainability context. The mapping does not seek to offer a detailed critique of the extant literature but to highlight significant phases of the relationship and interaction between supply and value chain management and sustainability concept.

A lot of interest has been shown in this subject area over the past two decades but there is no evidence supporting a view that scholars gravitated around a central theme at the onset of sustainability concept development. The reason for such a historical pathway could be attributed to the dual focus of scholarship on the subject; with one strand of research focussed on changes in supply and value chain to accommodate sustainability and the other anchoring scholarship on organisational level inference to sustainability, using organisational theories.

Despite the lack of an obvious common theme(s) from the 1990s, Touboulic and Walker (2015) teased out chronologically a set of themes that defined supply and value chain management and sustainability research from 1996 to 2010. Scholarship on the subject was expressed as descriptors or as an additional factor instead of substantive definition. This was a key feature of most of the studies undertaken before the year 2000. One of the earlier descriptors was the green supply chain theme by Green et al. (1996). It aimed at drawing attention to a new way of thinking about supply and value chain management, especially industrial procurement from the perspective of environmental sustainability. The 'green supply' phase was followed by environmental supply chain dynamics (Hall 2000). This was the era when the scope of environmental innovation and sustainability discourse had expanded to supplier firm. Hence, the need for customer facing organisations to be engaged with the issue of sustainability. The next phase 'green procurement or purchasing' emphasised the need for supplier organisations to be actively engaged to reduce environmental impact.

Following the initial broadening of the scope of environmental innovation to embrace supplier organisations, the increasing notion for corporate responsibility had gathered momentum among stakeholders. Consequently, supply and value chain management within environmental management context was viewed to be connected to sustainable development, for as long as businesses were made answerable for social and environmental impacts emanating from their respective supply and value chains. In line with the exigencies of the time emphasis was placed on the need for businesses to place ecological and social factors at the centre of their corporate strategy and extend it to their suppliers down the chain (Wolters 2003). Two years after Wolters' (2003) recommendation for organisations to embed sustainability at the centre of its operations, Carter (2005) suggested five distinctive facets of procurement social responsibility as: (1) the environment, (2) diversity, (3) human rights, (4) philanthropy, and (5) safety.

By the mid-2000s, integrating environmental thinking into supply and value chain management had been established as a necessity. This trend was epitomised by the strand of literature that emerged from 2005 and beyond. For instance, Srivastava (2007) coined a definition for green supply chain management as the act of 'integrating environmental thinking into supply-chain management, including product design, material sourcing and selection, manufacturing processes, delivery of the final product to the consumer as well as end-of-life management of the product after its useful life'. Similarly, Carter and Rogers (2008) focussed on 'the strategic, transparent integration and achievement of an organisation's social, environmental, and economic goals in the systemic coordination of key inter-organisational processes for improving the long-term economic performance of the individual company and its supply chains'.

Recalling the dual historical pathway that characterised integration of sustainability into supply and value chain management, scholars in the late 2000s provided a variety of definitions underpinned by single, dual, or multiple sustainability themes (see examples by (Eltantawy et al. 2009; Walker and Brammer 2009; Laura and Michael 2009; Tate et al. 2010)). Carter and Easton (2011) suggested that sustainability thoughts involving proper management of social and environmental issues have evolved from what they termed 'standalone' themes, through the notion of social responsibility, and finally to the concept of sustainability.

A middle phase of this uncoordinated evolution of supply and value chain thoughts was characterised by attempts to capture sustainability under the ambit of corporate social responsibility. Environmental and social issues such as diversity, philanthropy, human rights, and safety were positioned under the umbrella of corporate social responsibility portfolio of supply and value chain management research and practice. However, corporate executives perceived corporate social responsibility activities collectively did not yield financial rewards. This economic anxiety of the business sector appears to have been resolved with the inclusion of the triple bottom line of John Elkington (an author, advisor, and serial entrepreneur) into developing sustainable supply and value chain thoughts.

It served as a unique vehicle to convey the essence of sustainability knowledge and practice to the business sector in the language that businesses understood best—explicitly factoring economic performance. In practical terms factoring the triple bottom line opened many possibilities to organisations. These included cost savings connected to sustainable packaging, material reuse, and recycling; lower health and safety costs;

financial benefits associated with better working condition such as lower turnover; safer warehousing; reduced disposal costs accruing from the implementation of ISO 14000 standards, amongst many better cost-saving benefits. Carter and Easton (2011, 48) expressed these sentiments as follows: 'Rather than suggesting that firms identify and engage in social and environmental activities which will hopefully help, or at least not harm, economic performance, the triple bottom line explicitly directs managers to identify those activities which improve economic performance and dictate the avoidance of social and environmental activities which fall outside of this intersection.'

A major consolidation phase in the supply and value chain vis-à-vis sustainability discourse was reached after the ground-breaking work of Carter and Rogers (2008) on the prerequisites for a sustainability embedded supply and value chain management. They described strategy, risk management, organisational culture, and transparency as factors that could promote or inhibit decision making towards integrating sustainability into supply and value chain management. These earlier studies served as the basis for the current discourse around sustainable development that considers a concurrent consideration of social, environmental, and economic factors.

The next generation of sustainability incorporated supply and value chain management studies focussed more on how the integration process can be done effectively. The work of Roy et al. (2018), for example, captured the 'how' question quite well with the development of a 'landscape of the principal facets' of sustainable supply chain management. These themes offered a blueprint that is akin to a typical planning process stages which straddle across intention to transit from traditional to embedding sustainability phase, through implementation models, management systems for inter-organisational dynamics, and performance to contingency programmes. It is the reason why some supply and value chain management scholars are actively accentuating the call for significant, comprehensive, and endearing changes in our approach to supply and value chain management curriculum. It is presently expected that supply and value chain management thinking will effectively factor sustainability to engage current and future students with the requisite sustainability orientation and skills to enable them address successfully the complex economic, ecological, and social issues posed by unsustainable supply and value chain management systems and networks. The need to quickly engage education curriculum is fundamentally aligned with the viewpoint that integrating sustainability into supply and value chain management is not a destination, but an ongoing endeavour for business and society.

The review of the evolution and scaling-up pathways to sustainable supply and value chain management encourages learners to appreciate the dynamics of supply and value chain management discipline within the context of sustainability. It does prompt students to the fact that integrating sustainability into supply and value chain management curriculum has huge implications for business and society. It is critical for students to appreciate that getting engaged with sustainability discourse will foster resolving an old and growing problem that requires knowledge, passion, and creativity. Several drivers have contributed to catapulting sustainability to prominence and key amongst them are the continuous need for raw materials and energy resources, climate change issues, and stakeholder understanding and pressure for environmental and the social actions. The intricate nature of sustainability challenges students to recognise the urgency of capturing ESD scheme within supply and value chain management curriculum.

The Case for Integration: Supply and Value Chain Management Education and Sustainability

Sustainability has gained prominence in higher education and in business schools globally. It has become one of the topics covered in many supply and value chain management modules in higher education. However, it has not been fully integrated into supply and value chain management curriculum. Several reasons account for the lack of urgency on our part as supply and value chain management academics. Firstly, the need to change a programme designed for a specific knowledge and skills provision in the specialised area of traditional supply and value chain management, to focus on shaping a sustainable business and society threatens scholars' sense of identity. Thus, the need for supply and value chain management curricula to be re-oriented to meet the goal of sustainable education as captured in the Bonn Declaration could be a source of anxiety for established academics in the field, particularly considering the time and resources required to foster multidisciplinary collaboration with other faculties and industry.

Secondly, there seem to be lack of appreciation that the interrelationships and interdependence between business and society are a critical matter and our passive posture impedes momentum towards integration. Hence, the rather low presence of sustainability in the current supply and value chain management curriculum. Traditional supply and value chain networks have been associated with production-oriented systems configured primarily towards achieving economic goals. Therefore, the ingrained assumptions for scholars and practitioners in this field regard economic imperatives for effective and efficient supply and value chain system as an overarching priority over other considerations such as environmental and social issues. Such a perspective impedes the ability and purpose to initiate and pursue business and educational curriculum innovations that capture environmental and social objectives. Therefore, there is the need to challenge our shared philosophical assumptions about the supply and value chains systems within the realities of our contemporary society. It cannot be overemphasised that sustainable supply and value chain management is underpinned by the believe and recognition that supply, value addition, and purchasing activities are of strategic importance to corporate survival as well as resolving sustainability challenges.

Thirdly, the challenges associated with the process of sustainability integration across modules, programmes, and departments as well as engaging business sector collaborators ought to be recognised. Admittedly, sustainability as an emerging academic field attempts to address a complex challenge with huge implications for business and society at local and global levels. Both Komiyama and Takeuchi (2006) and Blackstock and Carter (2007) concede that incorporating sustainability into curricula generally is a new discipline that requires deployment of competencies such as 'systems-thinking, anticipatory, normative, and strategy-building methods in participatory, deliberative, and adaptive settings' to succeed.

In terms of ontological, epistemological, and methodological paradigms, Brundiers and Wiek (2011) suggested that the field of sustainability questions the underlying assumptions, values, and ethos of established disciplines. Furthermore, internal barriers within educational and business organisations, be they faculties or departments, make it difficult to form and manage effectively partnerships required for curriculum development and its delivery.

Despite these challenges, the shear level of the potential for positive or negative influence of supply and value chain management activities demands a sense of urgency for incorporation. If our students who are tomorrow's supply and value chain professionals are to subsist with the growing sustainability challenges, we need to appreciate the enormity of the challenge and identify innovative curriculum content and pedagogy to develop their capabilities, through a transformative learning experience.

Grounding Supply and Value Chain Management Curriculum in Sustainability

Beyond developing innovative curriculum content and adopting appropriate pedagogy, it is essential to set the right context to engender interest and readiness of students to engage with sustainable supply and value chain management discourse. The public sphere is inundated with sustainability-related news and information, and there is evidence of incorporation of sustainability principles into schools' practices and processes. However, students that we meet at higher education level have varied levels of interests and insights about the sustainability agenda. This ranges from very little or greater awareness and understanding of sustainability. The challenge is that students that are aware of the subject mostly do not appreciate the urgency and the implications on personal responsibility. Students tend to have a high preponderance to deny control to act and defer the responsibility for seeking solutions to others. This connotes reluctance to consider major lifestyle changes, even to the point where sustainability values may not influence students' actual behaviours as new professionals after graduation.

To establish the appropriate disposition of higher education students to sustainability, it is important to explain from the onset that the business environment per International Standard Organisation's ISO 14001 consists of the surroundings in which a business operates, including air, water, land, natural resources, flora, fauna, humans, and their interrelationships. This serves to raise sustainability discussion out of the domain of undertaken a behaviour change for the benefit of future generations. The shift from shareholder perspective to stakeholder theory is also an important discussion to have with students at the early stage. Drawing students' attention to the growing magnitude of ecological challenges at local, regional, national, and global levels is also essential. Citing notable corporate visions that factored sustainability has been another effective means of drawing attention to business sector involvement with embedding sustainability in their operations. For example, John Kirkpatrick, Head of Sustainability, Lendlease Europe, stated that 'Sustainability allows us to attract and keep talent. And it encourages the best suppliers to work with us'. Apart from the cost factor, the need for stakeholder collaboration because sustainability is an issue that extends beyond the confines of a single business, as far as supply and value chain management is concern, generates interesting debates for helpful deliberations among students.

Sustainable Supply and Value Chain Management Concept

There is a need to showcase to students the cardinal changes in theoretical approaches over two decades in the speciality and operations of traditional supply and value management due to the emergence of sustainability. Rightly capturing the trajectory of the strategic shift to sustainable supply and value chain management (SSVCM) will demonstrate to students the centrality of purchasing, supply and value addition activities to long-term business performance and resolving sustainability challenges. It is important to acknowledge that there is no consensus on definitions of sustainable supply and value chain management in the extant literature because of the complicated nature of the subject and the inherent challenges associated with developing a common framework across different industries (Pullman et al. 2009). It is also important to explain to students that value chain concept builds on supply chain principles and both have sustainability implications.

An important distinguishing feature of the various conceptualisations on sustainable supply and value chain management that integrates the triple bottom line worth highlighting to students, is the debate as to whether management's engaging in sustainability is discretionary or mandatory. It is prudent to encourage students to keep the meaning of sustainable supply and value chain management open and be receptive to new ideas that will emerged from areas yet to be explored.

Curriculum Development for Sustainable Supply and Value Chain Management

Higher education curriculum design and management is subject to programme development policies and procedures. Business schools in the UK must ensure compliance with the set policies and procedures crafted based on the Quality Assurance Agency (QAA) for higher education framework. The subject benchmark statement for business and management defines what can be expected of a graduate in the subject, in terms of what they might know, do, and understand at the end of their studies. These are the guidelines that were followed in the three cases of embedding sustainability into supply and value chain management modules at undergraduate (year 1 and year 3 respectively) and postgraduate (MBA) levels that is reflected upon in this section.

The first-year mandatory 'Introduction to Sustainable Logistics and Supply Chain Management' module captured the essence of sustainability as a central plank of today's supply and value chain management education and business management. As an integral part of a BSc Logistics and Supply Chain Management programme, the module was designed to encourage students to be critical and engage with sustainability as they progressed along a pathway that expanded the scope of supply and value management topics beyond year one topics such as introduction to sustainable logistics and supply chain planning; sustainable purchasing principles and process; sustainable transport fundamentals; and green facilities design and management.

The third-year specialist pathway module 'Sustainability for Supply and Value Chain Management' was optional. The main import of the module was to emphasise employee, managerial, and personal responsibility for sustainability across the supply and value chain management discipline. A conscious effort was made to derive practical sustainability implications cases from the topics covered as part of the module delivery. Industry stakeholder speakers were drafted in to deliver sustainable supply chain management and sustainability innovation topics. The guiding principle was to prepare students to appreciate the need to be involved with the sustainability agenda at the level of an employee, a manager, or an individual after graduation. As an optional specialist module in year three, emphasis was placed on critical thinking and employability skills such as developing environmental management and social objectives for a supply chain facility and/or logistics schemes.

The Global Logistics and Supply Chain Management MBA pathway module 'Corporate Strategy and Sustainability' fully encapsulated the idea that the success of an organisation's supply and value chain management programmes is dependent on the extent of integration of sustainability into their systems. This MBA module was important to prompt students who were all professionals from different fields of endeavour about the urgency for sustainability intervention from corporate executives. It also factored the need for students to have professional and transferable skills to begin to make an impact even whilst on the programme. Part time MBA students were encouraged to integrate sustainability criteria into a familiar supply and value chain process at work, while full time students were provided an avenue to undertake a similar project with the university's procurement, human resource, and operations departments. The real-world project to design a strategy for effective management of sustainable supply or value chain, from input supply to final consumption, was supported by respective industry partners.

All the modules had preamble which typically read as follows (with slight changes depending on the module, the level, and its unique focus):

This module (Introduction to Sustainable Logistics and Supply Chain Management /Sustainability for Supply and Value Chain Management/ Corporate Strategy and Sustainability) is designed and delivered to ensure that students are enabled to examine the domain of supply and value chain management thoughts from sustainability perspective. It seeks also to develop students' capacity to adapt sustainability thinking to specific supply and value chain management contexts through interactive teaching and learning sessions, using study activities such as mind mapping, real-world learning projects, case studies, sustainability agility dairy completion, blended learning, etc. to develop relevant and appropriate knowledge, competencies and skills for academic and professional careers in supply and value chain management. The module design, delivery and assessment promotes a strong knowledge and research skills acquisition by supporting individual and group learning during lectures, tutorials and group work sessions. The module topics are selected and systematically delivered to draw attention to resource limitation and increasing ecological and social challenges to encourage current and future supply and value chain management professionals, managers and staff to fully engage with sustainability. The overall purpose of the module is to promote concurrent consideration of economic, social and environmental factors (triple bottom line) to achieve effective, efficient and sustainable supply and value chain management.

Like other business and management modules, these sustainability embedded modules were designed with knowledge and understanding as well as skills and attributes learning outcomes. Thus, learning outcomes set across the three modules presented below, indicate a variety of outcomes with some more suitable to the introductory module, others match the aim and objectives of the third-year undergraduate module and some suitable to corporate strategy and sustainability MBA module:

Examples of knowledge and understanding learning outcomes include:

By the end of the module, students should be able to:

1. Define and explain sustainable supply and value chain management concepts.
2. Distinguish between traditional and sustainability embedded supply and value chain management.

3. Describe some of the fundamental elements of sustainability embedded logistics and supply and value chain management systems.
4. Provide critical awareness of the methodologies used to determine the extent to which a given logistics and supply and value chain system is sustainable.
5. Provide a basic understanding of the science of sustainability and its interphase with social discourse for policy intervention and regulation as it influences logistics and supply and value chain management.
6. Examine sustainability principles that underpin strategies to achieve sustainable supply and value chain management.
7. Identify the range of activities in logistic and supply chain and derive their sustainability implications.
8. To gain an understanding of sustainability innovation in logistics systems and supply and value chains and appreciate their usefulness in providing a competitive advantage to the business.
9. Understand the drivers for a strategic approach to sustainable supply and value chain management.
10. Appreciate the value of sustainable collaboration within supply and value chains.
11. Identify strategies for partnerships and collaboration with industry, governmental and educational partners, and so on.

Examples of skills and attributes learning outcomes include:

By the end of the module, students should be able to:

1. Investigate the role and responsibilities of stakeholders including supply and value chain managers, entrepreneurs, international institutions, governments, consumers, and educational scholars in promoting viable and successful sustainability embedded supply and value chain systems.
2. Become more critical in tackling complex sustainable logistical and supply and value chain decision problems.
3. Design a strategy for effective management of sustainable supply or value chain, from input supply to final consumption.

4. Plan and work individually and as a team member to resolve a real-world sustainability challenge associated with supply and value chain management.
5. Evaluate the management of a sustainable product's life cycle 'from cradle to grave' using reverse logistics principles.
6. Apply research skills to retrieve, review, and critique sustainable supply and value chain management journal articles and industry reports and regulatory information on environmentally and socially sound strategies,
7. Demonstrate an ability to critically evaluate current supply and value chain management practices and recommend areas for potential sustainability principles integration,
8. Produce a well-written, referenced, and supported academic report on contemporary supply and value chain management with the context of sustainability.
9. Gain a valuable experience at group work and oral presentation on selected sustainable supply and value chain management issues.
10. Take responsibility for active and personal engagement with sustainability activities on campus (year 1 and 3) or as a supply and value chain management professional (MBA level), and so on.

Pedagogy and Delivery Methods

The underlying rationale for integrating sustainability into supply and value chain curricula at higher education is to engage students with sustainability mindset and influence positive actions through the provision of a comprehensive array of sustainability competencies. The goal is to facilitate learning to ensure that module and programme aims are fully met. However, it also essential to ignite a lifelong learning ethos to prepare students to pursue more sustainability knowledge and skills in their professional careers. To realise this vision and objectives our teams (in all the three cases for year 1, 3, and MBA level curricula) have followed a transformative, participatory, and collaborative pedagogical paradigm with emphasis on critical thinking and analysis of the interphase between supply and value chain management and sustainability, drawing on real-world cases to engender strategic sustainability initiatives and to highlight the centrality of personal involvement.

To ensure that students are challenged to engage actively, think critically, and reflect on their own and external perspectives, our teams used cohort group lectures and tutorials delivered by interdisciplinary teaching group, project and problem-based learning, mind mapping concept, case study, and virtual learning environment (studynet, moodle, blackboard, etc.). These were complemented by online materials, module updates, audio-visuals, and the novel sustainability agility dairy that encourage students to record industry news updates with sustainability implications. Students are encouraged to write their personal reflective commentary on the news items recorded to be presented at the end of the course. Invited guest lecturer provides understanding of the practical supply and value chain management context within which integrating sustainability principles occur.

Students at all levels have found the simple activity for meeting sustainability goals through partner or supplier selection exercise interesting and insightful. They are set a task to identify a real-world case for partner or suppliers' selection. The next step is for students to set the relevant economic, environmental, and social objectives and use them as a benchmark to assess potential partners or suppliers using a scaling system. Final selection is done based on partner or supplier ranking. Mind mapping about how to differentiate between traditional and sustainability embedded supply and value chain management systems has proven popular with undergraduates. The book by Grant, David B., Alexander Trautrims, and Chee Yew Wong (2013)—*Sustainable logistics and supply chain management: Principles and practices for sustainable operations and management.* London; Philadelphia; Kogan Page Limited, has also been an important recommended reading for these modules.

A cardinal principle adhered to by the team is a commitment to continuous review of pedagogy and methods, particularly to reflect any higher education policy change, and factor feedback and recommendations from students, delivery team, and external examiners. The next section covers how sustainability is integrated throughout the supply and value chain management curriculum.

Reframing Supply and Value Chain Management in Sustainability

The embedding process starts with an introductory session on sustainability as a general 'new business' concept to generate interest and map students' previous knowledge and understanding on the issue. Subsequent sessions are tailored to reframe supply and value chain management curriculum in sustainability. This process normally commences with sustainability embedded definitions of supply and value chain management followed by a discussion on sustainability implications of the key motives behind supply and value chain management, such as value proposition as a competitive factor and responsiveness versus efficiency issues. Typical topics from which sustainability implications are derived include logistic systems, supply and value chain, facility location operations, distribution including transportation, inventory schemes, sourcing, procurement, technology, value chain design, organisational and governance structure, supplier and customer relationship management, demand management, and supplier chain partnerships.

A key point that is emphasised to students is the need to take a strategic approach to have a comprehensive plan to integrate sustainability across the entire supply and value chain systems and networks to avoid partial efforts becoming counterproductive. While the supply and value chain management curriculum area is broad with multiple sustainability implications, it does highlight the need for stakeholder engagement beyond a specific business to properly deal with sustainability challenges associated with supply and value chain management—a point that is emphasised to students.

Concluding Commentary

There are several factors driving the rise to prominence of sustainability—natural resource depletion, climate change issues, stakeholder interest amongst others. The evolutional pathways to scaling up sustainable supply and value chain thoughts and management of social and environmental issues took a complex and unstructured route. Thus, arriving at a consensus to integrate sustainability was rather driven mostly by external pressures beyond scholarly ambition within the field. On the part of industry stakeholders there is the realisation that 'green' supply and value chain management is an important strategic objective for organisations looking for multiple benefits from sustainability embedded operations. These benefits could reflect in the form of cost savings, stronger brand recognition, and competitor differentiation (Roehrich et al. 2017).

It is common knowledge that supply and value chain managers and professionals are critical actors with the potential to produce either positive or negative sustainability impacts through their supplier collaborations and selection, warehousing and plant operations, transportation and carrier services chosen, and product package selection. But the requisite sustainability embedded curriculum to continuously provide the needed sustainability conscious human resource is lacking. Indeed, Silvestre (2015) opined that integrating sustainability into supply and value chain management is not 'a destination', but an 'endless journey characterized by trajectories of progress' as a result of the complex, radical, and evolving nature of the issues at play.

HEIs as agents of change have in principle recognised the need to promote more sustainable futures through curriculum development and delivery. Indeed, HEIs are a major stakeholder towards the realisation of UNESCO's GAP on education for sustainable. However, their commitment to implement the declared principles of sustainability into curriculum has been questioned because the integration process seems to lack momentum. A complete adoption of sustainability into management curricula (integration) has not been the popular option attempted in many HEIs. What has been done in most cases is the superficial bolted-on approach that is characterised by delivering a set of sustainability-related topics as supplementary information to the subject matter of a given business management discipline.

An effective supply and value chain management curriculum that provides a shared understanding of sustainability concept and its implications for current and future business practice, with the requisite knowledge and skills to challenge students and encourage critical approach to supply and value chain management discipline and practice, is urgently required.

The kind of curriculum that will foster 'sustainability literacy' (Stibbe 2009), which entails applying interactive learning methods that are fundamentally different from traditional rote learning, to engage students in actual life problem solving projects needed in a resource finite and ecologically challenged world. It is the most potent vehicle to build the capacity of future business leaders who will go on to create sustainability innovations that will factor ecological and social goals that are viable and profitable.

Whereas, all stakeholders are convinced of the need for urgent accommodation of sustainability in the curriculum, it is important to point out that HEIs particularly in the United Kingdom are also working to satisfy competing interests of meeting the immediate need of students and developing and delivering a curriculum that addresses the needs of the general society. The integration is also inhibited by the shear diversity of the field of sustainability and the absence of tried and tested adaptable pedagogical models for curriculum design (Stephens and Graham 2010). The lack of consistency in the application of the integration concept and the limited leveraging across the three domains of educational philosophy—curriculum design, teaching, and learning (Figueiró and Raufflet 2015)—is another challenge.

Despite the prevailing challenges to integration, supply and value chain networks are still responsible for a greater proportion of the adverse ecological and social impacts from business operations. Again, the globalised nature of distribution channels has complicated the effects of supply and value chain networks on the environment and socio-economic development across the world. It thus highlights sustainability innovation as both a competitive factor and sustainable development variable. HEIs are expected to equip students to be able as graduates to creatively and successfully navigate the complex sustainability challenges associated with supply and value chain management. Therefore, a set of clear, distinctive, deliberate efforts to fully embed sustainability into supply and value chain management curriculum for students' development is an urgent matter.

References

AASHE, Association for the Advancement of Sustainability in Higher Education. 2010. Sustainability Curriculum in Higher Education: A Call to Action. Accessed May 10, 2018. www.aashe.org/files/A_Call_to_Action_final%282%29.pdf.

———. 2014. Stars Technical Manual: Version 2. Accessed May 12, 2018. www.aashe.org/files/documents/STARS/2.0/stars_2.0_technical_manual_-_administrative_update_two.pdf.

Accenture. 2010. Our Journey Forward 2010–2011 Corporate Citizenship Report Summary. Accessed May 10, 2016. https://www.accenture.com/........ Accenture-2010-2011-Corporate-Citizenship-Our-Journey-Forward.pdf.

Blackstock, K.L., and C.E. Carter. 2007. Operationalising Sustainability Science for a Sustainability Directive? Reflecting on Three Pilot Projects. *The Geographical Journal* 173 (4): 343–357.

Blanco-Portela, Norka, Javier Benayas, Luis R. Pertierra, and Rodrigo Lozano. 2017. Towards the Integration of Sustainability in Higher Education Institutions: A Review of Drivers of and Barriers to Organisational Change and Their Comparison Against Those Found of Companies. *Journal of Cleaner Production* 166: 563–578.

Brundiers, Katja, and Arnim Wiek. 2011. Educating Students in Real-World Sustainability Research: Vision and Implementation. *Innovative Higher Education* 36 (2): 107–124.

Carter, Craig R. 2005. Purchasing Social Responsibility and Firm Performance: The Key Mediating Roles of Organizational Learning and Supplier Performance. *International Journal of Physical Distribution & Logistics Management* 35 (3): 177–194.

Carter, C.R., and P.L. Easton. 2011. Sustainable Supply Chain Management: Evolution and Future Directions. *International Journal of Physical Distribution & Logistics Management* 41 (1): 46–62. https://Doi.org/10.1108/09600031111101420.

Carter, Craig R., and Marianne M. Jennings. 2002. Logistics Social Responsibility: An Integrative Framework. *Journal of Business Logistics* 23 (1): 145–180.

Carter, C.R., and D.S. Rogers. 2008. A Framework of Sustainable Supply Chain Management: Moving Toward New Theory. *International Journal of Physical Distribution & Logistics Management* 38 (5): 360–387.

Dubey, Rameshwar, Angappa Gunasekaran, Thanos Papadopoulos, Stephen J. Childe, K.T. Shibin, and Samuel Fosso Wamba. 2017. Sustainable Supply Chain Management: Framework and Further Research Directions. *Journal of Cleaner Production* 142: 1119–1130.

Eltantawy, Reham A., Gavin L. Fox, and Larry Giunipero. 2009. Supply Management Ethical Responsibility: Reputation and Performance Impacts. *Supply Chain Management: An International Journal* 14 (2): 99–108.

Etse, Daniel, and Coral Ingley. 2016. Higher Education Curriculum for Sustainability: Course Contents Analyses of Purchasing and Supply Management Programme of Polytechnics in Ghana. *International Journal of Sustainability in Higher Education* 17 (2): 269–280.

Figueiró, Paola Schmitt, and Emmanuel Raufflet. 2015. Sustainability in Higher Education: A Systematic Review with Focus on Management Education. *Journal of Cleaner Production* 106: 22–33.

Fiselier, Evelien S., James W.S. Longhurst, and Georgina K. Gough. 2018. Exploring the Current Position of ESD in UK Higher Education Institutions. *International Journal of Sustainability in Higher Education* 19 (2): 393–412.

Green, Ken, Barbara Morton, and Steve New. 1996. Purchasing and Environmental Management: Interactions, Policies and Opportunities. *Business Strategy and the Environment* 5 (3): 188–197.

Grindsted, Thomas Skou. 2011. Sustainable Universities: From Declarations on Sustainability in Higher Education to National Law. *Environmental Economics* 2 (2): 29–36.

Hall, Jeremy. 2000. Environmental Supply Chain Dynamics. *Journal of Cleaner Production* 8 (6): 455–471.

Karatzoglou, Benjamin. 2013. An In-depth Literature Review of the Evolving Roles and Contributions of Universities to Education for Sustainable Development. *Journal of Cleaner Production* 49: 44–53.

King, Andrew A., and Michael J. Lenox. 2001. Lean and Green? An Empirical Examination of the Relationship between Lean Production and Environmental Performance. *Production and Operations Management* 10 (3): 244–256.

Komiyama, Hiroshi, and Kazuhiko Takeuchi. 2006. *Sustainability Science: Building a New Discipline*. Springer.

Krause, Daniel R., Stephan Vachon, and Robert D. Klassen. 2009. Special Topic Forum on Sustainable Supply Chain Management: Introduction and Reflections on the Role of Purchasing Management. *Journal of Supply Chain Management* 45 (4): 18–25.

Lans, Thomas, Vincent Blok, and Renate Wesselink. 2014. Learning Apart and Together: Towards an Integrated Competence Framework for Sustainable Entrepreneurship in Higher Education. *Journal of Cleaner Production* 62: 37–47.

Laura, Spence, and Bourlakis Michael. 2009. The Evolution from Corporate Social Responsibility to Supply Chain Responsibility: The Case of Waitrose. *Supply Chain Management: An International Journal* 14 (4): 291–302. https://doi.org/10.1108/13598540910970126.

Lozano, Rodrigo, Rebeka Lukman, Francisco J. Lozano, Donald Huisingh, and Wim Lambrechts. 2013. Declarations for Sustainability in Higher Education: Becoming Better Leaders, Through Addressing the University System. *Journal of Cleaner Production* 48: 10–19.

Melnyk, Steven A., Robert P. Sroufe, and Roger Calantone. 2003. Assessing the Impact of Environmental Management Systems on Corporate and Environmental Performance. *Journal of Operations Management* 21 (3): 329–351.

Mulà, Ingrid, Daniella Tilbury, Alexandra Ryan, Marlene Mader, Jana Dlouhá, Clemens Mader, Javier Benayas, Jirí Dlouhý, and David Alba. 2017. Catalysing Change in Higher Education for Sustainable Development: A Review of Professional Development Initiatives for University Educators. *International Journal of Sustainability in Higher Education* 18 (5): 798–820.

Pullman, Madeleine E., Michael J. Maloni, and Craig R. Carter. 2009. Food for Thought: Social Versus Environmental Sustainability Practices and Performance Outcomes. *Journal of Supply Chain Management* 45 (4): 38–54.

Ramos, Tomás B., Sandra Caeiro, Bart Van Hoof, Rodrigo Lozano, Donald Huisingh, and Kim Ceulemans. 2015. Experiences from the Implementation of Sustainable Development in Higher Education Institutions: Environmental Management for Sustainable Universities. *Journal of Cleaner Production* 106: 3 10.

Roehrich, Jens K., Stefan U. Hoejmose, and Victoria Overland. 2017. Driving Green Supply Chain Management Performance Through Supplier Selection and Value Internalisation: A Self-determination Theory Perspective. *International Journal of Operations & Production Management* 37 (4): 489–509.

Rowe, Debra. 2007. Education for a Sustainable Future. *Science-New York Then Washington* 317 (5836): 323.

Roy, Vivek, Tobias Schoenherr, and Parikshit Charan. 2018. The Thematic Landscape of Literature in Sustainable Supply Chain Management (SSCM) A Review of the Principal Facets in SSCM Development. *International Journal of Operations & Production Management* 38 (4): 1091–1124.

Seuring, Stefan, and Stefan Gold. 2012. Conducting Content-analysis Based Literature Reviews in Supply Chain Management. *Supply Chain Management: An International Journal* 17 (5): 544–555.

Shephard, Kerry. 2008. Higher Education for Sustainability: Seeking Affective Learning Outcomes. *International Journal of Sustainability in Higher Education* 9 (1): 87–98.

Shrivastava, Paul. 2010. Pedagogy of Passion for Sustainability. *Academy of Management Learning & Education* 9 (3): 443–455. https://doi.org/10.5465/amle.9.3.zqr443.

Silvestre, Bruno S. 2015. A Hard Nut to Crack! Implementing Supply Chain Sustainability in an Emerging Economy. *Journal of Cleaner Production* 96: 171–181. https://doi.org/10.1016/j.jclepro.2014.01.009.

Srivastava, Samir K. 2007. Green Supply-Chain Management: A State-of-the-art Literature Review. *International Journal of Management Reviews* 9 (1): 53–80. https://doi.org/10.1111/j.1468-2370.2007.00202.x.

Stephens, Jennie C., and Amanda C. Graham. 2010. Toward an Empirical Research Agenda for Sustainability in Higher Education: Exploring the Transition Management Framework. *Journal of Cleaner Production* 18 (7): 611–618. https://doi.org/10.1016/j.jclepro.2009.07.009.

Stibbe, A. 2009. *The Handbook of Sustainability Literacy Skills for a Changing World*. Totnes: Green Books.

Tate, W.L., L.M. Ellram, and J.F. Kirchoff. 2010. Corporate Social Responsibility Reports: A Thematic Analysis Related to Supply Chain Management. *Journal of Supply Chain Management* 46 (1): 19–44. https://doi.org/10.1111/j.1745-493X.2009.03184.x.

Touboulic, A., and H. Walker. 2015. Theories in Sustainable Supply Chain Management: A Structured Literature Review. *International Journal of Physical Distribution & Logistics Management* 45 (1/2): 16–42. https://doi.org/10.1108/IJPDLM-05-2013-0106.

UK National Commission for UNESCO, (UKNC). 2013. Education for Sustainable Development (ESD) in the UK—Status, Best Practice and Opportunities for the Future. March 2013 Report. Accessed May 12, 2018. https://www.unesco.org.uk/wp-content/uploads/2015/03/Brief-9-ESD-March-2013.pdf.

Vachon, Stephan, and Robert D. Klassen. 2006. Extending Green Practices Across the Supply Chain: The Impact of Upstream and Downstream Integration. *International Journal of Operations & Production Management* 26 (7): 795–821.

Walker, H., and S. Brammer. 2009. Sustainable Procurement in the United Kingdom Public Sector. *Supply Chain Management: An International Journal* 14 (2): 128–137.

Wals, Arjen E.J. 2014. Sustainability in Higher Education in the Context of the UN DESD: A Review of Learning and Institutionalization Processes. *Journal of Cleaner Production* 62: 8–15. https://doi.org/10.1016/j.jclepro.2013.06.007.

Wolters, Teun. 2003. Transforming International Product Chains into Channels of Sustainable Production: The Imperative of Sustainable Chain Management. *Greener Management International* 43: 6–13.

9

Sustainability, Management Education, and Professions: A Practitioner Perspective

Simon Graham

Introduction

The business of business is changing radically, and so the skills required by the people who lead corporations are also changing. As business increasingly sees itself as a positive agent for social, environmental, and economic change, so the skills and experiences needed by business leaders need to reflect the new reality. Business schools create business leaders. How should they react to this new need?

Each generation of business leaders lives through a period of change, and it is by capitalising on that change that businesses thrive (Matai 2011). The growth of corporate success is, to a large extent, the story of meeting the challenges of change. For example, the successful companies of the industrial revolution were those that responded to the new opportunities that technological and social change gave. Indeed, they were often those that led the change. A similar experience has been more recently seen with the Internet and social media revolution, where

S. Graham (✉)
De Courcy Alexander, London, UK
e-mail: simon.graham@decourcyalexander.co.uk

© The Author(s) 2019
K. Amaeshi et al. (eds.), *Incorporating Sustainability in Management Education*,
https://doi.org/10.1007/978-3-319-98125-3_9

successful businesses have led the change to new business models (Serrat 2017).

Today, the world is challenged by unprecedented global societal, economic, and environmental challenges. This means that corporations are looking beyond traditional business models, including models of corporate responsibility. Traditional corporate action to "to do good" has evolved from many different complementary angles. The first case stems from a sense of social responsibility, and possibly dates from the beginning of the corporation (see, e.g., Pierson 1959, 323ff). The root of the argument is, in the words of Paul Polman, ex-CEO of Unilever, "The purpose of business is first and foremost to serve society" (Ignatius 2017). This concern drives activities like philanthropy and demonstrations of moral leadership that have increasingly been seen in the world stage (cf. Anderson 1986). Such activities are frequently driven by the CEO of an organisation or strategic, marketing, or Corporate Social Responsibility (CSR) departments.

In contrast, for many organisations, the main drive for sustainable action does not come from a sense of moral obligation but from other business drivers. For example, many companies see a wider business case for sustainability. There are multiple cases of new opportunities that open with sustainability, greater supply chain resilience, reduced risk, lower operational costs, and improved staff morale (e.g., Graham 2013; Grubnic et al. 2015; Ignatius 2017). The author's own experience is that businesses that understand and gain from sustainability are those that combine a wide sense of morale obligation and understanding of the huge business opportunity with a desire to demonstrate leadership not just in their industry but beyond.

The societal role of universities and educators in society is something that dates back hundreds if not thousands of years. However, the business school, a more recent creation, is in many ways unique, located on the tectonic fault line between the academic and business community. (Gardiner and Lacy 2005, 179)

Business education has also claimed to be at the forefront of promoting social responsibility for many decades (Rive et al. 2017). There has been a sharp rise in the number of courses at business schools that look at Corporate Social Responsibility (CSR), ethics, and sustainability, many claiming to cover all three subjects seriously as part of their programme (see, e.g., Christensen et al. 2007). At the same time, researchers have increasingly found sustainable business a rich mine of information for a range of research areas. For example, fields like operational and risk management are ripe for sustainability, and there are many studies around supply chains and other complex operational scenarios that can be used to demonstrate the business case for sustainable activity (e.g., Crates 2016; Gold and Schleper 2017).

Given all this development, how successful have business schools been at encouraging sustainable business practice and empowering the next generation of sustainable business leaders?

The iconic course for many business schools is the MBA and so it seems sensible to start here. The degree is widespread and used frequently as a benchmark for business leadership and there is evidence that MBA-qualified business leaders run corporations that are more sustainable than their competitors (Slater and Dixon-Fowler 2010). As the same time, it has been under attack as being too focused on profit over ethics (Rasche et al. 2013). To understand the issue more deeply, the author undertook a small study of sustainability professionals who had engaged with MBA programmes. Many were graduates themselves of MBA programmes or had recruited those with MBA qualifications to work under them in their companies. They included both practitioners and consultants who worked for companies of all sizes from very large multinationals to micro-businesses, and included people who worked in the USA, Europe, and Asia.

Based on this research and hundreds of years of cumulative experience, it is clear that there are some things that business schools need to do to really become the place that fosters the sustainable leadership that business needs in the coming decades. These needs can be divided into five areas, which are not listed in order of priority. They can be defined as the six Cs of Curriculum, Context, Communication, Collaboration, Connection, and Challenge.

Curriculum: Ensure Sustainability Is Central

We are faced with a paradox: Is education the problem or the solution in working toward a sustainable future? At current levels of unsustainable practice and over consumption it could be concluded that education is part of the problem. If education is the solution then it requires a deeper critique and a broader vision for the future. (UNESCO 2005, 59)

For many of the MBA graduates, one of the major aspects of the course to them was that sustainability was felt to be peripheral to the main point of the degree; as one graduate said, "a bit of shoehorning in sustainability and CSR with intangible value of the firm." Many spoke of their courses treating sustainability as an add-on and not treated as seriously as subjects such as marketing or strategy. While it was noted that the flexibility that electives offered meant that there was an opportunity for more depth, it was generally agreed that, "it was quite elementary," with one graduate saying, "there was nothing I learnt that you or I did not learn within a few months on the job." For many, when asked what they would change most about their experience it was that sustainability needed to be more integrated into the course.

This challenge has been identified globally (Jamali and Abdallah 2015). In an overview of studies of business schools worldwide, Setó-Pamies and Papaoikonomou (2016) found that overall coverage of CSR and sustainability was very poor. In Spain, only 25% of business schools offered CSR and ethics as stand-alone courses while in Belgium, only 12% of schools included CSR at undergraduate level. Many of the courses themselves are driven by staff with an interest in the subject rather than an overall business school strategy (Stubbs and Schaper 2011). At the same time, studies have found that top-performing schools more frequently include ethics, CSR, and sustainability (Christensen et al. 2007), but frequently the subject is elective rather than core (Rasche et al. 2013). While the situation is improving, there is evidence that it is still only the leading business schools in each nation that are engaging with sustainability (for a Portuguese example, see Branco and Delgado 2016). Those which do, demonstrate the "potential of postgraduate MBA courses to promote sustainability within the private sector, especially if sustainable development is embedded across the curriculum" (Annan-Diab and Molinari 2017, 79).

Business schools should consider sustainable business core to their curriculum and not rely on elective modules to teach CSR.

Curriculum: The Centrality of Sustainability to Business

> It becomes more central everywhere. Imagine doing a ten year discussion of the future strategy of whatever organisation it is and ignoring issues of sustainability. Are you mad? (A member of UK business school faculty quoted in Brammer et al. (2012))

Not only were concerns raised about the position of sustainability in the curriculum, but also by the presentation of sustainability in business. The idea that embedding sustainability in business strategy brings business success has been current for decades (e.g., Elkington 1994) and there is increasingly large evidence that businesses of all sizes and across a wide range of industries are embracing sustainability as a core strategy (Graham 2013).

Business schools frequently focus on business strategy (Brammer et al. 2012) and so have a huge opportunity to demonstrate the strategic value of sustainability. However, there is evidence that the majority of schools do not encourage this way of thinking (Matten and Moon 2004). As one graduate said, "There was no clarity on [the] strategic importance [of sustainability]." One graduate noted that while their strategic module covered a wide range of issues, including marketing and pricing, it did not touch once on larger social, economic, or environmental issues. In fact, as one graduate mentioned, even when the term "environment" was used, it was restricted to phrases like "competitive environment" with no connection to issues like biodiversity or climate change.

One MBA graduate particularly mentioned a module that was offered as part of their course that was promoted as covering sustainable business. However, they felt that in this case, sustainability was included, was treated as a means to an end rather than a subject of interest in itself: "The focus was on how to run a business that sells sustainable stuff rather than how to run a business sustainably."

By putting the strategic nature of sustainable business central to the course, this also means that the student experience is enhanced. In fact, as Michael Page, Dean of Rotterdam School of Management at Erasmus University said, "If you only place ethics, CSR, and sustainability into functional courses, the faculty may only pay lip service to the topics" (quoted in Christensen et al. 2007, 356).

Business schools need to understand the fact that responsible business is of interest in itself and not treat sustainability as a means to an end. The curriculum needs to demonstrate that sustainability is now core to business strategy for many successful firms and to teach students the reasoning that leads to successful sustainable business strategy.

Context: Clearly Show the Value of Sustainable Business

> Sustainability has to be strategic and incorporated into all the operations, decisions and programmes across the whole business. Therefore the role of academics is to educate students of all levels to understand that there is more to creating a sustainable business than recycling, turning off a light switch or donating money to an ecological charity. (Williams 2012)

Part of this stems from a fundamental understanding of the role of business in society. For many business schools, sustainability is considered part of corporate responsibility, responsible business, and CSR which are themselves considered part of ethics (Rasche et al. 2013). Thus, they focus on *why* businesses should be sustainable rather than *how* this can be facilitated (Cullen 2017). As one graduate said, "the course will need to show them how sustainability can give them and their business the edge over the competition, instead of a compliance millstone this is now a business opportunity that could differentiate their business into new untapped markets and generate extensive goodwill in the market."

To do this requires a real engagement with sustainable business beyond ethics and CSR. As one graduate said, there is a huge opportunity for schools to demonstrate the importance of "mainstreaming by embedding sustainability in day-to-day business processes." This is not to say that business schools need to teach modules on environmental risk management or legal compliance, although there may, as graduate put it, "exist a requirement for many business executives to first understand the very basics of how the planet functions." Rather schools need to give their students the skills to understand good sustainable practices and the importance of these in a business context (Elkington 1994). As one graduate said, "I wish my MBA prepared me for thinking in an analytical way about sustainability."

Business schools should be places where students learn how to be successful sustainable business leaders and provided the wide range of tools that they will need in the complex business environment that they go to after graduation.

Context: Champion Best Practice

It has been long recognised that involving businesses in business schools enhances the student experience (Haski-Leventhal and Concato 2016). Case studies are a useful teaching tool that enables students to better understand how the theories they learn are realised in the business world (McCarthy and McCarthy 2006). Many schools use case studies, either presented in class, through multimedia, by visiting speaker, or through site visits. This meant that the course could provide, as one graduate said, "something a bit more real life focused as opposed to academic." Case studies are often those of well-known companies like Exxon Mobile and Rio Tinto, and can be used to highlight the challenges that businesses face in sustainability as well as good practice.

There are many great examples of sustainable businesses, many of which are not well-known brands (e.g., Grubnic et al. 2015). Providing the students with a wider range of case studies also broadens them to see potential employment and business opportunities. Business schools are also well known for bringing in external speakers, taking students on trips to see businesses, and encouraging students to undertake placements and internships. By building relationships with sustainable businesses, students will therefore see how sustainable leaders build their companies.

There is a particularly strong need to dig deeper into companies. Companies are prone to either underplaying or overplaying sustainable achievements. The former, aptly named "greenhushing" by Font et al. (2017), is likely to be increasingly common as more organisations engage in the right actions but feel that their customers prefer not be told about sustainability benefits. The latter is exemplified by what is termed "eco-bling" by Liddell (2008), where environmental projects focus on the visible rather than the material. A wider and more derogatory term, "greenwash," has been used for decades to describe examples where companies seem to talk about sustainable actions as an alternative to effective action. Cutting through the greenwash, eco-bling, and greenhush to find the companies that are truly engaged in sustainable business is something that requires the proven academic skills of systematic research and critical analysis. It also means that academics need to spend time speaking with the pioneers of sustainable business.

Once formed, the relationships need to be ones of high levels of trust between the companies, universities, and students. As Rive et al. (2017) rightly say, "Socially responsible cooperation between business schools and companies is considered a win-win game when the game rules have been clearly defined" (p. 240). For one thing, the companies need to feel able to speak openly about times where they have found the journey difficult. Becoming a leader in business is not easy, and that is true as much for sustainable leadership as any other field. And students gain more when businesses feel able to explain the less photogenic sides of their journey as well as the successes. Sometimes, this experience is best served by connecting with business leaders who are no longer employed by the companies that they transformed as this can sometimes enable them to have a more balanced perspective, but schools should balance this with a need to keep the student experience relevant and timely in the fast moving world of sustainable business.

Business schools need to create solid partnerships with sustainable leaders with corporate experience to help their students to see the practical implications in business.

Communication: Demonstrate Integrity Through Sustainable Practice

The issues of greenwashing and greenhushing are issues of credibility and business schools are confronted with similar challenges. In addition to the challenge that they promote unsustainable business models, many schools have also been challenged on the integrity between their teaching and their practice. In the area of sustainable business, this is most usually directed at the university rather than the business school, and often around specific issues like the Living Wage or Fossil-Fuel Divestment. There is evidence that business schools that have more success embedding sustainability and CSR into curricula are aligned with institution which have research into sustainable issues (e.g., Christensen et al. 2007) but it is, to some extent, just as important that the institution "walks the walk." Similarly, there are some good examples of programmes run by business schools using community and social engagement as part of their student offering like Burgundy School of Business's Pédalogie par l'Action Citoyenne, winner of a 2016 Trophée des Campus Responsable.

However, there is less evidence of schools are leading the charge in sustainable operations. Two global respected global standards for building energy efficiency, for example, are BREEAM (Building Research Establishment Environmental Assessment Method) and LEED (Leadership in Energy and Environmental Design) and buildings that hold high rating in these schemes are often held up as exemplars for sustainable construction and operation (Cole and Valdebenito 2013). However, a search of the US Green Business Council website found that only four business schools in the USA have LEED Platinum buildings, including Harvard Business School's McCulloch Hall, with the Peking University HSBC Business School in China standing alone in the rest of the world. As of the end of 2017, no business school in the world was housed in a building ranked BREEAM Outstanding.

For students, this is becoming critical. Increasing access to information and a desire for accountability is driving a generation of students to ask more questions of institutions, particularly about how they are run. They often consider sustainability as important as finance in their decision making (Graham 2015). It is therefore critical that business schools engage with sustainable activity in their operations as well as their teaching and research if they are to become leaders themselves in sustainability and to show credibility to their students. This will then ensure the students receive the integrated and inspirational education that will foster them as leaders in sustainable business.

Communication: Cover the Complexity

Along with this greater access to and demand for data comes an acknowledgement of the complexity of life. This is particularly important in business and sustainability where simplistic answers can often lead to misunderstandings. In the words of one respondent the purpose of an MBA is to "understand the motivations, constraints and opportunities those businesses face on the path to sustainability." Business schools are increasingly engaging with the complexity of sustainability and are using this to teach the soft skills that are required by the corporate life as much, or more, than skills in marketing and finance (Wright and Bennett 2011). "Graduates increasingly need to have the ability to question assumptions; to understand that the way things have always been done is not necessarily the best way for business or for society to continue, and to explore alternatives. Students should be open minded, culturally aware, willing to listen and learn. They should be able to ask the right questions [and] deal with complexity" (Weybrecht 2017, 89).

To engage with complex issues like this requires an understanding of the depth of sustainability as well as its breadth. This means that, as well as helping students to see how sustainability empowers business strategy, business schools need to show how it helps to answer the complex questions where business interacts with society, the economy, and the environment. There is evidence that students engage well with this type of activity (e.g., Deer and Zarestky 2017), and that business schools can enhance the student experience by including sustainable leadership as a key part of their learning objectives.

To do this will require pedological transformation. Business schools will need to look at sustainability anew and see how it can inform how they teach business and its complexity.

Collaboration: Break Down Barriers Between Disciplines

What if we had courses that brought together examples from not just the business world, from political sciences, law, from environmental studies, so students get a richer appreciation of the challenges they will confront when they graduate? Indra Nooyi, ex-CEO PepsiCo (quoted in Annan-Diab and Molinari 2017, 73)

At the same time, there has been a steady growth in collaboration across subjects to improve students' understanding of the challenges of sustainable business. Much of this has taken place outside business schools, for example, between engineers and sociologists (Byrne and Mullally 2016), but there are many opportunities for business schools to also engage in the multidisciplinary work that underpins sustainable business. Many of the leading schools are also showing leadership in this field. For example, Christensen et al. (2007) found that the University of Michigan aimed to "develop a deeper understanding of sustainability issues by exploring areas such as engineering, health, law, ethics, anthropology in addition to the traditional MBA and MS disciplines" (p. 363).

For sustainability professionals, this multidisciplinary approach is critical. "The greatest soft skill that I have learnt in this job is the ability to talk to people across the company in all departments." "Sustainability crosses all the barriers in the business, and so I need to be able to talk to everyone in language they understand." It is therefore essential that business schools encourage their emerging leaders to manage multidisciplinary projects and understand the implications of working with people across business, in operations and manufacturing, design and procurement, marketing, and government affairs.

Business schools need to work across disciplines to help students to engage with sustainable business and teach them the skills that they will need in their later working life.

Collaboration: Create Community

Few companies can afford large sustainability teams and in consequence the role of sustainability practitioner can often be very lonely. Practitioners often work alone or, if they are part of a team, it is rare to work alongside another person with knowledge and experience in the field (Graham 2014). Staff who work in isolation often have lower productivity than those working in teams, and this can be the case even when the individual is theoretically part of a team but completes their tasks alone (cf. van Dick et al. 2009). This means that sustainability staff may be disproportionately dependent on support from outside their organisations. While such excellent networks exist for knowledge sharing these are frequently limited in geographic scope. Therefore, business schools have a large opportunity to be community builders.

However, currently, the opportunity to create such a network for each school is limited. Traditionally, the number of sustainability executives in most MBA programmes is small. As one graduate commented, "I was very much an exception as a sustainability professional on my MBA programme." However, the interest and awareness of sustainability amongst students in business schools is increasing dramatically (Haski-Leventhal and Concato 2016). As this interest grows, it can be nurtured by alumni and cohort connections, but also through networks that transcend the schools. This is one area that the UN Global Compact and its Principles for Responsible Management Education (PRME) initiative mentioned earlier in this book can help. The PRME community includes over 650 institutions representing over 85 countries and is organised across 14 regional chapters (Haertle et al. 2017). Its principles include an objective to "facilitate and support dialog and debate among educators, students, business, government, consumers, media, civil society organisations and other interested groups and stakeholders on critical issues related to global social responsibility and sustainability." And part of this could be to support the creation of a network of business school graduates who are actively working in sustainable business.

Business schools need to work together to foster connections between sustainable business professionals across sectors to continue to share knowledge and experience even after they graduate.

Connection: Cultivate Passion in the Cohort

The course must be able to generate a real and personal connection with the candidate relating to the environment and sustainability based on their own personal motivations be that for the environment, for their career, their family or their company. (Tertius Beneke)

Business schools have been challenged by the need to engage emotionally with students and provide them with a values education that goes beyond profit (Rasche et al. 2013). Sustainable business provides exactly this opportunity. Many programmes base their offering on providing a vehicle for students to combine their passion for social justice with an understanding of business (Christensen et al. 2007). Indeed, students of sustainable business frequently start from a position where they are driven by purpose like a passion to solve a particular social problem (Deer and Zarestky 2017). Being a sustainable business leader brings a new level of meaning and purpose. As one graduate put it, "Who [else] in their day job can say that they contribute to sustaining their life support system?" This passion has the knock-on effect of also enabling sustainability leadership to be more embedded in the school (Brammer et al. 2012).

Business schools can go beyond this, however, and inspire a generation that as yet does not understand the part that they can play in transforming business. A new generation of potential students is rising that sees business as a sustainable leader and is prepared to take their place in this if given the right tools (Graham 2015). These students are often not excited by traditional business graduate school courses and so are new and untapped markets.

To inspire a new generation means looking afresh at the focus of business schools. In the words of one graduate, it means "combining facts with emotional and behavioural awareness." The school needs to take a strategic approach to recruiting, retaining, and inspiring passionate people. It also means exploring the full breadth of sustainable practice to find points where students can connect.

Critically, it also means engaging students with an understanding of how sustainable business leadership will enable them to achieve their own personal goals. As one graduate said, "they are doing an MBA, they want to excel, they want to be the best they want to achieve and if this is their driver and goal they cannot achieve this without understanding sustainability." Sustainability is increasingly a key to business success for many companies and, as one graduate said, "If they want to excel and be the best they will need to know how sustainability works."

Business schools need to engage with the emotions and imagination as much as the intellect to inspire students.

Challenge: Explore Alternatives to the Consensus

This is a vision that challenges business schools to examine their relationship to society, to the business community, and to the higher education landscape. It will mean thinking, organizing, and acting in ways that have thus far been unusual or underdeveloped. It will mean incorporating new models and strategies and devoting renewed attention to economic, environmental, and personal well-being for all populations around the world. (AACSB 2017, 3)

More fundamentally, there is a need for business schools to radically look at business through a new lens. Sustainability gives business schools the opportunity to reassert their legitimacy as positive agents in society (Snelson-Powell et al. 2016). It gives them a positive agenda to encourage their students and funders that they too can be part of the solution to the great social, economic, and environmental challenges of the age. It can be the catalyst for change that is needed in the discipline (Fisher and Bonn 2017).

For the emerging sustainability professional, this is critical. The path to being a sustainable business is not simply to do the same things that have always been done a little bit better. It is to rethink the way that business operates. As one graduate said, "Business schools have not caught up with the fact that we need to do business differently." As Paul Polman said, "We needed a new economic model; we also needed a different business model. Not one based on being 'less bad' or on occasional acts of benevolence, but one where business has a positive impact on society in all it does" (Ignatius 2017). That means a radical rethink of what it means to do business. It means redefining what business means.

For business schools, this means looking beyond traditional business models to new paradigms like circularity and the sharing economy. They need to, as one MBA graduate said, "banish the thought that financial capital is the only capital or resource that an organisation uses" and include raising awareness of critical business issues like natural capital. It means looking beyond short-term shareholder value and business cases to the wider purpose of business as a societal good. It also means, in the words of another MBA graduate, looking at the "many problems we have yet to properly face including income inequality and the rise of the precariat." For many business schools, it will mean challenging the very models of economic prosperity and corporate success on which they base their curricula.

Particularly, it means starting to challenge business itself about its mission. Business schools have a critical role in empowering the next generation of business leaders to see their role as providing a new vision for business. As the world needs more sustainable businesses, it is incumbent on business schools to give their graduates the tools they need to become these leaders. They move from seeing sustainability as a peripheral activity to one that transforms business and creates a space where they can thrive. They need to see how they can create a community of corporations that can be positive agents for change and to create companies that are actively working for social, economic, and environmental good.

Challenge: Cultivate Transformational Individuals

One of the key roles of business schools is to create responsible business leaders (cf. Williams 2012). The school must therefore foster the skills that will enable their graduates to become the change-makers who are needed to transform business for the better. This means going beyond, in the words of one graduate, an "understanding how business works and how business leaders think." It means having the tools to understand the challenges that corporations face and the opportunities that sustainability and business afford for each other. Fundamentally, this means perceiving the student not as a business person who needs to understand sustainability but as a student of sustainable business.

> The purpose of the company is not to enrich its shareholders, but to enable sustainable value creation for its various stakeholders (including investors) in the short, medium and long term. (Jyoti Banerjee)

The first step in this is to reconcile the different languages of business with sustainability and CSR. As one graduate commented, an MBA offers the opportunity for the student to gain "the tools and vocabulary to speak with decision makers and line staff in 'traditional' companies and organisations, and understand the motivations, constraints and opportunities those businesses face on the path to sustainability." For many graduates, this is essential, as communication is key to so much of their success in business. However, it is also a key skill for entrepreneurs creating new opportunities.

The next step is to empower students to actively engage with others to create solutions. As one graduate put it, "how to be stakeholder-informed, not stakeholder-driven." Businesses frequently end up being reactively sustainable by responding to stakeholder concerns. True sustainable leadership relies on being informed by the non-consensus of complex stakeholder webs and uses this to create a strategic agenda that exceeds the social, economic, and environmental needs of all.

It also requires that leaders be able to take their own path, and that is the third step. Business schools should challenge their students. As one graduate said, "Sustainability challenges centre on the person and person's perspective." By challenging traditional business models and silo-driven ways of working, business schools can demonstrate how business leaders can transform the world. By demonstrating how successful businesses are sustainable, both through their own actions and through the case studies that they show, they can light a path to guide the entrepreneur. And by showing leadership through community collaboration and communication, the school itself can be a beacon for sustainable leadership itself.

To achieve this requires a revisioning of the business school. Business schools are not a crucible for leadership. They are the nursery for the next generation of business leaders. Their corridors are the place that business inspiration can be found. Their halls are where the complex economic, environmental, and social challenges that business face can be understood, and where emerging business leaders can learn the skills to transform the corporate world into sustainable business.

Acknowledgements Thanks are given to the many experts who have helped with this chapter, particularly Jamal Gore, James Farrell, Jyoti Banerjee, Jonathan Horrell, Tertius Beneke, and Toby Abbott.

References

AACSB. (2017). *A Collective Vision for Business Education.* Tampa, FL: AACSB.
Anderson, Jerry W. (1986). Social Responsibility and the Corporation. *Business Horizons* 29 (4): 22–27.
Annan-Diab, Fatima and Carolina Molinari. (2017). Interdisciplinarity: Practical Approach to Advancing Education for Sustainability and for the Sustainable Development Goals. *The International Journal of Management Education* 15 (2): 73–83.
Brammer, Stephen, Annie Powell and Andrew Millington. (2012). Embedding Sustainability in Business Schools: The State of the Art in Teaching & Learning, Research, and Operations. In *Research Paper Series No. 60-2012,*

ed. Robert Caruana. Nottingham, UK: ICCSR Nottingham University Business School.

Branco, Manuel Castelo and Catarina Delgado. (2016). Corporate Social Responsibility Education and Research in Portuguese Business Schools. In *Social Responsibility Education Across Europe*, ed. Duygu Turker, Ceren Altuntas, and Samuel O. Idowu, 207–227. Cham, Switzerland: Springer International Publishing.

Byrne, Edmond P. and Gerard Mullally. (2016). Seeing Beyond Silos: Transdisciplinary Approaches to Education as a Means of Addressing Sustainability Issues. In *New Developments in Engineering Education for Sustainable Development*, ed. Walter Leal Filho and Susan Nesbit, 23–34. Cham, Switzerland: Springer International Publishing.

Christensen, Lisa Jones, Ellen Peirce, Laura P. Hartman, W. Michael Hoffman and Jamie Carrier. (2007). Ethics, CSR, and Sustainability Education in The Financial Times Top 50 Global Business Schools: Baseline Data and Future Research Directions. *Journal of Business Ethics* 73 (4): 347–368.

Crates, Emma. (2016). *Building a Fairer System: Tackling Modern Slavery in Construction Supply Chains*. Bracknell, UK: CIOB.

Cullen, John G. (2017). Educating Business Students about Sustainability: A Bibliometric Review of Current Trends and Research Needs. *Journal of Business Ethics* 145 (2): 429–439.

Deer, Shannon and Jill Zarestky. (2017). Balancing Profit and People: Corporate Social Responsibility in Business Education. *Journal of Management Education* 41 (5): 727–749.

Elkington, John. (1994). Towards the Sustainable Corporation: Win-Win-Win Business Strategies for Sustainable Development. *California Management Review* 36 (2): 90–100.

Fisher, Josie and Ingrid Bonn. (2017). Sustainability and Undergraduate Management Curricula: Changes Over a 5-year Period. *Australian Journal of Environmental Education* 33 (1): 18–33.

Font, Xavier, Islam Elgammal and Ian Lamond. (2017). Greenhushing: The Deliberate Under Communicating of Sustainability Practices by Tourism Businesses. *Journal of Sustainable Tourism* 25 (7): 1007–1023.

Gardiner, Louise and Peter Lacy. (2005). Lead, Respond, Partner or Ignore: The Role of Business Schools on Corporate Responsibility. *Corporate Governance: The International Journal of Business in Society* 5 (2): 174–185.

Gold, Stefan and Michael C. Schleper. (2017). A Pathway Towards True Sustainability: A Recognition Foundation of Sustainable Supply Chain Management. *European Management Journal* 35 (4): 425–429.

Graham, Simon. (2013). Business Lessons from Independent Companies. *Croner's Environment* 53: 7–9.

———. (2014). What can Sustainability Execs Learn from the Geeks That have Inherited the Earth? *BusinessGreen*, August 12. Accessed March 27, 2018. http://bit.ly/2BCR8c4.

———. (2015). Bridging the Generation Divide. *Croner's Environment* 59: 10–12.

Grubnic, Suzana, Christian Herzig, Jean-Pascal Gond and Jeremy Moon. (2015). A New Era–Extending Environmental Impact to a Broader Sustainability Agenda: The Case of Commercial Group. *Social and Environmental Accountability Journal* 35 (3): 176–193.

Haertle, Jonas, Carole Parkes, Alan Murray and Ross Hayes. (2017). PRME: Building a Global Movement on Responsible Management Education. *The International Journal of Management Education* 15 (2): 66–72.

Haski-Leventhal, Debbie and Julian Concato. (2016). *The State of CSR and RME in Business Schools and the Attitudes of their Students*. Sydney, Australia: Macquarie Graduate School of Management.

Ignatius, Adi. (2017). Future Economy: The Opportunity of Sustainability. *Harvard Business Review*, November. Accessed March 27, 2018. http://bit.ly/2hW1VbU.

Jamali, Dima and Hanin Abdallah. (2015). Mainstreaming Corporate Social Responsibility at the Core of the Business School Curriculum. In *Handbook of Research on Business Ethics and Corporate Responsibilities*, ed. D.E. Palmer, 275 296. Hershey, PA: IGI Global.

Liddell, Howard. (2008). *Ecominimalism: The Antidote to Eco-bling*. London: RIBA Publishing.

Matai, D.K. (2011). What is The Key to Survival in a Constantly Changing Environment? *Business Insider*, March 30. Accessed March 27, 2018. http://read.bi/2CJFpaS.

Matten, Dirk and Jeremy Moon. (2004). Corporate Social Responsibility. *Journal of Business Ethics* 54 (4): 323–337.

McCarthy, Patricia R. and Henry M. McCarthy. (2006). When Case Studies are Not Enough: Integrating Experiential Learning Into Business Curricula. *Journal of Education for Business* 81 (4): 201–204.

Pierson, Frank Cook. (1959). *The Education of American Businessmen: A Study of University-College Programs in Business Administration*. New York: McGraw-Hill.

Rasche, Andreas, Dirk Ulrich Gilbert and Ingo Schedel. (2013). Cross-Disciplinary Ethics Education in MBA Programs: Rhetoric or Reality? *Academy of Management Learning & Education* 12 (1): 71–85.

Serrat, Olivier. (2017). *Knowledge Solutions*. Singapore: Springer.

Setó-Pamies, Dolors and Eleni Papaoikonomou. (2016). A Multi-Level Perspective for the Integration of Ethics, Corporate Social Responsibility and Sustainability (ECSRS) in Management Education. *Journal of Business Ethics* 136 (3): 523–538.

Slater, Daniel J. and Heather R. Dixon-Fowler. (2010). The Future of the Planet in the Hands of MBAs: An Examination of CEO MBA Education and Corporate Environmental Performance. *Academy of Management Learning & Education* 9 (3): 429–441.

Snelson-Powell, Annie, Johanne Grosvold and Andrew Millington. (2016). Business School Legitimacy and the Challenge of Sustainability: A Fuzzy Set Analysis of Institutional Decoupling. *Academy of Management Learning & Education* 15 (4): 703–723.

Stubbs, Wendy and Jan Schapper. (2011). Two Approaches to Curriculum Development for Educating for Sustainability and CSR. *International Journal of Sustainability in Higher Education* 12 (3): 259–268.

UNESCO. (2005). *UN Decade of Education for Sustainable Development 2004–2005*. Paris, France: UNESCO.

van Dick, Rolf, Patrick A. Tissington and Guido Hertel. (2009). Do Many Hands Make Light Work? How to Overcome Social Loafing and Gain Motivation in Work Teams. *European Business Review* 21 (3): 233–245.

Weybrecht, Giselle. (2017). From Challenge to Opportunity—Management Education's Crucial Role in Sustainability and the Sustainable Development Goals—An Overview and Framework. *The International Journal of Management Education* 15 (2): 84–92.

Williams, Terry. (2012). The Role of Higher Education in Creating Sustainable Leaders. *The Guardian*, March 2. Accessed March 28, 2018. http://bit.ly/2E0QaqU.

Wright, Norman S. and Hadyn Bennett. (2011). Business Ethics, CSR, Sustainability and the MBA. *Journal of Management & Organization* 17 (5): 641–655.

10

Three Faculty, Two Business Schools, One Goal

David Roger Grayson, Ron Ainsbury, and Saulius Buivys

This chapter explains how three faculty—David Grayson, Ron Ainsbury, and Saulius Buivys connected with two business schools: Cranfield School of Management, UK (Grayson, Ainsbury) and Rotterdam Business School (RBS), Netherlands (Buivys, Ainsbury)—have collaborated over a decade with the single goal of improving the effectiveness and impact of the teaching of corporate responsibility (CR) and sustainability amongst graduate management students (MBAs and other management Masters).

D. R. Grayson (✉)
Cranfield School of Management, Cranfield, UK
e-mail: david.grayson@cranfield.ac.uk

R. Ainsbury
Rotterdam University of Applied Sciences, Rotterdam, Netherlands

S. Buivys
Rotterdam Business School, Rotterdam University of Applied Sciences, Rotterdam, Netherlands

© The Author(s) 2019
K. Amaeshi et al. (eds.), *Incorporating Sustainability in Management Education*,
https://doi.org/10.1007/978-3-319-98125-3_10

- We set out the development of three tools, seven steps, Jigsaw Target, and Stages of Maturity (SOMAT) and explain the evolution in their use as an integrating model.
- We describe their use in the teaching of Business Responsibility and Sustainability in the international MBA and Masters students in two business schools: Cranfield School of Management (UK) and RBS (Netherlands).
- We report on the use by graduate students of the RBS to use the tools to analyse businesses and the reaction of businesses to results of the analysis.
- We offer the integrating model as a potential tool to aid the teaching of Business Responsibility and Sustainability in other business schools both with pre-work and with post-work experience Masters students and to form the basis of future research on embedding the principles of responsible business.

This chapter is divided into the following sections:

1. Introduction to Cranfield and the RBS
2. The Seven-Step Model
3. The Jigsaw Target and SOMAT
4. Conclusion and Further Research/Development.

Introduction to Cranfield and the RBS

Cranfield University

Cranfield University is a British postgraduate and research-based public university specialising in science, engineering, technology, and management. Cranfield's School of Management offers postgraduate degrees, such as a highly ranked MBA, as well as executive education and development programmes. It was a founding partner of the ABIS (Academy of Business in Society) and was one of the earliest global signatories of the UN PRME (Principles of Responsible Management Education). As such, the School's sustainability journey has been captured in several UN PRME Communications on Progress.

The Doughty Centre for Corporate Responsibility was an action-research centre within the Cranfield School of Management from 2007 to 2017. The centre worked closely with academia, business, and other partner organisations and networks to teach, research, and publish (books, articles, reports, and practical how-to guides). In addition, the centre took on a limited number of consulting assignments and runs bespoke courses and workshops for business. It is now part of the Cranfield Sustainability Network.

Rotterdam Business School

The Rotterdam University of Applied Sciences comprises nine teaching institutes (some 36,000 students) and five research centres. A wide variety of programmes is offered with the focus of education closely connected to developments in the metropolitan region of Rotterdam.

The RBS is the international arm of the HR Business School at the Rotterdam University of Applied Sciences. The RBS offers three bachelor's degrees and three master's degrees.

For a number of years the RBS has used an "Inside-out Outside-In" approach to development of study programmes and teaching to ensure that students are exposed to real-life issues as part of their learning. Businesses are actively engaged in the education process by providing real-life questions and challenges they are facing (outside-in) to students who are expected to deliver innovative advice and solutions (inside-out).

This approach has allowed RBS to evolve the way in which we teach graduate students about being a responsible business. The three master's degrees are structured with specialist topics built on a base of a number of core modules. One of the original core topics was "Business Ethics and Policy". This was expanded into a course titled "CSR" (corporate social responsibility) which itself evolved into "Managing Corporate Sustainability" in which we focus the students on embedding sustainable business practices into everyday operations of businesses, large and small.

The Seven-Step Model

The Model

In 2001, David Grayson and Adrian Hodges developed a Seven-Step framework for companies wishing to manage social, environmental, and economic (SEE) risks and opportunities. This was part of their book *Everybody's Business: Managing Risks & Opportunities in Today's Global Society* (Grayson & Hodges 2001).

They subsequently developed and refined the model and this was published in *Corporate Social Opportunity!: Seven Steps to Make Corporate Social Responsibility Work for Your Business* (Fig. 10.1) (Grayson & Hodges 2004).

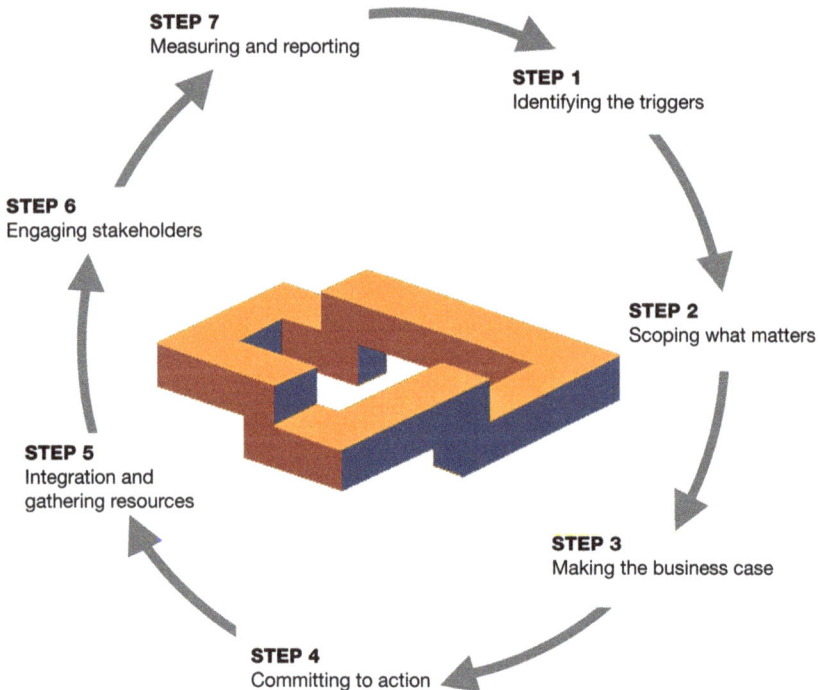

STEP 7
Measuring and reporting

STEP 1
Identifying the triggers

STEP 6
Engaging stakeholders

STEP 2
Scoping what matters

STEP 5
Integration and
gathering resources

STEP 3
Making the business case

STEP 4
Committing to action

Fig. 10.1 The seven steps

Seven steps has been used as a teaching model, first in Cranfield University, and then at the RBS (Table 10.1).

Testing in the Classroom Phase

Cranfield

When David Grayson was appointed to set up and run the Doughty Centre for Corporate Responsibility at Cranfield School of Management in 2007, one of his first initiatives was to establish a new MBA course elective on managing a sustainable business. This used the Seven-Step model as the spine of the course. This elective was run on circa 12 occasions with both the full-time and executive MBA students between 2008 and 2014 by when it had been superseded by a core, compulsory course.

Table 10.1 The seven steps

Step 1:	It is about how a combination of changes in the external environment and heightened expectations from stakeholders cause triggers that impact an organisation. These triggers can stimulate revision of organisational strategies and operational practices.
Step 2:	Scoping what matters is about identifying the material impacts that an organisation has.
Step 3:	Making the business case is about how to build the justification for the proposed new organisational strategies, informed by organisational considerations and by overall organisational goals and business drivers.
Step 4:	Committing to action is about the adoption of new strategy and the implications/links to organisational values, leadership, governance, organisational purpose, and the value of making public commitments.
Step 5:	Integration and implementation are about putting the new strategy into practice and embedding across the organisation in strategic business units and functions.
Step 6:	Engaging stakeholders involves engaging both internal and external stakeholders in implementation of the new strategy, including partnering with other companies, non-governmental organisations (NGOs), academia, and public bodies.
Step 7:	Measuring and reporting are about collecting and disseminating data on the implementation of the new strategy and using this to trigger further progress and a further iteration of the seven steps for continuous improvement (see Fig. 10.1).

RBS

In 2012 Saulius Buivys, inspired by David Grayson's approach towards CSR as presented in the seven steps book, replaced an existing RBS course "Business Ethics and Policy" with a new course "Corporate Social Responsibility" as a core module for the three RBS Master programmes: MCE—Master in Consultancy and Entrepreneurship, MFA—Master in Finance and Accounting, and MLM—Master in Logistics Management.

The module description read: "Through following a 7-step approach to Managing Sustainable Business, this practical, "how-to" course aims to equip students interested in promoting responsible business with the tools and techniques needed to embed sustainability into business purpose, strategy, and practice. These include identifying and assessing the triggers for taking a more socially responsible approach to business, scoping a company's most material environmental, social, and governance (ESG) issues, and how to build the business case for corporate responsibility. These topics were covered in six lectures (28 contact hours).

Students were originally assessed by means of an examination focused on analysing a specific CR case study. We decided that this was limiting the range of competences that we could assess. We changed to an assignment. This allowed students to practise and demonstrate a wider range of learning: specifically, analysis, critical review, application and operationalisation of theoretical frameworks, and team work. This course ran successfully for three years.

Feedback from Students and Businesses

General reaction of the students in both Cranfield and Rotterdam was positive. They liked the highly participatory nature of the course delivery and appreciated discussions on a variety of tools which could be used to integrate responsible business elements into strategy.

This inspired Buivys and Ainsbury to develop a case study based on the Seven-Step model which was integrated into teaching and has allowed students to understand even better how the Seven-Step model could work in a company.

The Jigsaw Target and SOMAT

Developing the Jigsaw Target

At the annual ABIS Colloquium held at Cranfield University in 2008 Cranfield doctoral student David Ferguson, who had developed his PhD thesis looking at embedding sustainability in the UK subsidiary of EDF (EDF Energy), presented the concept of the bullseye target—a set of parameters which could be aimed at by responsible managers.

This model encompassed all the elements that were later cited in the 2010 Accenture/UN Global Compact survey of CEOs of companies which are signatories to the UN Global Compact: such as board oversight; sustainability embedded in strategy and operations of subsidiaries; embedded in global supply chains; participation in collaborations and multi-stakeholder partnerships; and engagement with stakeholders such as investors.

Grayson and Ainsbury subsequently refined the Ferguson model. They explicitly incorporated the importance of leadership ("top down") and employee engagement ("bottom up"). They also included more operational enablers such as knowledge management and training for sustainability; engaging a wide range of stakeholders other than just investors (important though it is better to explain to investors how sustainable development will change the strategy of business and to cultivate stewardship i.e. long-term shareholders rather than share-traders) and the role of the specialist CR/sustainability function (Fig. 10.2).

For a long time, Grayson and Ainsbury called this the "Bulls-eye" model after a shooting or archery target, where the aim is ultimately to score a bullseye—the centre circle of the target. They came to recognise, however, the inherent weaknesses of this term, as it suggested a static and disconnected set of components.

In applying the metaphor to business, Grayson and Ainsbury realised that an organisation must actively manage both the inner and the outer rings while aiming at the centre: the bullseye. Consultees on earlier drafts of their 2014 paper, "Business Critical: Understanding a Company's Current and Desired Stages of Corporate Responsibility Maturity",

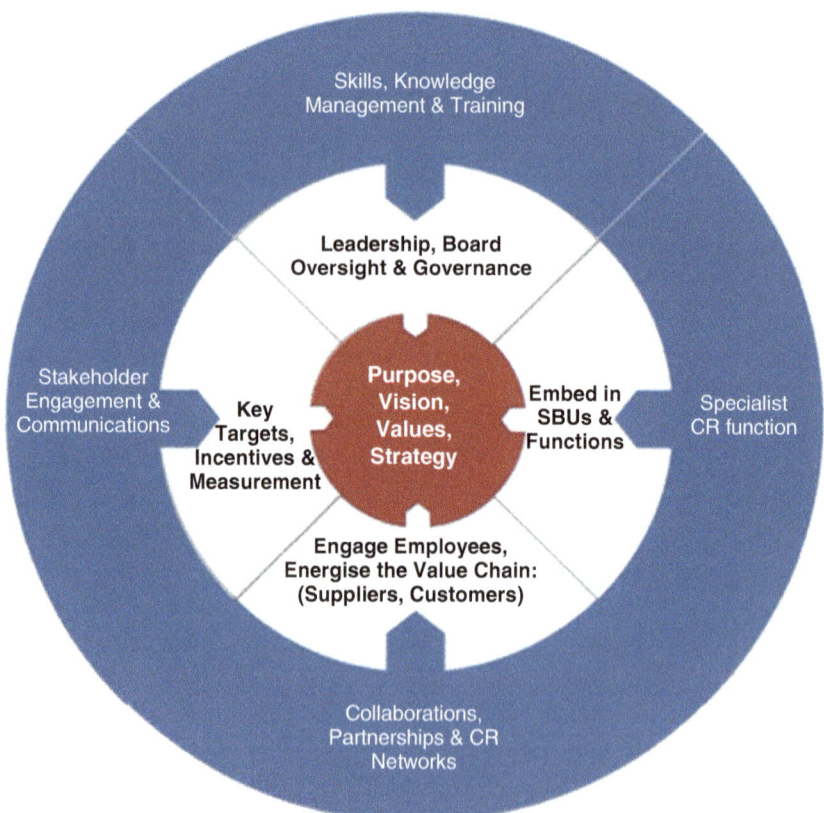

Fig. 10.2 The Jigsaw Target

suggested a pyramid as an alternative. In the end, they retained the "target" but added in a "jigsaw" motif to suggest the inherent inter-connectivity between all the elements. They are not independent of each other. Thus, for example, collaborations/partnerships/networks (Operational) should relate to Energising Value Chain (strategy); Management Skills, Knowledge & training (operational) should relate to Engaging Employees (strategy); Communications and stakeholder engagement (operational) should relate to key targets and measurement, incentives (strategy); specialist function (operational) should relate to embedding in strategic business units and functions (strategy), and so on. In order to achieve sustainability all components of the model need to be aligned. Further information can be found on the Jigsaw Target, in Ainsbury R., Grayson D, Business Critical, Doughty Centre for Corporate Responsibility, Cranfield 2014.

Developing Stages of Maturity (SOMAT)

There have been several attempts to provide a definition for the activities of a company that are focused on more than just the immediate needs of its business model.

Generally speaking, while different epithets are used to describe stages, there is more or less agreement that the spectrum commences on one end where companies are in denial of any responsibility other than to make profit and take no responsible action whatsoever, while at the other end are companies who are, in some way, transforming the way they (and others) do business.

The first stage is one where the response of the business is a type of denial. "This has nothing to do with me or my business." This stage is variously described as Reactive, Defensive, or Rejection. Dunphy adds a variation of denial, calling out a group as Stealthy Saboteurs—entrepreneurs with no hint of ethics who see an opportunity to climb on board and take advantage of the new.

The second stage is where the company moves to a more defensive posture and seeks to comply with the minimum change that either meets regulation or what is perceived as enough to satisfy the more active stakeholders. This stage is described as Defensive, Compliance, or Engaged.

The third stage is where management sees a direct business benefit in some form (e.g. reducing cost by reducing waste or energy consumption). Clarkson describes this stage as "accommodative"; "managerial" is used by Zadek. Dunphy calls them "Efficient", Mirvis and Googins call this stage "Innovative", and Kramer and Kania would call this the start of the "Offensive" stage.

The fourth and fifth stages are where the company is becoming pro-active in some way. Clarkson merely has one group he calls "Pro-active". Most other writers set out two separate stages—the first, where companies believe that there is some form of competitive advantage to be gained by being pro-active—these seek out opportunities to use responsibility as a lever for corporate reputation and strategic advantage. This stage is described as strategic, pro-active.

The fifth stage is where the company has realised that complex social problems may not be solved by one company working alone, there is no competitive advantage, that business value is at stake unless the whole industry works together. Companies in this stage may variously be described as Civil or Champions. Some posit that this stage is an ambition, an horizon that is never reached for as a company approaches the standards change.

Cranfield's Doughty Centre was developing and refining its own model for embedding sustainability since it began. Zadek's model of SOMAT was adapted by the Doughty Centre as the basis for a one-day Change-Management workshop it ran for CR professionals, on behalf of the UK CR coalition Business in the Community from 2008.

At the same ABIS Colloquium, where David Ferguson presented his embedding bullseye, Professor Dexter Dunphy spoke of the six-phase model he and others had developed in Australia, colourfully describing phases with titles such as "bunker wombats", and "transformative futurists" in addition to "stealthy saboteurs" mentioned earlier (Dunphy et al. 2003).

Inspired by Zadek and Dunphy, David Grayson experimented with a five-stage model, "SOMAT". The SOMAT model was used by the Doughty Centre in a major consulting assignment for The Crown Estate in 2008–2009, working with their senior management team to develop a sustainability strategy for the organisation. In turn, the SOMAT framework combined with the Jigsaw Target led to the development of a practitioner workshop that was first used with companies in 2009 at a conference organised by the Australian Centre for Corporate Public Affairs in Melbourne. Grayson's experience using the enlarged model (Jigsaw Target and SOMAT) to analyse the evolution of the sustainability strategy of the UK retailer Marks & Spencer was presented at an international conference in Bocconi, Milan in January 2011 and was subsequently published as a case study in The *Journal of Management Development* (Grayson 2011). The same model was then used to explain Unilever's evolution (Grayson & Exter 2012).

Meantime, Ron Ainsbury, who had been appointed a visiting fellow of the Doughty Centre in 2009 and commenced guest lecturing at RBS in 2010, started to collaborate with Grayson on the development and embedding of SOMAT and the Jigsaw Target. Their findings were presented and discussed at a workshop hosted by Legal & General. Legal & General then hosted the launch of their occasional paper (Ainsbury and Grayson 2014) summarising progress at an event in May 2014. An abridged version of the paper was subsequently published by Ethical Corp in their monthly magazine in August 2014 (Ainsbury and Grayson 2014).

Cranfield's Stages of Maturity

Stage 1: Denier—not recognising any responsibility for a company's SEE impacts;

Stage 2: Complier—following laws and common business practices in dealing with SEE impacts;

Stage 3: Risk Mitigator—identifying material SEE impacts and reducing negative impacts to mitigate reputational, financial, regulatory, social "licence to operate" risks;

Stage 4: Opportunity Maximiser—reducing negative SEE impacts but also now systematically seeking business opportunities from optimising positive impacts the business has;

Stage 5: Champion—both embracing sustainability in its own value chain, but also collaborating with others and advocating public policy changes to create sustainable development.

Using the Models in Teaching

Experience at Cranfield

The SOMAT and Jigsaw Target models have formed a key part of teaching with some 500 senior executives participating in the Cranfield Development Programme. They have helped to provoke discussion and reflection amongst the executives about where their own organisation currently is and where it aspires to be on SOMAT. The models have also been used in MBA, executive MBA and specialist Masters in Management & Corporate Sustainability and other MSc courses as key tools to understand attitudes towards CR, as well as actual performance.

Experience at the Rotterdam Business School

It has been at RBS, however, where a fuller and more extensive use of the models has evolved over the last seven years. As a visiting lecturer at RBS, Ron Ainsbury was asked to present a course on business ethics to executive MBA students. As he explored updating the course content he was interested to consider whether or not SOMAT and the Jigsaw Target would make sense in smaller companies outside the UK. He decided to do trial of an assignment: "analyse the company you work for using SOMAT and the Jigsaw Target".

The feedback from the executive MBA students was positive. First, there was no difficulty at all in understanding the main concepts. Second, the students found that using the Jigsaw TARGET components allowed them to see just how pervasive was their company's approach to being responsible and sustainable.

Ainsbury shared this experience with RBS Research Lecturer Saulius Buivys. They agreed that the subject should have a higher profile within the Masters programmes. Buivys successfully argued the case with his Graduate Department peers. Together they designed a new course, Managing Corporate Sustainability (MCS) (56 contact hours) to replace the CSR course (28 contact hours).

Managing Corporate Sustainability (MCS)

The MCS course is taught over a period of eight months with content of the course divided into three parts.

Part 1

During this first part, Ainsbury provides an introduction to the basic concepts of being a responsible and sustainable enterprise in the twenty-first century. There are six face-to-face sessions where key concepts are introduced and explained with students pointed to additional reading. Each session is designed to be interactive with students being encouraged to explore answers to selected questions online during the class.

The first lesson explores the evolution of CR, reviewing the social and environmental issues that face the world in the twenty-first century, and how these are affecting, or have the potential to affect, business value. Therefore, just as businesses are already doing with economic and commercial risks—the potential impact of ESG risks need to be assessed, a response strategy developed and embedded into operations.

The second lesson introduces the concept of purpose and the discussion centres around the purpose of various businesses. Students explore why businesses start and look at the driving forces behind contemporary start-ups that have grown exponentially—typically with a social purpose embedded.

The third lesson then introduces the concept of SOMAT and the TARGET—essentially culture change, change in any management process typically requires leadership setting direction and goals, and then a business builds on successive stages of development as they proceed along the new path.

The fourth lesson explores collaboration and the need for various disparate groups to work together in order to produce solutions to social and environmental problems. A contrast is made between typical business issues—which require internal cooperation and potentially some outside resources to resolve—but are usually relatively straightforward—and typical social and environmental issues which are complex and often require multiple stakeholders to work together to affect a solution.

The fifth lesson discusses the opportunities for new business models—using social and environmental issues as spurs for innovation. Several current examples of entrepreneurs and new business models emerging are set out and a challenge issued to the students—if these entrepreneurs can do this what could they do in their home countries?

The sixth lesson reviews the current literature setting out the business case for being a responsible business.

Part 2

The second part of the course is delivered by Buivys via three four-hour workshops during which students are taught how to identify opportunities arising from sustainable and responsible business practices and how to incorporate these practices into every aspect of running the business.

The main objective of the first workshop is to set a stage and provide guidance and tools in writing a case study and teaching notes on evaluation of CR in the company. During this workshop participants discuss how to develop and write cases study and teaching notes. Students also revise their understanding of the SOMAT model which was discussed during the first part of this subject. This is crucial as the model is required to be used by students as a core tool while working on their group assignment (more detailed information about this assignment is provided later in this chapter).

The main focus of the other two workshops is the Grayson and Hodges Seven-Step model which provides guidance on how to integrate elements of responsible and sustainable business into various aspects of business. Buivys starts with covering the first three steps of the model which includes: identifying the triggers and opportunities, scoping what matters, and making the business case during the third workshop. The remaining four steps—committing to action, integration and gathering resources, engaging stakeholders, and measuring and reporting—are covered in the fourth workshop. These workshops are designed to be closely linked with the knowledge gained during the first part of the course taught by Ainsbury. However, if the first part is based on knowledge building, the second part of the course is focused on operationalisation of it. Buivys uses an extended teaching case he and Ainsbury developed: "The Path to a Sustainable SME: The van Houtum Story" (Ainsbury & Buivys, 2013) to illustrate and check student's understanding of the model through these workshops.

Part 3

In part 3, students are grouped according to their degree specialty and attend two workshops in which the issues relating to managing responsibility and sustainably specific to their degree programme[1] are discussed.

MCE:

- The Circular Economy: what opportunities for new business models?
- Social and Environmental issues: what new business opportunities? New business models such as B-Corps?
- What role can consultants play in helping their clients become more responsible and more sustainable?

MFA:

- Assets pricing in the circular economy
- Carbon pricing
- Corporate governance and ethics

MLM:

- Sustainable supply chain management

Assessment via Assignments

Students are assessed via two assignments. The first is an individual assignment and is set and supervised by Buivys. Each student is given a tailored question and needs to respond by presenting a 4000-word essay on the assigned topic. A typical essay might be to research six companies that are taking the lead in the student's home country, choosing six companies that are leading the way in being more responsible or sustainable using the taught models.

The second is a group assignment where the JIGSAW Target and SOMAT come into play.

Students are given a detailed briefing paper to help them to prepare their assignments. The students are required to self-form teams of three (although by special request lecturers allow teams of two and four), choose a company with certain criteria as a guide, analyse the company using the JIGSAW Target and SOMAT, and then write up the results as a case study.

The structure of the assignment has been modified over the past two years. At first students were just asked to provide the assessment. As an improvement, Buivys then introduced the concept of writing the assignment as a case study—complete with teaching notes. This step provides useful, extra learning experience for students as they were forced to consider how they would use their company assessment to teach other students at least three critical lessons related to MCS.

Ainsbury and Buivys have added a requirement that students provide their assessment to the company and ask the company for feedback on their assessment.

Final Course Workshop

A final workshop is held in part 3, after students have submitted their group assignment. This session provides an opportunity for students to share their experience in conducting the research, writing the case, and teaching notes. It is an opportunity to explore their experience in using the Jigsaw Target and SOMAT tools in their evaluation of their case companies.

A modified version of this three-part programme was also taught by RBS as blended learning (online webinars plus local tutors) to students in Brazil as a result of a collaboration negotiated by Buivys with INEPAD— Instituto de Ensino e Pesquisa em Administração in Ribeirão Preto.

Feedback from Students and Businesses on SOMAT and TARGET

The RBS team's experience has been very positive.

- The Jigsaw Target and SOMAT are very useful tools for allowing students to analyse a company and assess its responsibility performance.
- Students have found that analysing a company in this way helps them understand better the complexities of being a responsible business.
- With modest adaptations,[2] the models can be used effectively with SMEs and NGOs.
- Companies that have been analysed have found the analysis illuminating and helpful.

Enterprises Studied

A total of 119 different enterprises have been studied by MCS students since 2014 with one Netherlands family business being studied twice by two different student groups.

Due to the spread of students, most of these businesses were in either the Netherlands (35) or Brazil (35) with 26 coming from Asia, 15 from other European nations, 6 from Central & South America, and 3 from Africa, making the total of 120 assignments.

Most of the enterprises (69) were private or family owned, while 9 were government-owned enterprises, 2 were NGOs, and the remaining 40 were local subsidiaries of or joint venture with multinational businesses.

Student Evaluations

Students are regularly asked to evaluate their experience in using the TARGET and SOMAT to evaluate their chosen company.

Overall, students respond positively to the SOMAT and TARGET describing these as "very useful" tools.

> SOMAT
> "This tool provides an indication of which direction (the business needs) to move."

> TARGET
> "All the elements in the model provide a yardstick to measure if the company is sustainable or not."

The experience of most students has been that being required to apply the Jigsaw Target and SOMAT to a live company gave them a much better understanding of the principles of responsibility and sustainability as covered in formal lectures. Moreover, being required to write up their case study, complete with teaching notes, was found to be a good way of checking what they have learned. The case-studies also add to subsequent teaching experience.

Business

The TARGET model and the SOMAT model have proven to be broadly applicable across a wide range of enterprises—with a few recommendations on what adjustments might need to be made when applying the model to SMEs.

Company Feedback

In recent iterations of the assignment RBS has asked for feedback from individual companies that have been analysed, and who have received a copy of the student analysis. This feedback is emailed directly to the course supervisor. The response from most companies has been positive.

Vietnamese Bank:
Your report … gives us an overview of our comprehensive performance on all activities. The teaching note has pointed to a few significant issues that we are considering. Almost all of the student recommendations sound acceptable. However, there are a lot of challenges to implement sustainability. As you know, every business wants to earn profit to pay to its shareholders.

Indian Software business:
We appreciate the detailed analysis and synthesis of the materials which will support us to embed sustainability in the long run. Some of the recommendations can be implemented with immediate effect but to implement some other recommendations will take a certain period of time.

Bangladesh Enterprise
We want to become a role model of corporate sustainability in Bangladesh. We have been planning for this sustainability strategy to embed in our corporate culture—we think we are on right track to achieve this. The corporate responsibility target model developed by Doughty Centre for Corporate Responsibility is very interesting. Our Managing Director has talked about integrating CSR into core values, strategic and operational stages as well. We understand to be a role model in corporate sustainability we need to make overhaul changes in board oversight & corporate governance, incentives & performance measurement, key target, and last but not least leadership to align with our sustainability implementation target.

Vietnam Medium-sized Enterprise
It is very interesting that there is a model to help us having a holistic view about our plan, what we are doing, and what we can do to improve our sustainability strategy. We are actually thinking of applying this model to our company not only in this sustainability plan but also in other plans since it provides detailed information.

From a Dutch SME

We are very satisfied with the research and analysis. Taking part in the assignment with the students made us realise that we are on the right track but that there are improvements that can be made to become even more successful in terms of corporate sustainability.

Vietnamese mid-sized enterprise

I spent some time reading the model of sustainability and the five stages. I am interested in the explanation of each definition.

From a Dutch family business:

We're very satisfied and pleasantly surprised by the analysis and assessment of the students. Even though the period in which they assessed our organization was relatively short, they managed to get to the core of our CSR-policy. Their transparent and constructive way of reporting and their useful tips help us getting better insight in our efforts and shortcomings.

The model is very clear and useful for understanding what action is needed or advised and on what timescale. The visualization of the model in a manageable table also works very well when informing staff and management on how we're doing and where we can improve.

From a Vietnamese SME

I think the model is interesting tool to assess our current sustainability progress and help us have higher understanding of corporate sustainability.

Further Potential Developments

There are several exciting areas for further development.

- First, the models appear to be substantial tools and could be further refined and tested.
- Second, the use of these models as the basis of a practical assignment, combined with the requirement to present results as a teaching case to share learning with other students, has proven to be a successful method of embedding an understanding of the concepts of CR and sustainability.

- Last, the models have the potential to be further developed as an analytical tool enabling companies to develop their own SOMAT paths to the Jigsaw Target.

Refining the Models

A recent publication by Bain & Company, "Achieving Breakthrough Results in Sustainability", based on a survey of 300 companies engaged in "sustainability transformations" coupled with detailed interviews with heads of sustainability for major companies that have been recognised for their results, provides verification of several aspects of the Jigsaw Target and the change of mindset required to progress through the SOMAT.

Bain developed four guidelines which echo elements of the Jigsaw Target and the seven steps (Table 10.2).

The most common suggestion from our students related to differences between what one expects for a large corporation versus what might be the case in small to medium-sized enterprise, for example, the role of a specialist manager for CR.

Several of our Asian students felt that there might be different kinds of "Denier/Complier" and suggested the following (Table 10.3).

There is potential to work with others on testing and refining the model and the table of guidelines that are used. One area where we can develop the concept further is the description of Champion. In our view there are no "Champions". Our concept is that Champion is a moving

Table 10.2 Bain versus Jigsaw Target

Bain & Co	Jigsaw Target	Seven steps
Making clear public commitments with quantitative targets	Key targets, incentives, and measurement	Step 4
CEO leadership	Leadership, board oversight and governance	Step 4
Change throughout the organisation	Engage employees, energise the value chain	Step 5
Incorporate sustainability into daily decision-making	Embed in strategic business units and functions	Step 5

Table 10.3 Students' suggested modification of Denier & Complier Stages

Denier:	Regards rules, regulations, and standards as an impediment to making a profit
Evader:	Businesses actively seeking loopholes or shortcuts around rules and regulations
Forced Followers:	Forced to comply with rules and regulations but without real conviction and no vision
Complier:	Complying with rules and regulations as a minimum standard for risk management

target. A company breaks new ground but then others follow and what was once Champion behaviour becomes the norm.

After further study, we also suspect that our existing models do not give sufficient emphasis to organisational culture and culture change to embed sustainability successfully.

Refining the Teaching

All three authors are interested in helping lecturers in other institutions to build capacity in teaching these models.

For lecturers interested to include in their teaching programme a SOMAT/TARGET assignment and have students choose a company, analyse the company (including interviews with company personnel), produce a report on the business, discuss findings with the company, and report on the company's feedback.

We will be able to provide:

1. Brief PowerPoint presentation setting out the concepts
2. Detailed assignment description
3. Marking rubric for the assignment.

We need to emphasise that the concept of SOMAT is a continuum rather than a series of easily categorised, discrete stages. Companies may be assessed as being at different stages for different elements of the Jigsaw Target.

Developing the Consulting Possibility

Feedback from companies has been positive with many appreciating the "snapshot" provided by the student analysis. Some responses suggested that it would be nice to have more measures that they could use as a benchmark. There is potential for collaboration in setting out what might be benchmarks. There might also be the possibility of developing "how-to" manuals for each of the elements of the Jigsaw Target.

Conclusion

As pressure from mainstream investors as well as other stakeholders on businesses to embed sustainability grows, so too will the capacity of business schools around the world to teach the subject effectively need to grow. We hope our experience with students from more than 30 countries across the world can help build that capacity.

Notes

1. See explanation in Section "Testing in the Classroom Phase".
2. For example, a few SMEs have need of a corporate relations specialist, but might need to have someone dedicated to the function as part of a broader role.

References

Ainsbury, Ron, and Saulius Buivys. 2013. The Path to a Sustainable SME: The Van Houtum Story, The Case Centre 713-003-1.

Ainsbury, Ron, and David Grayson. 2014. Towards Sustainability Maturity, Ethical Corporation, August.

———. 2014. Business Critical: Understanding a Company's Current and Desired Stages of Corporate Responsibility Maturity, Doughty Centre for Corporate Responsibility Occasional Paper.

Dunphy, Dexter, Andrew Griffiths, and Suzanne Benn. 2003. *Organizational Change for Corporate Sustainability*. London: Routledge.

Grayson, D. 2011. Embedding Corporate Responsibility and Sustainability: Marks and Spencer. *Journal of Management Development* 30 (10): 1017–1026.

Grayson, David, and Adrian Hodges. 2001. *Everybody's Business: Managing Risks & Opportunities in Today's Global Society*. Dorling Kindersley.

———. 2004. *Corporate Social Opportunity!: Seven Steps to Make Corporate Social Responsibility Work for Your Business*. Greenleaf Publishing.

Grayson, David, and Nadine Exter, eds. 2012. *Cranfield on Corporate Sustainability*. London: Greenleaf Publishing.

Index

© The Author(s) 2019
K. Amaeshi et al. (eds.), *Incorporating Sustainability in Management Education*,
https://doi.org/10.1007/978-3-319-98125-3

239